D1129195

More Praise for Ann Va
and *OASIS Conversations*

"As an HR Executive who has experienced several career transitions, I have learned the importance of real collaboration and engagement. At the World Bank Group, Ann Van Eron has been an essential person in making this happen, and in her book, *OASIS Conversations: Leading with an Open Mindset to Maximize Potential*, she shows how this occurs. I highly recommend this book for every executive who wants to make change real."

—Sean McGrath, Ph.D., SVP,
World Bank Global Human Resources

"We all face challenges relating to people with different perspectives. *OASIS Conversations* offers practical tips on how to be open-minded and work effectively with others—at work, at home and in life. I am glad to have experienced the OASIS process with Ann Van Eron and recommend her process for other leaders interested in improving relationships with their teams and colleagues, boosting morale and making their workplaces more effective, efficient and enjoyable."

—Jennifer Flake, Executive Director—Communications,
Ford Motor Company

"I have worked with Ann for over twenty years across several organizations; she has consistently encouraged individuals to confront the challenges with open and direct communication using the OASIS model. She not only teaches it but practices OASIS in life, making her a highly effective and sought after communicator and coach. Many have found her approach of open communications to be simple, useful, and practical, both in the workplace and in their personal lives. It is clear that OASIS can help foster a better approach to communication for all."

— Sunita Holzer, EVP, Chief Human Resources Officer,
Realogy Holdings Corp. (previously with Chubb,
American Express, and GE Capital)

"The beauty of this book—which is practical at the same time—is that Ann Van Eron, with her vast experience as an executive coach and organization change consultant, has provided an easy-to-remember-and-follow rubric, OASIS, yet allowed for flexibility and individuality in its implementation. Call it "structured agility." Whether one aspires simply to be more socially intelligent or a more effective change leader—or both—following Ann's advice and suggestions will lead the way for such a worthy journey and set of goals."

—W. Warner Burke, Ph.D., Edward Lee Thorndike Professor of Psychology and Education, Editor, *Journal of Applied Behavioral Science*, Teachers College, Columbia University

"The OASIS Conversation process is valuable for leaders today. Ann Van Eron's OASIS process has been extremely well-received by United Nations leaders and staff globally. People routinely report successful results using the memorable and practical process. It is great that more people will now have access to this critical skill for emotional and social intelligence."

—Maryel Jansen,(retired) Manager, Learning, Leadership and Organization Development, United Nations

"Ann Van Eron has helped my team achieve a higher level of performance through her coaching on the OASIS model. Her methods are based on leading edge science and are easy to understand and practice. Developing these skills will help anyone become a better listener, establish better relationships, and achieve superior results."

— Colleen Moynihan, Oshkosh Corporation Senior Vice President, Quality & Continuous Improvement

"Ann observes that our personal and professional worlds are increasingly VUCA (volatile, uncertain, complex, and ambiguous). In her new book, she describes OASIS Conversations as a structured way to be present and effective through vulnerability and openness in inevitably difficult social, family, work, and community contexts. Ann asserts that we can be taught to be emotionally smarter, and she provides clear instruction for her proven method. Ann has modeled herself and taught me about vulnerability and openness, and I believe her book will make this path available for others."

— Raymond E. Crossman, Ph.D., President, Adler University

"I worked with Ann and her OASIS concept in the last few years both at IFC and the World Bank during significant reorganizations and general resistance to change. I was very impressed with how her notion of 'positive intent' changed the way I and many of my colleagues now look at the change process. Assuming a positive intent and trying to put yourself into the shoes of another colleague to try to understand how things look from the other side has changed the way I work with people. I don't think that any modern organization can survive without practicing OASIS, and I am very grateful to Ann for introducing it to me. I am also glad that wider audiences will now have access to this concept through Ann's new book *OASIS Conversations*."

— Nena Stoiljkovic, VP Global Client Services,
International Finance Corporation

"Ann Van Eron taught me the OASIS method at a critical time in my career, moving from manager to director level. She taught me to really connect with my team, peers, and leaders. The OASIS method has been a safe haven for me in an uncertain world. Ann's approach and her coaching showed me the value of checking my own assumptions by observing first and really paying attention to the person in front of me. It has helped me in many areas as diverse as dealing with performance issues on my team, to influencing peers on strategy, to communicating with senior executives and board members on talent issues. With the playing field ever-changing and our companies driving even more innovation to keep up, our past success and experience mean less today, and yet there is incredible power in cultivating a disciplined practice of opening to the present moment and building confidence that you can lead others to what is needed now. OASIS provides me a mental framework to do just that, to stay open and agile, to be creative amidst change. It helps me connect, gain perspective from different angles, and be more confident in taking action, especially when bold steps are required, as they often are in leadership today. Ann is a wise coach with an approach purpose-built for the volatile environment so many of us find ourselves leading in today."

— Kelly Wojda, Director of Diversity & Talent, Caterpillar

"Ann Van Eron's OASIS process is easy to remember yet incredibly powerful for people in all walks of life. The beauty of OASIS is that it offers a visually memorable model we can 'see' in our heads even when we are in the midst of difficult interactions and that can guide us through conversations—whether or not we are able to plan them beforehand. Using and internalizing the OASIS process enables us not only to achieve better results but also to strengthen our relationships with others. Given years of teaching MBA students from multiple cultures about leading and influencing with integrity, I firmly believe that the skills and open mindset fostered by the OASIS process are among the most valuable assets that leaders, and indeed all of us, can have."

—Mary Trefry, Ph.D., Sacred Heart University,
USA and Luxembourg

"*OASIS Conversations* is a must read for all leaders who want to influence others and deliver compelling results. To help navigate the challenges in today's innovative, complex, volatile world, Dr. Van Eron has contributed a truly valuable, actionable approach to creating open-minded conversations that yield an oasis of possibilities and ultimately greater impact."

—Nisha Advani, Ph.D., former head of Executive Talent
and Organization Development, Genentech

"While many books and much research emphasize the need to be emotionally and socially intelligent, Ann Van Eron shows us *how* to be so in a practical and memorable way. The OASIS process enables leaders to be engaging and create a positive and productive environment amidst diversity. I am glad to have experienced OASIS with Ann, and I highly recommend the process for all."

—Frances Sinha, Human Resources Director,
Human Rights Watch

"Dr. Van Eron has spent years researching and refining her approach to ensure people have the most productive conversations possible, even when feeling uncomfortable. *OASIS Conversations* gives you the framework and steps you can easily follow to get the results you desire."

—Dr. Marcia Reynolds, author of *The Discomfort Zone: How Leaders Turn Difficult Conversations into Breakthroughs*

"The OASIS Conversation process provides relaxed awareness of self and others, through shared understanding in interaction. The process and metaphor are invaluable in flowing through barriers of mind and culture, thus enhancing freedom of interaction and communication. The OASIS Conversation skills can be used for all ages and works in families, classrooms, and meetings. OASIS goals to enhance emotional intelligence, reduce conflict, and develop a better sense of self, and appreciation and understanding of others are applicable in most human interactions. I have found them useful in graduate classroom teaching, conference seminars, and curriculum meetings, as well as in my daily interactions."

—Dolores G. Norton, Ph.D. Samuel Deutsch Professor Emerita
The University of Chicago

"For many years, my leadership style has been dominated by achieving results, and when faced with opposition or challenging relationships, I have relied on blunt force to drive through the resistance. Ann introduced to me the OASIS model...which despite its simplicity, ultimately became a powerful tool that helped me manage conflict and difficult conversations in a much more positive manner. It gave me a process & discipline to proactively think through the biases and lenses that others look through and ultimately build capabilities to constructively manage differences. My career has been focused on change...and with all change comes resistance; finally, I have a structure to help me recognize that people have different needs and that gives me a structured process to pause and move from simply reacting to fostering a positive interaction."

— David Herbert, CFO Caterpillar Electric
Power Division, Caterpillar Inc.

"Early in my career, I used to shy away from tough human conversations: Ann's OASIS model helped me understand what to improve and the results for me have been magic."

—Erika Ratcliffe, Organisational Improvement Consultant,
Market Lead, Kepner-Tregoe Europe

"The OASIS process offers a pathway to break the us-versus-them pattern of escalating reactions, defensiveness, and lack of progress. While this destructive pattern is increasing in our culture, our politics, and our world, this book offers us the skills to step back and SHIFT the direction to possibilities and solutions. *OASIS Conversations* will feed people's hunger for something different. Learning the OASIS model increases our awareness of how we are pulled into destructive patterns. With this new self-awareness and armed with OASIS skills, we are able to shift our mindset and the nature of our conversations. It is then that old reactive patterns lose their pull on us. Ann Van Eron has demystified the magic of her skills in this book so people all over the world can SHIFT the conversation in these volatile times. Thank you, Ann."

—Pat Ruzich, Ruzich Consulting/High-Performance Coaching

"The importance of having an open mind and being curious about the other person's point of view is so important. Assigning inaccurate motives to others gets in the way of productive solutions, so many times. The OASIS Moves can help both sides suspend judgment, understand the facts, and find solutions that are win-win for both sides."

—Robert Trefry, former CEO of Bridgeport Hospital and
Yale-New Haven Health System; Board Chair of
United Way and Executive Coach

"Ann's approach is about truly connecting with people based on finding common ground and synergies. In today's fast-changing, socially-connected world, leaders need to connect with everyone around them to maintain and grow their circle of influence. This connection requires the leader to influence people who have different opinions and experiences. It is easy to read about emotional intelligence and talk about being open. Actually, being open and connecting requires identifying your own personal path and then actually walking that path every day until it becomes habit. I have found Ann's OASIS approach to be a refreshing way to evolve my leadership skillset."

—Nehal Trivedi, Senior Vice President,
Title Resources Guarantee Company

"Ann is, without a doubt, the best executive coach I have had in my career across the public and private sectors. She made me realize that to be a good leader and change manager, you need to carry the team and bring about a cohesiveness and purposefulness in the team. All leaders and teams will benefit greatly from the coaching and open mindset shared in *OASIS Conversations*."

—Anita George, Senior Director, World Bank Group

"I have had the pleasure to work with Dr. Van Eron for more than a decade. In that time, I have been impressed by her mastery of both classical and modern approaches to communication and leadership. What truly sets her apart, however, is her empathy. She is the rare expert who demonstrates her power by listening, and doing so, she is able to teach colleagues and clients by understanding their needs. I am more successful in all of my endeavors because she has taught me so well what she practices so seamlessly."

—Brion Fox, Ph.D., Madison University

"I find OASIS a succinct process to follow. Open communication is an essential need to build connections and trust in business and life. It gives us insights in how we create win-win situations. The process is easy to remember and well set out. More importantly, clients enjoy using it. It is fun and rewarding because the effects are immediate and apply to all areas of life. I have personally benefited from it and would recommend it thoroughly."

—Shamim Nasser, Director, Discovering Potentials (London)

"Do you want a simple process to be the most effective leader you can be, creating the results you want? Ann Van Eron's *OASIS Conversations: Leading with an Open Mindset to Maximize Potential* shows you how with her powerfully proven, time-tested OASIS Conversation® method. Insightful examples from her worldwide leadership consulting engagements bring to life how to incorporate her winning process into our own lives and start benefitting right away."

—Joseph Vranich, President and Author,
Speaker—Spectrum Location Solutions

"If you lead people or aspire to lead people, you must read this book; otherwise, you'll shortchange your ability to realize your desired outcomes. Ann Van Eron has combined years of executive coaching and leadership consulting with brain science to produce compelling results around the world. Now, in her book *OASIS Conversations*, she distills those years of experience and scientific findings with her easy-to-use OASIS Conversation® process. Give yourself an advantage by buying this book."

— Marie Meade, Senior Account Manager,
Verizon and Founder of Computious.com

"*OASIS Conversations* is a readable, practical guide to holding conversations that work. Ann Van Eron's process is easy to remember and will help you turn around challenging communication issues. I love the book and highly recommend it to everyone."

— Laurie Zuckerman, Executive Coach and
Organization Development Consultant

"OASIS is a powerful process for helping people, and leaders in particular, go deeper in understanding themselves, others, and issues and creating responses that reflect their awareness. Ann Van Eron demonstrates the power of creating an oasis with an open mindset to offer support and challenge for real change."

— Hassane Cisse, Director, World Bank

OASIS

CONVERSATIONS

Leading with an Open Mindset
to Maximize Potential

A Practical Pathway to Positive and Productive
Relationships for Unparalleled Results

ANN M. VAN ERON, PH.D.
Creator of the OASIS® Process

Open View Press
Chicago, IL

Published by:
Open View Press
www.OpenViewPress.com

ISBN: 978-0-9975136-0-8
E-book ISBN: 978-0-9975136-1-5
Library of Congress Number: 2016945129

Editor: Tyler Tichelaar
Cover and Interior Book Design: Bookwrights
Cover photo from 123rf.com
Every attempt has been made to source properly all quotes.

Printed in the United States of America
First Edition

For Joyelle, and all children young and old.

May an Open Mindset and the OASIS Conversation® process support us in experiencing open-minded connections, enjoying life, and creating a better world for everyone.

Acknowledgments

It would have been impossible to write this book or develop the OASIS Conversation® process without the help of many people.

Thank you to my many coaching and corporate clients; I have learned much from each of you. Thank you to my workshop participants all over the world; together, we explored what works best to support positive interactions and open-minded leadership.

As an avid reader and learner, I have many authors to thank for sharing their insights and perspectives. I have grown greatly from books and conversations to which I am indebted. I hope others will benefit from this book in the same way.

My thanks to my colleagues and friends who have heard about the dream of offering this book for a long time. Special thanks for their support goes to Kathleen FitzSimons, Kris Snow, Shamim Nasser, Pat Ruzich, Laurie Zuckerman, Trish Montagnino, and Lou Schwartz. Thanks to Tyler Tichelaar for your patient editing.

Finally, thank you, my family, for your support.

Observation

Awareness
(of assumptions, emotions, and background)

Shift
(to being open)

Importance

Solution

Contents

Introduction

Envisioning an Oasis of Positive and Productive Interactions

o·a·sis /ō'āsis/ *1. a fertile or green area in an arid region (as a desert). 2. something that provides refuge, relief, or pleasant contrast.*

— Merriam-Webster Dictionary

Do you live and work in environments with misunderstandings, miscommunication, and mistrust? Are you finding interactions with others challenging and a drain of your energy?

Are you having impactful conversations with colleagues and others that inspire innovative and creative solutions, or do you feel like you're just overwhelmed by the pace of work and life and the challenges of influencing others?

What will help you be more successful in our fast-changing, diverse global world where the "rules" continue to change?

Sometimes it's difficult to believe there are any positive answers to these questions and issues. After all, turbulence has become such a constant that the U.S. military coined the term "VUCA world" to characterize our current environment of continual volatility, uncertainty, complexity, and ambiguity.

Add to this situation that we have become a truly global society and in our own workplaces, schools, and even homes, we have an increasingly diverse mix of cultures and viewpoints. These days, four generations are often in a workplace, not to mention in our communities. These and many other converging trends are causing us to rethink our tried and true ways of communicating. We are recognizing that we need to be open to new possibilities amid the turbulence. Most of us, whether in a formal leadership position, or as a parent, teacher, partner, or subject matter expert, think we are open-minded. Yet, in reality, we are all naturally biased and our judgments impact our interactions.

1

Thus, even when we are well-intentioned, we often find ourselves feeling frustrated, and quite frankly, at a loss as to how to "get through" to those who differ.

A lot of energy is wasted because we misunderstand each other, make uninformed judgments, and have difficulty coming to agreements—causing both relationships and results to suffer. For most of us, communicating with others is one of the most challenging aspects of our professional and personal lives.

What we need most are open-minded leaders who are emotionally mature and self-aware, and who are willing to pause and withhold judgment long enough to arrive at a new understanding of "what is." This often requires a shift to being open and a mindful response that allows for heretofore impossible solutions. If you are reading this book, I suspect you are wondering how you can be that leader—how you can go from draining interactions to creating an engaging workplace or environment and moving it forward into successful and dynamic new possibilities.

In the past, leaders were expected to manage by command and control. Today's leader needs to learn how to operate in uncertainty and to grapple with problems he or she can no longer solve with an easily issued directive. People all over the world are less apt to follow orders or be coerced into complying. Instead, leaders need to influence and to collaborate. Furthermore, the complex dilemmas we all face require many diverse inputs and views to solve. Leaders need to be open-minded and know how to have impactful conversations with diverse others (everyone) to be effective and successful. Leaders need to learn and innovate, without relying on past answers. Leaders require resiliency and openness to new ways of working and co-creating, and they must build relationships across different groups and boundaries.

How can you be a leader who builds relationships and bridges over the boundaries that seem to exist between people? You do it by having mind-opening conversations. All meaningful change, innovation, and results happen through conversation. That's what this book is really all about—conversing with people—not just commanding or telling them, but listening to them, being curious about them, dialoguing with them, and coming to understanding and agreements that are mindful of everyone involved. It requires being open-minded when interacting with someone with a different perspective (i.e., everyone).

As a leader of the future, in these pages you'll learn how to adopt an open mindset, be open to potential opportunity, and engage in mindful OASIS Conversations that will lead to shared goals and solutions. A critical need for leaders and a key focus of this book is knowing how to stop, suspend judgment, and shift to a more open perspective and stance. Leaders need to create an oasis of possibilities. This book will show you *how* to keep yourself from reacting based on your judgment and learn how to respond thoughtfully from a place of openness and curiosity. You will learn a concrete set of skills that can transform almost every interaction into a satisfying and productive one. Once you attain the critical skill of open-minded conversations, you will be more successful in all of life's facets. Open-minded conversations are core to creating successful environments and the relationships that are critical for creating impactful outcomes. OASIS Conversations involve being aware and non-judgmental with an intent to create an oasis-like environment for exploring, learning, agreeing, and co-creating. It is through mind-opening conversations that leaders align people of diverse perspectives around a shared vision, agree on responsibilities and processes, and ensure understanding, agreement, and accountability.

An open mindset and collaborative behaviors are key to realizing the potential available in our new world. In a word, we need to "open-up"—that is, we need to be open-minded, open-hearted, and to embody openness to ourselves, others, and opportunities. Becoming open requires being mindful of our reactions and judgments, catching ourselves, and shifting to being open to creating solutions with others.

In my work, as an executive and team coach and consultant in organizations, I continually hear about the challenges leaders face when they are unable to influence others effectively. Dealing with others who hold different views or with individuals who seem closed to new and different ideas is often one of the greatest challenges leaders face. They experience frustration and waste time and energy when their efforts to influence are futile.

Organizations have begun to emphasize the importance of collaboration in our diverse world. Those who once succeeded by obtaining results at any cost are now being penalized if they are unable to work effectively with others. Leaders are expected to be emotionally and socially intelligent.

By applying the practical, proven OASIS conversation process provided in these pages—whether you are an executive, professional, manager, teacher, parent, partner, thought leader, or a neighbor, you will be more emotionally and socially intelligent and be more confident about being a positive influence in your interactions.

In this book, you will learn the OASIS Moves for effective conversations with anyone in any situation. Each of the moves draws you closer to experiencing an oasis or a respite where positive and productive interactions can thrive. Research supports that when we are in such an open state, we are more creative and can envision new opportunities. Cues will help you to remember the moves when you need them. You will learn each component of the OASIS Conversation process:

- setting your intention and building rapport
- separating observations from assumptions
- becoming aware of assumptions, emotions, and background conditioning
- shifting from judgment to openness
- identifying what is important to you and others
- developing options and agreeing on solutions

You will benefit from understanding that people have different definitions of respect. You will discover how to work with resistance and difficult situations. You will learn how to embody an open mindset and assess both your inner climate and the relational and social environments in which you move. Finally, you will learn tips for creating habits that use the OASIS Conversation skills.

A mindset is a way of thinking that influences a person's perspective, attitude, and behavior. An open mindset is the belief, perspective, and behavior of being present and aware of "what is" and also anticipating "what is possible or unfolding." An open mindset involves being responsive and welcoming rather than reactive and dismissive. An open mindset involves being curious, compassionate, appreciative, non-judgmental, and optimistic. What are some results for leaders who embody an open mindset and engage in OASIS Conversations? Many report the ability to be centered and present amid turbulence. Open-minded leaders grow to trust themselves. They are able to cultivate the emotions related to high performance. Open-minded leaders have the ability to identify compelling goals and inspire others to see possibilities and become engaged. They are able to create positive climates and cultures that support open conversations enabling positive outcomes. With the mindset of openness, leaders approach others with genuine curiosity and thoughtfulness; they are more apt to ask rather than tell. Open-minded conversations facilitate more engagement, more innovation, and positive results. Embracing the open mindset and OASIS conversational skills will support you in being an effective and successful leader who fulfills your potential and makes a difference in your sphere of influence.

Examples of When to Engage in Open-Minded OASIS Conversations

For a long time, I have been trying to figure out how leaders can create an environment where people with different viewpoints can work together in a satisfying way that still allows productivity to skyrocket. As an organization development consultant, executive coach, and leadership development expert for over twenty-five years, I find challenging situations that consume a lot of energy to be the norm. Let me give you some examples of how this is the case both in the workplace and at home.

At Work

- Detail-oriented Melissa works on a team with Joe, who typically focuses on the big picture—details annoy him.
- Anita, an executive star at a Fortune 100 company, feels that her boss is not supportive of her ideas. She feels exhausted and unappreciated.
- Jeff, who sees himself as creative, considers deadlines a target rather than a fixed point. He reports to Robert, who rules by strict deadlines.
- Managers from a paper company complain that their new teammates from a merger speak French in front of them instead of English. They assume their counterparts are talking negatively about them. The colleagues, speaking their native tongue, believe they deserve a break from the challenge of speaking a second language for hours at a time and see no reason for their teammates' concern.
- While a company president has exceeded his target goals, his

board of directors questions his forthrightness in sharing information. He spends a lot of energy feeling undervalued and not trusted.

- Despite the adage that "the most valuable asset is a truly satisfied customer," few customers in airports or retail clothing stores believe they receive effective service or that their complaints are heard.

At Home

- Some family members differ in how they value saving versus spending money. Others have preferences about how the dishes should be washed. More seriously, they may differ about the nature of the religious beliefs they practice and the best way to raise children. In the realm of everyday matters such as housekeeping, Jerry labels his partner a "pack-rat" and in return is called a "neat freak."
- Neighbors have become polarized over a proposal for a museum to be built in their community that would replace a park. They resort to name calling and labeling each other as "racist" rather than exploring the range of options together.
- A great divide exists where people cannot talk freely to their neighbors and family members who support different candidates and different political solutions.

Few of us have formally learned the skills to have effective conversations that address challenging issues such as these and result in satisfactory interactions. The OASIS Moves detailed in this book will give you a way of assessing what is needed in an interaction and how to create a positive and productive interaction for unparalleled results. Each move represents a component found in productive conversations. Each move has a kinesthetic action that helps you move closer to creating an oasis of possibilities. My hope is these moves will enable you to interact more effectively with others and experience more impact and confidence in influencing others as these moves have done for many others around the globe.

Understanding the following principles has supported me and others in experiencing more effective interactions:

- We all see and experience the world differently based on our backgrounds and conditioning.
- We naturally pay attention to different things.
- We all want respect, yet we each have different definitions of respect.
- We are naturally biased and tend to judge others to protect ourselves.
- When we are in judgment and closed, others naturally become closed and defensive.
- We have a basic human need for empathy and understanding.
- Emotions are contagious.
- When we help others to feel understood, they relax, are more open, and can envision more possibilities.
- When we are clear about our agreements, things go more smoothly and significant change is possible.
- When we have open-minded conversations, we are more satisfied and productive.
- Conversations enable real and substantial change.

One challenge is that we fail to remember these principles when we most need them. OASIS Conversations is a way to recall them and engage in satisfying and productive interactions. The good news is that you can create the habit of engaging in open-minded conversations for better results. You will find OASIS Moves particularly useful in those challenging conversations when you disagree with or misunderstand another person's viewpoint or behavior. You might believe that you are "right" and the other person is "wrong." If you feel particularly strong about your viewpoint, it is time to call on the OASIS Conversation pathway to support you. You can also use the process to assess what is needed in your interactions.

Proven Results

The OASIS Conversation process has been tested with leaders all over the world in organizations such as the United Nations, Cleveland Clinic, GE Capital, Chubb Insurance Group, New York-Presbyterian Hospital, Ford Motor Company, Caterpillar, International Finance Corporation, the World Bank, Consumers Union, and a wide range of nonprofit and private organizations. Many participants have reported significant shifts in how they interact, greater productivity, and more fulfillment. People report that the tools and concepts are easy to remember and they continue to embody an open mindset and employ the OASIS Moves in their daily interactions. Many report that learning the OASIS Conversation Moves has been life-changing. I wish the same for you.

Using OASIS Moves, Jim and Harold, executives of a Fortune 100 company who had been feuding, came to understand each other. Jim was the head of information technology at the corporate headquarters and Harold was responsible for information technology in the company's key business operation responsible for implementing new technology to meet customer demands. Because they could not agree, Harold essentially duplicated Jim's corporate efforts. They ran into a firewall problem that could not be solved by the two of them. Many consultants were brought in at great expense. Finally, I spent a few days with the two of them and taught them the OASIS Conversation process. At first, it was difficult for them to be in the same room. After learning and using OASIS, they created a workable solution that could not have been imagined previously, resulting in multimillion dollar savings.

A consumer goods company acquired a previous rival, but the two company's leaders did not see eye-to-eye. The sales forces continued to compete with one another rather than working together. After learning and using the OASIS Conversation process, leaders came to agreement on fundamental issues, which allowed them to stop wasting energy fighting, gain significant market share, and increase their bottom-line.

Carli, an executive at a Fortune 50 company, contemplated leaving after twenty years of success because she was exhausted from the lack of support by her manager. She believed he did not like working with her, was withholding information, and was not including her in some meetings. She assumed it was because she was a woman and direct in her communication. After some coaching, she tried the OASIS Moves and discovered he was angry because he learned she was complaining about him. After their mindful conversation, he became one of her best supporters. They found common ground and began working well together. Within a short while, Carli was promoted, based on her manager's support.

People using OASIS Conversations in workplaces report that they are enjoying their peers, working more effectively, experiencing less stress, and feeling more engaged at work. Others tell about promotions and advancement in their careers. For instance, Mark went from low performance ratings and almost losing his job to becoming a partner in a major consulting firm. Maddie, a law firm partner, said she now knows how to work more successfully with her staff. Rather than fire a staff member recently, she had an OASIS conversation with him, clarified their expectations of each other, and celebrated his growth into a strong performer. She confesses that she fired many before him when she was unaware of what else she could do. Now she knows the process and can function more effectively.

Others have forged new business partnerships and developed creative innovations, resulting in significant savings and profit. People from different and often differing departments successfully had meaningful conversations, came up with a plan, and took effective steps to support the organization's success. Companies gained significant market share and became more competitive. Many managers conducted fruitful conversations with their staff and colleagues, despite contentious interpretations about expectations. In one organization, some of the most talented staff were leaving because of the leader's demanding expectations. After a meeting using OASIS Moves, Julie, the leader, and her team came to a shared understanding that gave greater flexibility to individuals, but still helped them achieve organizational goals.

Companies acknowledge more satisfactory customer relations and enhanced employee engagement scores. Many individuals report more energy and better health. As you may be aware, the correlation between stress and poorer health has been well-documented.

In one company where OASIS was introduced, 99 percent of managers reported continuing to use the OASIS Conversation process three years after taking a workshop. Ten years later, participants continue to praise the value of OASIS and how the process has improved their work environments. Another client had an outside firm conduct focus groups, interviews, and surveys to assess the impact of its training programs. Programs that taught OASIS Conversations have consistently received the highest scores and praise, even years after people take the workshop. In fact, the organization expanded the OASIS courses to most levels and locations across the world. A Wall Street firm was concerned about low engagement scores and mistrust among staff and management. After OASIS Conversation workshops, post-scores on employee engagement and satisfaction surveys skyrocketed. Tensions between departments and within areas were greatly reduced. The leaders of a Fortune 100 company engaged in OASIS Conversations dealt with longstanding issues and found common ground. The alignment of the senior team positively translated into a smoother running company and better results.

OASIS Conversations have proved valuable across cultures, functions, and levels. It has been shared in many countries around the globe. It has also worked in diverse organizations from manufacturing, financial services, health care, government and non-governmental agencies, privately held companies, and technical and consulting firms.

People using OASIS Moves share that they have more confidence and skill in all of their conversations, and thus, their personal lives are more enjoyable. One couple developed a solution to their ongoing and annoying skirmishes over the use of their TV's remote control! On a much deeper level, many parents enjoy more genuine conversations with their children. Some report having some of their most meaningful connections with adult children, family members, and friends after having used the process.

Finally, the OASIS Conversation pathway will support you in being more emotionally intelligent. Daniel Goleman, author of books and articles on the subject, defines emotional intelligence as the capacity to understand your own and others' emotions, as well as the capacity to motivate and develop oneself and others to improve work performance and enhance organizational effectiveness. Goleman's review of research across various disciplines shows that being emotionally intelligent is a critical ingredient for success. Ninety percent of the difference between outstanding and average leadership is linked to emotional intelligence. Research suggests that emotional intelligence may be the best predictor of success in life, much more than cognitive intelligence or IQ. While there is strong support for emotional intelligence, less information is available on *how* to be emotionally intelligent. The OASIS Conversation process will show you *how*. You will learn how to be more self-aware and to manage your own emotions. You will also become aware of others' emotions and views and be better able to relate to them and create results together.

I am glad to be on this journey with you. I welcome hearing your thoughts and what you learn as you experiment with this process. Please share your insights with me at Ann@Potentials.com.

With regards,

Ann Van Eron
Ann Van Eron, Ph.D.

CHAPTER 1

What Are OASIS Conversations?

An Overview

*"It all depends on how we look at things,
and not on how they are themselves."*

— Carl Jung

An OASIS Conversation is a powerful, five-step, easy-to-grasp process for creating a positive environment and communicating productively with others to produce agreements, solutions, and fulfillment. Each of the "moves" involves an internal awareness and choice of action. Over time, the process becomes seamless for its practitioners, and it is what we do naturally in successful interactions. Knowing the components enables you to assess what may be needed to ensure a positive and productive interaction. The acronym stands for:

O = **Observation**

A = **Awareness** (of assumptions, emotions, and background)

S = **Shift** (to being open)

⌒ = **Importance**

S = **Solution**

OASIS is also a metaphor. What would be possible if you could create the experience of an oasis in your interactions? What if you could turn the desert of miscommunication that exists between you and others into an oasis where you can meet and have a refreshing conversation—one that allows you each to understand where the other is coming from so you can develop empathy and insight and reach mutually beneficial agreements? You and your partners would feel more relaxed and refreshed understanding "what is" and be open to new possibilities.

Let's explore OASIS Moves in detail.

O = Observation

The first move of the OASIS Conversation process is identifying what is observed or heard—separating the data from our assumptions or interpretations. For a reference point, think about the suspenseful '60s TV series *Dragnet*. "Just the facts, ma'am," the main character, a police investigator, would say when interviewing a woman about a particular crime. To observe takes practice. Read the following example.

Imagine you have a regularly scheduled 9:00 a.m. staff meeting and one of your team members arrives at 9:30 a.m.—again. You immediately feel undermined in your authority. After all, this is the third time in a row he has been late. You might think, *He clearly does not respect me.* You wonder whether other team members are watching your reaction. You note that others are also beginning to come late and are not expecting to start right away. After all, if he comes late, why can't they be late? They know he's critical to the meeting and that it probably won't start without him. So you ask yourself: Will anyone turn up on time for next week's meeting? I had to get up early to be here on time. What makes him think the rules don't apply to him?

Your emotions have to do with your judgment of the situation and the assumptions you have made. However, they are *not* the observable data or the facts. Your observation (without interpretation) is simply that a staff member arrived at 9:30 a.m. three times in a row when the meetings were scheduled for 9:00 a.m.

A = Awareness of assumptions, emotions, and background, all of which prompt us to judge the situation

After noting your observation(s), it's important to be aware of the assumptions, emotions, and background experiences that influence your thinking. These are separate from your observation and lead to judgment.

Assumptions: You might assume that the person who arrived at

9:30 doesn't care about being on time or is not committed to the team. Or you could assume something's wrong. Regardless, it is important to be aware.

Emotions: You might notice tightness in your chest and feel angry or disappointed when the team member arrives at 9:30 instead of 9:00. Identify your emotions by noting your sensations and by completing the sentence "I feel _____" with one word. Using this example, you might notice, "I feel disappointed."

Background: You might have had the background experience of working with another colleague who was often late, so you are reminded about that person's lack of reliability. Maybe you recall a parent telling you it is unacceptable to be late. Your background includes your past experiences, standards, and expectations.

S = Shift (to being open)

Notice your internal reaction or signal. Then stop, step back, suspend reacting to your judgment, and shift your perspective and stance to being more open. Most of us have a physiological reaction when we are judging and believe the other is wrong. We also have an internal voice or conversation that says, among other things, that we are "right" and the other "wrong." We can learn to identify our judgment signals. At this point, it is critical to substitute judgment with openness to and curiosity about the other person's perspective. This involves activating a different part of the brain that is creative and open to possibility. Others sense when we are open rather than judging.

Perhaps you have judged the team member who arrived late as unreliable. You may be thinking, "I am right and he's wrong." Often, people experience a recurring signal when they make judgments. Internal signals vary from person to person. Yours could be a tightening of your stomach or jaw or another physical cue. If your emotions are strong, the OASIS Conversation process has strategies for cooling down. When you notice your judgment signal, remind yourself to assume positive intent and remember your intention to create an OASIS experience with the other person and become open to the possibilities.

I = Importance

Now that you're open, you are ready to communicate. When you say, "I've noticed that for the past three weeks, you've arrived at 9:30 for the 9:00 a.m. meeting," you are calm and not being accusatory. As you ask questions of the other person and listen actively, the task is to focus on what is important to you, what is important to the other person, and what is important to you both. You seek understanding.

What you discover is that your team member has been late because he has another meeting at 8:00 a.m. in a distant building across the corporate campus. Your colleague sent you an e-mail some time ago and assumed you recalled he would be attending these other meetings. You don't recall the e-mail and recognize that you don't always read all of your messages. You share that you have missed the input of this individual and that his absence has had an impact. Perhaps others are coming late because they think if he can, they can too; others may simply be irritated that he is late. You also are wasting valuable time by repeating important information when he comes in—time you don't have to waste because you are two days behind on project Z.

This move of the OASIS process is about increasing understanding. You end up with a statement like, "We are both committed to our team working well and making headway on this project. Given that it is important for you to attend the other meetings and it is important for me to have you included in our team discussion and update, what are our options?" If it were not a misunderstanding and oversight, as in this case, you would still want to understand what was going on for the other person and express your needs and what is important to you. When joint goals exist, there is incentive to find a solution.

S = Solution

After you understand what is important to all involved, you then explore possible options and solutions. You could change the time or location of the meeting, your colleague could call in from a cell phone, the staff member could provide a written report that could be read, etc. This is where you both agree on what each of you will do—what concrete behavior or action each of you will take. Your team member may agree to poll other staff members about their availability for an alternate meeting time. You may agree to change the meeting if the rest of the team can make another time. What could have become a negative situation now has become an opportunity to connect with each other.

Many managers and teammates have struggled over such situations. One of my clients, Jim, actually fired a staff member publicly when he was late for the third time to a staff meeting. Jim, the manager, was new to the organization and intuitively "knew" he was not being respected by this longtime employee. Engulfed by his anger, Jim told the staff member to leave immediately. This action cost Jim a lot in respect with his other colleagues, since everyone but Jim knew the staff member had a long-standing arrangement to arrive late because of family obligations. (Luckily, this issue was re-addressed in a more positive way soon after.)

The OASIS Conversation process works in many complicated situations because it helps you to understand your response and to remain open-minded so you can understand others without judgment and come to a mutually satisfying agreement. If an employee is coming late to meetings because he or she doesn't value meetings and you believe they are important, the process will support you when you talk about it with him or her.

In contrast to the example above, Mike, a group leader, was able to slow down and be open to hearing why his staff member, Julie, was having difficulty getting to meetings on time or at all. Julie was in sales, so she was often on the road and meeting with clients at the meeting time Mike had established. After exploring what was important to each of them, they agreed that reaching sales targets was most important. Mike needed to be kept informed and provided information, while Julie needed to meet with key clients when they were most available—hence, the conflict around meeting time. They agreed on an arrangement that worked for both of them so each felt respected and valued. In this case, Julie would inform Mike in advance if she would not be at a meeting and she would provide a written update. She took responsibility for getting information from her coworkers. By using OASIS Moves, Mike and Julie had a conversation that saved their relationship. Both felt satisfied and they achieved their business goals.

OASIS Conversations enable us to complete the circuit that connects us with others. Just as incredible power exists in an electrical connection, equal or greater power exists in those magical moments of human connection. OASIS Conversations empower us to create those magical moments every day, which means more creative, productive, and harmonious relationships. Then, we actually experience an *oasis* with each other. I personally use these skills daily—with my colleagues, family, clients, and neighbors, and they have made a wonderful difference in my life. My clients in organizations around the globe report the same satisfaction and positive results. Your own sustained practice will allow you to use OASIS Moves increasingly quickly and effectively in ever more challenging moments. The process works when conversing with one person or with a group. Think carefully about some of your most challenging interactions as you read the rest of this book. Next, plan your conversations with the people involved.

In summary, you will benefit from this book when you:

- Learn the OASIS Conversation process, and work to incorporate it into your life.
- Practice using OASIS Moves in your interactions.
- Commit to creating an environment of openness and respect.
- Discover your questions.
- Reinforce the concepts.

In the next chapter, I will define and investigate the meaning of respect, a critical ingredient for effectively influencing others and producing results. Then we will examine how to prepare for OASIS Conversations. The chapters that follow explore each of the OASIS Moves: Observation (O), Awareness (A), Shift (S), Importance (I), and Solution (S). Then, in Chapter 10: Putting It All Together, you will review a successful OASIS Conversation and learn how to work most effectively with resistance. Next, we will explore how to work with especially challenging situations where there are struggles. We will highlight some stances that support having an open mindset. Finally, we will explore ways to build the OASIS Moves habits and provide support for your journey.

CHAPTER 2

Respect

The Foundation of OASIS Conversations (Intent Does Not Equal Impact in a World of Differences)

"The basic building block of good communication is the feeling that every human being is unique and of value."

— Author Unknown

OASIS Conversations

Have a clear intention, plan when possible, and build rapport.

O = **Observation**

A = **Awareness** (of assumptions, emotions, and background)

S = **Shift** (to being open)

⁀⁀ = **Importance**

S = **Solution**

The head of a large division of a multinational organization asked me to work with his group. Productivity had plummeted and staff members were complaining that they didn't feel respected. Employee surveys reported that engagement and morale were low and trust for the leader and of each other was a huge negative. The leader didn't know what to do since the climate seemed to be worsening. His encouraging talks no longer worked.

My private interviews with his staff members confirmed the same results—they did not feel respected. Most seemed surprised when I asked them to explain their experience of disrespect. They found it so obvious. Their concerns included fellow workers not saying hello and goodbye, passing in the hallway with no acknowledgment, gossiping, talking or laughing too loudly, not informing others when taking breaks, arriving late for meetings, not looking people directly in the eye when talking, and not listening. Other issues were using the microwave to cook food like stuffed cabbage or popcorn, the smells of which some found offensive, bringing up irrelevant topics in meetings, which wasted time—and the list continued. Most assured me they had made efforts to be respectful of their colleagues. They could not understand the "rude" behavior of some of their peers.

I then met with team members in groups to explore their concerns. I asked them to observe my behavior and notice their responses as I simulated entering their workplace during a typical day. I took my briefcase and walked into their office without looking up or acknowledging the other team members. I proceeded directly to my desk, turned on my computer, and began reviewing my email.

Afterward, I asked participants what they experienced. One person said, "You got it right! That's how it is here." Most said they found my behavior disrespectful or rude. Some suggested that I should have said, "Good morning!" I asked whether all agreed. One team member, Pat, said she saw my behavior of entering, including not saying good morning, as quite respectful. (Others had told me that she enters their workplace in a similar way.) From her perspective, not saying good morning was the "right" thing to do in this work setting. The team members needed to review and approve documents. Office members had a flextime arrangement, which meant people started and finished at different times and took their breaks at will. Pat found it to be a burden to be constantly interrupted as people came in. She chose not to "disturb" others by saying good morning so no one's workflow would be broken.

Intent Does Not Equal Impact

Pat's logic made sense to her, and her intent was to support people. Unfortunately, others did not experience Pat's simple act of not greeting people as positive. Instead, the negative impact on some was palpable. For example, Shirley found Pat's behavior rude. She complained to others about Pat—saying Pat considered herself above the rest. Shirley then chose not to speak to Pat and encouraged her colleagues to follow her lead. Pat didn't understand why some of her colleagues seemed not to like her, but she certainly felt the cold hostility. Her response was to stay away from her coworkers. You can imagine the self-fulfilling prophecy for Shirley. She noticed that Pat did not engage with her much. This confirmed for her that Pat was arrogant. Shirley became even more closed to Pat and did not want to work with her. Others joined in, and without much discussion, the tension and mistrust in this office grew.

Soon individuals were bothered by a host of small infractions. Little discussion about the problem of low morale occurred. Team members just became more dissatisfied, and more disengaged. They did not extend themselves even in small ways to one another. In fact, not helping others became an unwritten norm. Many reported they no longer enjoyed coming to work and interacting with their colleagues. As you can surmise, this misunderstanding sucked up a lot of energy—energy that could have been devoted to getting the work done together. Sadly, this situation is not uncommon.

Trust Is Essential

We are constantly assessing our environments and interactions to determine whether we can trust others. This assessment can happen very quickly and intuitively. When we interact with others, we have biochemical and neurochemical responses. We read a person's energy and respond to electrical and other signals. We react based on our past experiences, and we decide whether we can or cannot trust the other. When faced with a threat or uncertainty, we are more likely to activate a part of the brain located in the amygdala that is associated with the survival response of fight, flight, freeze, or appease. We move to a state of distrust, becoming closed and protective. We all have experienced the negative impact of conversations where we and others are distrustful. On the other hand, we achieve connection and even fulfillment when we experience trust in an interaction. When the brain's prefrontal cortex is activated, we see possibilities, experience hope, and have productive and valuable interactions. Conversations can build a trusting environment, and trust supports positive and productive conversations. Also, negative conversations can create untrustworthy interactions.

Our amygdala is attuned to picking up threats. We assess and decide whether the other person is a friend or foe. When we choose foe, we close down, tend to believe we are "right" and the other is "wrong," and can get stuck in our viewpoint. From the place of distrust, it is hard to see another's perspective or to have empathy and demonstrate caring. This result happened to most members of this team—they lost creative energy for their work and became focused on surviving. When we pick up this negative, closed energy, we, in turn, often become closed ourselves. In reality, we are not in such life-threatening situations often. A critical skill is to be aware of our interactions and take steps to build trust and a sense of openness. Trust and openness are the foundation for having candid and connecting conversations that can generate positive results.

Assume Positive Intent

After the dialogue in our workshop using OASIS Moves, Shirley and her peers understood Pat's positive intention of not interrupting them by speaking to them in the morning. They relaxed a bit and became more open to her. Team members were able to forgive each other for some of their unsupportive behavior.

Most of us view a person's behavior, attribute a motive to it, and more often than not, tend to assume negative intent. Just the awareness of a person's positive intent can change the way we respond to that person. In turn, our response often changes how the person responds to us. Unfortunately, many people never discuss their assumptions. Misconceptions linger and impact relationships and outcomes. Sometimes, people are angry or upset and take actions that hurt others and themselves. People are often willing to forgive these acts once an OASIS Conversation occurs and a better understanding is reached.

As a facilitator, I worked with this team to air some of their different perceptions. After we discussed them, the team members developed new agreements about how to work together and help each other. The team developed a more positive environment and became more productive. Much less energy was drained away by being angry and distrustful of each other. When I followed up later, team members reported they felt more positive about coming to work and interacting with one another.

I feel sad to think about the huge amounts of energy wasted on these kinds of issues, which deplete people and take focus away from the work to be accomplished. We all know how draining it is when we believe coworkers or others don't respect us, don't support us, and may act against us. This environment creates distrust and suspicion of motives. I use the metaphor of the desert to refer to this kind of interaction. Trust is critical for effective relationships and creating positive results with others. It is valuable to be mindful of our interactions and to ensure that we work to create an open-minded and respectful climate. I think of such an open and generative state as an oasis. A useful question to ask yourself as you interact with others is, "Are we experiencing an oasis, or are we in the desert?" In other words, "Have we created an open and trusting climate or are we closed to one another?"

Saying Good Morning: Yes or No?

You might think it is obvious that people should say hello and there need not be ground rules about how to greet each other and work together. Everyone should know how to behave.

Interestingly, when I ask groups of people in various organizations whether they say, "Good morning!" to their colleagues, I hear a range of responses. In some parts of the world, like the South in the United States, people routinely greet each other in offices, and even strangers are greeted with enthusiasm in shops and on the street as they pass by. In some countries, such as France, office mates greet each other formally. They say, "Bonjour, Monsieur Bonhomme"—using surnames rather than first names—even when they have known each other and worked together for years. In some offices, people tend to get right to their email; they don't greet each other and that's accepted. In a New York company where I worked, most people did not say good morning. In a hospital, a manager greeted people in the morning, and one day, out of curiosity, counted the number who responded. He told me that number was less than 30 percent! Since he is widely considered a friendly and well-liked person, I thought he might be exaggerating unintentionally. However, others verified this lack of responsiveness.

We learn the simple behavior of whether and how to say good morning from our early caregivers, families, and schools. We learn the norms in our workplaces by observing. For example, when my daughter was quite young, even before age three, I encouraged her to greet the doormen in our condominium in Chicago. Once when I was on a business trip, I called my husband and asked whether he was reminding her to say hello. He was. He had the same expectations of her, even though we had not discussed them. However, I noticed that other parents did not have the same standard for greetings from their children. For example, a mother in New York City told me she did not want to encourage her son to say hello to people. She worried about his safety. Once a workshop participant said she had moved from a small town where it was the norm to greet each other. One morning, she was on the street, saying, "Hi!" to her neighbors in a large city. A police officer patrolling on a horse said, "Lady, you are going to get in trouble if you say 'Hi' to so many people here." Another person said that no one spoke in the mornings in her home since her mother did not like to interact in the morning. Later, she kept the practice with her own family and in the workplace.

The point is that even for such a simple act as greeting people, most of us learned early from our caregivers and experiences what we consider the "right" behavior. Without thinking, we follow our habitual patterns. While our intentions may be positive, we are often unaware of our conditioned behavior's impact on others.

In one client organization, at mid-morning every day a senior level executive would walk around a nearby office of people who reported to him. His office was located on a different floor. He typically said very little and, according to him, was just trying to make himself available. Since he did not clarify his intentions, some staff members interpreted his behavior as "checking on them" and became angry at his perceived lack of trust. The manager was shocked when he heard this interpretation. I have also experienced situations where staff members were upset that their manager rarely visited or interacted with them. These people, in contrast to the others, expected a manager to come and inquire about their activities.

Whether it is frustration that dirty dishes have been left on the counter in the shared work kitchen or a complaint about someone not holding a door open for the person behind him, we each have different expectations for even the simplest behaviors. We are each influenced by what we have learned from our pasts.

Comedian Rodney Dangerfield always complained, "I don't get no respect." We may laugh at this statement because we'd rather laugh than cry. We crave respect. However, the challenge is that we each have a different definition of respect. For most Americans, respect is looking others in the eye when talking. Others, for example, some Asians and Africans, believe it is more respectful not to look elders or other highly respected people directly in the eyes. Some think it is respectful to use e-mail rather than call someone, so as not to disturb the person. Another feels disrespected when someone doesn't call. We each tend to think that our idea of respect is the "right" way while another way is "wrong."

What Is Respect?

This issue of respect is a funny thing. We each feel we know it when we see it. Universally, people agree that they want to be respected and that they share the belief that others should be respectful. Most report that they are respectful of others. We all feel we know what respect is, and yet, in countless conversations with people worldwide, perspectives and views differ about what specific behavior is respectful.

The Latin word "spect" means to see and "re" means again. Respect means to look again and see each person as an individual. Because of human nature, we initially may categorize someone as belonging to a certain group because of a certain feature such as his or her appearance. For example, we may label someone as a doctor or an administrator based on her clothes, or as young or old based on his hair color. Once we identify someone as an accountant, for instance, we then tend to believe we know what we need to know about the person. This is useful as a quick way of focusing. However, to be respectful, we need to slow down, take another look, and see a unique individual with many facets. It does not feel good to be categorized by a single dimension or even a few characteristics. For example, I don't want people to see me just as a consultant or an author. Also, I am not like other women, mothers, or people my age. I want to be seen and related to as a unique individual.

When we feel respected and appreciated for who we are, we have more energy and enthusiasm to bring to a workplace, school, community, or family. When we don't feel respected, our energy and attention is shifted to protecting ourselves. When we feel respected, we have more energy to respect and value others. When managers feel respected, they have energy to respect staff members who pass that energy on to clients and customers. This ripple effect has been demonstrated in organizations and communities and documented by research.

You may want to think of relationships where you do not feel respected and address those situations. The OASIS Moves will support you in having an effective conversation that results in agreement about what is respectful. In addition, the conversation itself will be perceived as respectful.

Our Background

We each assume we know what respect is, based on our personal experiences. Caregivers and teachers spend a lot of time emphasizing signs of respect. I often encourage my young daughter to say "Good morning!" and "Please" and "Thank you." I remind her about holding doors open for others, letting others help themselves first at a meal or get on the elevator first, telling people what she appreciates about them, and writing thank-you notes. Others reinforce my teachings by praising my daughter for her polite and respectful behavior. She experiences the benefit of being respectful. I'm confident that she will continue such behavior as she becomes an adult. She may also teach her children similar acts of respect.

However, not every child learns the same behaviors. Different actions are emphasized in different households and neighborhoods, depending on what seems most important—time and energy permitting. We need to appreciate that different forms of respect are emphasized in different families, communities, and cultures. For example, Nisha, who is from India, always brings a gift when visiting.

The golden rule has been taught in our schools and churches: "Treat others how you want to be treated." Actually, we need to "treat others how *they* want to be treated." I remember when a friend was very excited about the gift he had bought his wife for a holiday. He told me it was a set of car tires! That, by the way, was the very thing he had said he would love to receive. Reports were that she was not as excited about the tires as he was.

To respect another person, first have the intent to be respectful. We need to make an effort to see the person as a unique individual. Then we need to consider what is most important and what would best meet the other's needs. We can gather this information from observation or asking that person or others close to him or her. After taking action, we need to pay attention and observe whether the person receives it as a sign of respect, as we intended. If not, we can have an OASIS Conversation to learn more and determine what to do next.

The Mindset of Respect

It is useful to assume that others have positive intent and are not trying to hurt or bother us. We can then inquire to learn more. I believe each of us is generally doing the best we know how, based on our conditioning and perspectives, and we want to be appreciated for our situations. Adopting this mindset supports us in being more open and respectful. In turn, others are likely to be more respectful of us. This open mindset supports taking action together and working well with others at work, school, home, and in the community. Sensing we are respected allows us to relax, feel safe, and be more trusting. Respect in the workplace fosters trusting relationships. A trusting environment supports taking action together and living in harmony with others at work, home, and in your community. Trust is the glue that holds groups together to work through issues and create positive results together. Without trust, a lot of energy is devoted to protecting ourselves—energy that could be focused on innovation and action.

Respect and the Brain Connection

Brain research at the University of California, San Francisco[1] shows that we each have a neurological capacity known as "limbic resonance." This capacity allows us to sense when we are respected, trusted, or valued by others. The limbic region, one of the oldest parts of the brain, is sometimes referred to as the "reptilian" part. It registers whether we feel safe or we fear danger is lurking. When we feel respected, we get a cue that allows us to relax and coordinate with others. Scientists who examine the brains of people who respect one another see similar brain waves and what is called entrainment. This coherent pattern leads to resonance (or amplification) of these waves with an increased sense of trust. For this reason, showing people that we respect, trust, and value them generates positive results. Thus, learning how to respect others and communicate it effectively is an extremely valuable skill.

When we experience a sense of trust, it's called resonance. Distrust triggers dissonance. When distrust exists between people, scientists have observed that brain waves are not in sync and appear disparate.

---

1 For more information, see: Lewis, T., Amini, F. & Lannon, R. *A General Theory of Love.* New York: Random House, 2000.

People experience discomfort and spend their energy managing it rather than on working together. Research by the Heartmath Institute[2] shows that humans and mammals have the capacity to tune into others' inner states and experience a sense of trust (leading to amplification of brain waves) or distrust (leading to dissonance of the brain waves). When people feel respected and trusted, their limbic system gives them the message they are safe so they become more open to being and working with others and their ideas. Learning to respect others and build trust is critical for success.

I have worked with many organizations where dissonance and distrust have become the norm. People spend their time and energy talking about each other and about what is wrong, rather than being innovative and creating productive results. Luckily, I have seen trust and a positive environment created when they learn the OASIS Moves and start having effective conversations.

Use OASIS Conversations to Identify Respectful Behavior

Since our definitions of respectful behavior vary, we need to sharpen the skills of talking constructively with each other to learn more. OASIS Conversations will support you in promoting more respect.

I often work with teams to have OASIS Conversations about what they need to feel respected. In one company, a manager said she wanted people to walk into her office at the scheduled meeting time. This supported her in closing the meeting she was finishing and staying on time. Another manager in the same office found it more respectful for staff to wait outside his office even if he were running late. Another person said she would feel more respected if people did not "borrow" staplers and tape off of her desk without asking her. Someone else asked that people not speak to her as they approached her desk. Often, she was occupied and speaking on a phone headset. People were not aware of it since her long hair hid the phone. Another person experienced respect when her peers in the office pitched in and helped her finish a project at the end of the day. People who spend time together need to have conversations about what is important to them as signs of respect. A periodic review of how people are doing in supporting some of these behaviors will prove useful, too.

---

2 Learn more at www.heartmath.org/research

One work team in a hospital had been given the organization's lowest customer service score. The team members met and agreed on eight actions they could take to support more respect among their group. For example, they agreed to call each other by their first names and to greet people by name. They also agreed to walk clients to their next appointment. Within a year, this team had moved from the lowest to the highest rating and received an award for its customer service responsiveness! The actions the team members took were simple and cost the organization very little. All staff reported feeling better about coming to work and felt more valued. Morale, motivation, and employee engagement were significantly enhanced. What improved the situation was an OASIS Conversation and agreement among the team members on solutions.

It is important to recognize how the environment you create with others directly influences results. In a negative or disrespectful environment, less energy and attention are available for creativity and using team diversity to create positive results. Research reported in the December 2013 *Harvard Business Review* supports that the best solutions come from cohesive teams with diverse backgrounds and perspectives. Creating a positive environment is critical for success, and the OASIS Conversation process will help you to create a respectful environment.

Before we close this chapter, here are some practices for you to work on to become more respectful.

Practice

- Pay attention to what you identify as respectful behavior. Keep a list and then notice how your background experiences and conditioning influence you to identify, for example, holding doors open for others as respectful.
- Talk with people in your family, community, workplace, or school and listen to what each one identifies as respectful behavior. List items on a chart and agree on those you will try to emphasize. Later, come back and ask people how they are experiencing respect. Talk about what else is needed to support an environment of respect and trust.
- Pay attention to the people in your home, workplace, and community. Do you sense they feel valued and respected by you?

What do you notice? Which relationships could benefit from an OASIS Conversation to identify how to support an experience of respect?

In this chapter, we explored how everyone desires to be respected, but we cannot assume that everyone defines respect in the same way. By observing others and having open-minded communications with them, we can create an oasis of respect that will allow us to work together as a team to achieve our desired results.

Now that we understand what constitutes respect, let's examine the OASIS Moves in detail in the following chapters.

CHAPTER 3

Preparing for an OASIS Conversation

Have a Clear Intention, Plan When Possible, and Build Rapport

"Act as if what you do makes a difference. It does."

— William James

OASIS Conversations

Have a clear intention, plan when possible, and build rapport.

O = **Observation**

A = **Awareness** (of assumptions, emotions, and background)

S = **Shift** (to being open)

I = **Importance**

S = **Solution**

You can use OASIS Moves as a planning tool before holding conversations as well as a guide during interactions. One senior executive, who was known for being tough and not open to new ideas, went right from a briefing I gave on the OASIS approach to discuss a difficult situation with a member of his staff. He referenced a card[3] listing the OASIS

---

3   Visit www.OASISConversations.com to obtain a copy of the OASIS Conversation handout for an easy reminder of the process.

Moves prompts and followed the moves during the conversation. He had dreaded and postponed the conversation for a long time. Later, he sent an e-mail to me saying how much easier the conversation was because of the OASIS Moves and how glad he was to have achieved a mutually satisfying resolution. The executive became a believer in the OASIS Conversation process and recommended that all the executives and staff in the organization learn and use it.

At times, you will be faced with initiating a challenging conversation. Perhaps you don't feel comfortable with a particular person. You may have a difficult message to communicate or simply be unsure of how to bring up an issue. We all get stuck anticipating challenging conversations. When this happens, habitual conversation patterns take over with predictable outcomes.

How does Brian inquire about his concerns on a project? How does Sid ask for a raise? How does Marilee tell her husband she is upset about their finances and agree on action without creating discord? How does Chris talk to her brother about how to support their elderly parents? Some of us feel confident bringing up difficult issues; however, we are not sure why we are not getting the outcomes we want. Many of us do well with some parts of the communication process, such as offering our observations, but we are less skilled on other parts such as providing understanding.

We each have habitual patterns for how we communicate. Without awareness, we keep doing what we always have done and continue getting similar results. For instance, Liza yells when she is angry, while Pete, her spouse, says nothing when he is upset. Allie ignores people who have different views while Pamela uses logic to convince people they are wrong. Mack jumps to action before understanding concerns, and Zoey is dissatisfied because she somehow makes commitments she doesn't want to honor. All experience consequences from their habitual patterns.

Plan When Necessary

Conversations are most satisfying and productive when each move of the OASIS process is included. As you review the actions involved, pay attention to those you find natural and easy and those where you can use practice. I encourage you to experiment and notice how they work for you. You might want to find people to practice with you. That way, you can give each other feedback and begin to build the neural pathways for having OASIS Conversations. You are invited to go to www.OASISConversations.com to learn about practice groups.

Brain Connection

Neuroscience studies show that we have many neural connections (maps) in our brains that influence how we perceive situations and take actions. The more we use a neural pathway, the stronger it becomes and the more easily it is triggered. It is useful to be aware of what is important to you. By reinforcing these beliefs, you more readily act on them.

Neuroplasticity research shows that we can learn to create new patterns that will work better for us. Ideally, these new paths become habits that we can use without a lot of effort.

Our brains experience different states. We can be stressed and judgmental, or we can be in a more calm state where our brains feel more balanced. In the balanced state, our neural pathways communicate quickly and effectively; we feel whole and comfortable. We feel glad to be alive. In this state, we may feel a sense of being in the flow, and we can learn from our experiences and make adjustments as needed. When we consciously use the OASIS Moves, we are acting from this state, and the more often we do so, the more it will become a habit and seem natural. The practices at the end of each chapter will help you to exercise your brain muscles so you can act from this state with more ease.

Apply What You Learn

I want this book to be practical and useful for you. As you read, focus on people and situations where you can enhance your relationships and your outcomes. Perhaps you want to talk with your family members about helping with chores or you want to improve your relationship with your boss. Identify a specific situation where you would like to have a conversation. Then plan the conversation as you review each chapter. Here are three examples of such situations: 1) Tina feels her assistant is not committed to helping her and would like to develop a system in which they keep each other apprised. 2) Gretchen is upset with her new boss because she gave a coveted assignment to another professional. 3) John wants to know whether his contract will be renewed, and he wants feedback on his work.

Energy is being spent on making up stories and assumptions by each of those involved in these scenarios (all of which are real). By planning and coming to the interaction with an open, curious state, each person can help to keep the conversation focused on what will build the relationship and support productivity.

Develop an action plan for how you will have an OASIS Conversation. For example, become aware of your assumptions and emotions and what is important to you. After that, make an educated guess about what might be important to the person you plan to converse with. I promise that your preparation will pay off.

Use Reminders

I will give you cues to remember each move. To make it more real for you, I suggest you draw a map and take notes. The more you pay attention to the OASIS Moves, the more naturally they will be a part of how you communicate. My hope is that you will experience more satisfying interactions and get the results you desire.

By the time you finish reading this book, you will be able to remember each of the moves for having successful OASIS Conversations. The acronym, images, and physical reminders will support you in remembering them as needed. Of course, practice will best support you in remembering what works. You will be able to use OASIS Moves in the moment when faced with provocative statements or questions. When you feel the need, you can plan before particularly challenging conversations. It's always useful to practice or plan with a friend before high stakes conversations.

Bring a Clear and Positive Intention

Bring an open mind to your interactions. As you begin the journey of OASIS Conversations, I suggest you declare the following intentions: to bring an open stance commitment to building rapport and finding common ground, to be authentic, and to be present.

Call to mind your intention for an interaction. It's powerful to name your intention for a conversation, at least to yourself, the person you'll converse with, or others. By consciously declaring your intention, you are more likely to move toward this picture. For those more challenging relationships, it is useful to remind yourself frequently. For example, you might say to yourself, "Jeff and I are communicating clearly and building a trusting relationship. We experience an oasis together and create great results together." In addition to seeing a picture, it is useful to notice how you are likely to feel in your body as your intention is realized. Perhaps you notice yourself relaxing and feeling more playful as you envision your intention being fulfilled. As you shift your body position, you will be more open so Jeff is more likely to experience you as such.

When my intention is to create an oasis-like environment with my coworkers, I remind myself of my oasis image. An oasis is a refuge in a desert area made fertile by the presence of water. It is a peaceful place in the midst of turbulent surroundings. Perhaps you have been somewhere like that and have even called it an oasis. Or you may want to imagine a place in nature that you find beautiful and peaceful. I recall that I want to use the OASIS Moves and skills to create an open, respectful environment where my conversation partner and I are both relaxed and can understand what is most important. Then we can develop solutions where we both feel like winners. I want to build a satisfying community around me of people who can come to agreement on goals and actions. I want to understand others and to be understood. I envision satisfying and productive relationships.

Try to assume positive intent. Remind yourself that people are generally doing the best they know how. Even behavior you perceive as intended to hurt may not be what it appears. I find that often people are reacting to challenges in a system and simply don't know what to do. For example, some people feel that in a competitive environment, they need to be competitive. Make it your goal to stay open and create a sense of openness and curiosity in the interaction. Notice your judgment and hold off from taking any action you may regret later.

Be aware of the current situation as well as the long-term intent for a relationship. If a person has not completed a report she promised, try to figure out how to get it completed. How can such situations be avoided in the future? Every interaction can be an opportunity to strengthen the relationship and support achieving goals together. Once you have worked through a potential misunderstanding, disagreement, or even a failure to deliver on a task, the two of you have a history to draw on. You will have the confidence that you can work things out together as a team.

What is an oasis for you? A friend told me that when he was in Morocco, he would drive in the stark desert for miles, and then quite suddenly, he would see an oasis. Out of the hot bleak desert would emerge large palm trees, water, and a whole town of aliveness. The contrast between the arid desert and the green lush oasis really stood out for him. Janet, a friend, imagines a beach house in Sanibel Island, Florida, where she visits annually as a place of safety, nurturance, and rejuvenation. Develop your own picture of an oasis.

For me, an oasis conjures up an image of a holiday with palm trees, beautiful nature, warmth from the sun, nourishing fruit, and refreshing water. It is a place where I feel relaxed and open to possibilities. I like to feel that way in my conversations. When I am relaxed and open, communication is more satisfying and productive. My goal is to support myself in being open and in feeling like I am in an oasis of abundance. Such feelings are contagious and encourage others to be open, too. When we can stop ourselves from being closed or judging, then we can open ourselves to experience an oasis with others. I remind myself that I am confident and I can handle whatever comes up in a conversation. I trust that after learning the OASIS Moves, you will feel the same way.

Jackie, a leader I coach, was perceived by her coworkers as harsh, too quick, and unapproachable. Her intention was to create a more welcoming, oasis-like environment with her staff and colleagues. Her image of an oasis was relaxing in an outdoor café in Italy with friends. As she set the intention of experiencing such an oasis with her colleagues and learned the OASIS Moves, we saw dramatic improvement in her interactions. She was able to be calmer and refrain from making judgments, so people felt less defensive. Using OASIS, Jackie caught herself and refrained from responding with quick-witted barbs that made people feel inferior. Instead, she became interested and listened to colleagues. At first, they were surprised, but then they welcomed her listening and more open manner. Within a remarkably short time, her reputation became more positive. Her staff believed that she was really listening to them. She really was open for dialogue and their suggestions were taken. The whole tone of the department changed to being more relaxed. Soon even clients remarked that they sensed a difference—an openness to new ideas and innovation.

When you are skilled at creating this kind of experience in your interactions, you will be effective in creating the results most important to you.

Open Mindset

Make it your intention to adapt an open mindset where you are open to and appreciate "what is" and what's unfolding as well as are optimistic about what is possible. This involves having an open-mind (curious), open-heart (compassionate), open-gut (courageous), and open-hands (welcoming and non-judgmental). Your goal is to be responsive and welcoming rather than reactive and dismissing. After reviewing your intentions before an important conversation, notice how you feel and how you are presenting yourself. Ask yourself, "Am I open or closed?" If you feel closed, you may have your arms crossed. Others typically interpret this position as being in a closed-minded state. Sometimes, I find that I am anxious or in judgment of the other person. If I am closed, others are also more likely to become closed. If I am intent on a goal, I remind myself to focus on understanding before pushing for a solution. I try to relax myself, and then I open my heart and arms to supporting openness in the relationship.

An open-minded conversation literally means you are "open" to what the other person has to say. You are focused on gaining a clearer understanding of what he or she is telling you—without evaluating or judging. You cannot begin an open-minded conversation when you are convinced you're "right" and the other person is "wrong." An open mindset allows you to "hear" the other person with an appreciation for his or her perspective.

While there may be times when I feel like I am struggling with others in the desert, I try to keep myself open-minded and curious. Focus on expecting to find an oasis of connection, shared understanding, and positive results.

The challenge in dealing with our differences is that at times we each believe we are "right" while the other is "wrong." The human condition is to judge everything, whether or not we realize we are doing it. Since each of us filters everything we experience through our own unique background and perceptions of the world, judgment is inherent.

Without an awareness of this human condition, we may often misinterpret what we experience. Still, we regard our assumptions as indisputable fact! Such assumptions can translate to misunderstandings, disputes, and lost opportunities. If we own a business or are in management, the result is often compromised morale, productivity, and profitability. Make it your intention to have an open mindset. We will explore how to do this in the following chapters.

Build Rapport

Have the intention of connecting with people by building rapport and finding common ground with them. Build rapport before launching into giving feedback or stating a need. People who are socially adept find this process easy and natural. Others say that they don't find what they may call "small talk" easy.

Building rapport helps the person you are talking with to feel at ease and open to you and the conversation. By smiling and showing some interest, you help others feel safe and understand that you are not likely to hurt them. Inquire about or share information about something you have in common. Topics could be the weather, the commute, sports, children, vacations, something happening in the news, a company development, or health.

In workshops, I ask people to share something about themselves with the group. As we share about ourselves, we are a bit vulnerable. Invariably, in these brief conversations, participants begin to build rapport and feel connected. We often feel alone or feel that others don't connect with what we do. When we build rapport, we feel less alone and more connected with others.

It is human nature to feel connected when we have shared a similar experience. One participant felt connected with someone who went to his high school, even though they had never met and went at different times. They felt they shared similar experiences. We want to be understood. Even on small issues, having some shared experiences helps us feel understood and see another as more of a friend than a foe.

We look for these connections naturally. When we first meet someone, we look for common ground. For instance, when we learn we both have young children, we relax a bit since we feel more understood by this stranger. Strangers can easily talk about the weather since both are experiencing it. Even a brief comment about how nice it is finally to see the arrival of spring creates a sense of connection in an elevator conversation.

Find something you have in common with others. The following conversation openers will help:

- Do you come from a large family?
- Do you like action movies?
- Did you see the television show last night; can you believe the news?
- How about that player and sports team?
- I understand from Joe that you love photography, too.
- It sounds like your children have the same musical interest as mine.
- I see from the bag you're carrying that you also go shopping at….
- Do you like my shoes?

You don't always have to build rapport immediately before an OASIS Conversation. If you make the effort to talk with a person and connect with her regularly, then when it is time for your conversation, the other person will already know you are friendly. If a power differential exists between you—you are the person's manager, for example—remember to show interest in the other person. You will appear more human and show respect for the other person. People notice managers who show no interest in them and only see staff members as tools for getting work done; then they have less energy for supporting the manager.

How do you determine how much small talk is useful? Pay attention to the other person's behavior. Some people only like a little small talk before they will start to squirm or switch the subject to work matters. Follow their cue. Others will not seem relaxed and need more conversation to build rapport. Notice when a shift in energy occurs; then it is okay to shift subjects. This skill can be learned by carefully observing others.

Be Authentic

Focus on the goal of being authentic and true to yourself in your interactions while looking for win-win solutions. Years ago, I worried about spelling out these details of how to communicate because I thought some people might use them to manipulate others, but I don't worry anymore. When you are not interested in another person's needs and just your own, people seem to sense this pretty quickly. If people think you are using techniques to pull something over on them, or gain an advantage, they generally won't be supportive in return. Although using the process to create a situation where you win and the other person loses may work a few times, in long-term relationships, it won't. So explore your motives; make it your intention to be authentic. Reveal some of yourself, showing you are human, and have the goal of understanding others and coming to an agreement that will benefit those involved.

Tell the truth—as much of it as you know or can. Otherwise, you will lose credibility with people and they may not believe you next time. I remember a colleague who often exaggerated or simply said things that were not accurate. As people became aware of this pattern, they did not want to work with her, which caused a lot of problems for her and her coworkers.

Actually, if you have good intentions and state what is accurate, most people will be willing to work with you and grow to trust you. When you do make mistakes, acknowledge them, make amends, and move on. After a CEO apologized to staff for a difficult reorganization, staff members were able to stop fighting him and resume work. Most of the time, people will forgive you, recognizing that everyone does make mistakes occasionally. After all, we are all human.

When we are authentic and have integrity, congruence occurs with what we say (words), our posture or how we hold ourselves (body language), and our emotions or mood (tone). Seminal research by Albert Mehrabian[4] based on experiments dealing with communicating feelings and attitudes shows that when there is incongruity, people tend to believe body language or nonverbal behavior over spoken words. In fact, his research suggests that 7 percent of a message pertaining to feelings and attitudes is in the words spoken, while 38 percent of the same message is conveyed by the tone or emotion used in speaking those words. Finally, 55 percent of the message is conveyed by facial or body expression. The more you become aware of the connection between your emotions, your body language, and your words and thoughts, the better able you will be to check in with yourself and ensure more congruity. In addition, you will be able to understand others by paying attention to their words, emotions, and body language.

---

4 Mehrabian, A. *Silent Messages*. Belmont, CA: Wadsworth. 1971.

Be Present and Focused

With cell phone calls, e-mails, overbooked appointments on our calendars, and full personal lives, we are often multitasking. We try to squeeze more accomplishments into a limited time and may be left unsatisfied with their quality. This approach works for some of us, some of the time. Research conducted at Stanford University[5] shows that our division of attention may cause stress and burnout. Even multitasking's overall effectiveness is being questioned. The field of mindfulness and meditation is directed toward training us to keep attention on one thing at a time and to slow down our rapid pace.

The most impactful conversations generally require more devoted attention. Make sure you are paying attention to the other person as well as yourself.

You may think this sounds obvious; however, I have coached many managers and executives who focus primarily on themselves. They don't have much interest in the person they are speaking with. Terri, a marketing executive, kept most of her attention on how she was perceiving the world. She displayed little interest in her employees and did not inquire about how they perceived things. Since she had more experience in marketing, she did not believe her staff had much to offer. She thought they were just there to carry out her orders! Needless to say, her staff members were not motivated to support her or the organization. Once Terri learned how to shift her attention from herself and her thoughts to include others and be present and focused with them, she created a positive team environment and began getting better results.

> *"If you are present, you are alert, fluid, clear and able to welcome all things."*
>
> — Lao-Tsu

Be fully present for a conversation. If you are still mulling over the previous meeting, upset about an argument you just had, or thinking about the next task, you can't concentrate effectively. Learn to shelve the many other things competing for your attention. Direct your atten-

---

5   Reported in *Forbes* in October 2014.

tion to the person you are talking with and the current conversation. With practice, you will acquire the skill of shuttling back and forth between the other person and yourself. You'll pay attention to how you are reacting, share your own reactions, and still show interest and be curious about the other person's state.

Leaders who have developed the skill of paying attention stand out in the crowd. People appreciate getting your full attention and, in turn, they are more apt to give you theirs. Sometimes it seems like time stops when we are present with each other. More can then be accomplished and interactions become more satisfying. Leadership presence, a core competency that successful organizations emphasize, positively differentiates staff and managers from the competition.

Children can teach us about being present. When my daughter was five, she wrote in a school project, "I love my mother because...she keeps me from drowning in the pool and exercises with me." In fact, I was fully attentive with her during these two activities. I would intentionally let go of other concerns and give her my full attention. She experienced the difference.

Children are naturally present. They are often not worried about the past or future. They focus on what is happening in the moment. They exhibit and experience a contagious sense of aliveness and excitement. It's hard not to smile when interacting with young children and becoming fully engaged.

The OASIS Moves will support you in being more present in your interactions. Set the intention to be present and to listen to others as well as yourself. Stay in a curious and open state to see what you can learn. Remind yourself to feel your feet on the ground and notice that you are living in your body. Pause and breathe fully—allow your abdomen to fill with air, not just your chest. Notice your feelings as well as your thoughts. Feelings are like waves that move through your body and relax as you notice them. Ask questions of the other person and notice what you find interesting. Expect to learn something from an interaction and look for the learning.

Go Ahead: Try the OASIS Moves

Now that you have clarified your intentions, are present, and have built rapport, you are ready to plan for and have an OASIS Conversation. An OASIS Conversation is comprised of the OASIS Moves corresponding to each letter of the OASIS acronym. Each move or letter has a kinesthetic move to help you recall the component. In workshops, we reinforce the moves together. I use the terms OASIS Moves and OASIS Conversations interchangeably throughout this book. If you are a manager, you may use OASIS Moves to give feedback, receive feedback, delegate, follow-up, support motivation, and problem-solve. My leadership and team-building workshops use OASIS Moves as their foundation. You may also use OASIS Moves as a support in your conversations with family members, neighbors, and friends.

The following chapters will address each of the five OASIS Moves O—Observation, A—Awareness (of assumptions, emotions, and background), S—Shift (to being open), I—Importance, and S—Solution. For each move, we will examine what it is, its benefits, and how to practice it successfully. We will also explore challenges and offer opportunities to practice and develop new habits. Before you move on, however, be sure to practice what you have just learned.

Practice

- Make it a habit to state your intention to yourself to experience an OASIS and a climate of openness with colleagues, family members, and others.
- Choose to be present and attentive to someone today. Consciously put aside other thoughts and your phone or e-mail and enjoy the interaction. Notice how the other person responds and how you feel about the experience.
- Next, focus on building rapport with someone. Talk about current events, the weather, and other topics of interest. Notice how the other person is responding to you. Practice with someone and grow comfortable with a number of topics.
- Imagine being with someone you are open to—a child, a friend, a niece—and notice how you feel. Does your chest feel more open? How are you holding your body and arms? Now imagine yourself being open to another person; shift your body and practice being open in your posture and mindset. Practice the skill of being open-minded before you go into a meeting or a conversation.

- Identify a conversation you need to have, check that you have the right mindset of a clear intention, an open stance, and a readiness to be present and authentic.
- Identify ways to remind yourself of the OASIS Moves to keep the process real and useful for you.

CHAPTER 4

0 is for Observation

Is What You Observe a Fact or a Mirage?

"Observing without evaluating is the highest form of intelligence."

— J. Krishnamurti

OASIS Conversations

Have a clear intention, plan when possible, and build rapport.

O = Observation

A = Awareness (of assumptions, emotions, and background)

S = Shift (to being open)

ʃ = Importance

S = Solution

Observation in a Conversation

Describe behavior or facts without judgment.
"When I see…," "When I hear…," or, "I notice…"

Cue for Remembering O for Observations

The cue for remembering O, the Observation move of the OASIS process, is to hear or see an O, and in the process, notice your eyes or ears and reflect on what you are noticing. You might imagine pointing a flashlight on what you are noticing. You are aware that many possible things could attract your attention. The same applies to the person you are talking with. Clear communication begins with becoming aware of the raw data you are noticing and briefly separating it from your assumptions and interpretations. You are looking for concrete data that others would also observe if a video were recording a scene.

Let me tell you a personal story where communication was definitely not clear. On a cold winter night, I was in an SUV packed with eight family members as we drove to enjoy the holiday lights at the Washington D.C. Botanic Gardens. The trees were artfully wrapped with thousands of colored lights. Even flowers and rainbows had been created out of strands of lights. The effect was truly magical. As we neared the gardens, the line of cars waiting to enter increased. In the red Honda in line in front of us, a man was waving his hand back and forth. My sister Chrissy, who was driving, became irritated and wondered aloud, "What is his problem? I'm not doing anything wrong." The man continued to wave. My twelve-year-old nephew, Duncan, then asked, "Do you think we have a flat tire?" My sister, Lisa, then said, "Is someone's coat sticking out the door?" Jim, Chrissy's husband, gave his explanation. "The man must think the high-beam lights are on since the SUV Blazer we are in is taller than his compact Honda." Jim explained that he frequently receives this response when he is driving his truck. He told Chrissy to turn her high beam lights on and off to show him they weren't on. After she did this, the man opened his sunroof and slowly waved back and forth. Chrissy interpreted this gesture as, "Now he understands that nothing is really wrong and is apologizing."

When we reached the booth to pay, the attendant told us that the man in the car ahead of ours had already paid the $15 entrance fee for us. Chrissy interpreted this as "He is apologizing to us." Jim said, "The attendant must mean that Trish," (another sister who was in a car a few ahead of us with more family members), "must have paid." Ben, my fourteen-year-old nephew, smiled and stated, "It was a random act of kindness for the holidays."

We each saw the same observable data—a man in a red Honda in front of our SUV waving. Each of us made sense of his actions based on our background or past experience. Chrissy immediately worried that she had done something wrong—a lifelong habit learned in a large family. Jim assumed the driver was informing us that the high-beam lights were on based on his experience with his truck. Lisa had had her coat stuck in the car door in the past; just the day before, she had told a story about her friend's wedding dress hanging out the door on her way to her wedding and it getting quite dirty. Duncan had experienced a flat tire. Ben had seen bumper stickers and T-shirts encouraging people to commit random acts of kindness.

We each interpreted the observable data of the attendant saying "Your entrance fee has been paid" based on our stories as well. Once we were operating from our individual assumptions and stories, it was hard for each of us to imagine another interpretation.

After we parked, the man in the red Honda got out of his car and walked over to us. Chrissy generously explained that he had no need to apologize like that by paying, and Ben thanked him for his random act of kindness and wished him a happy holiday. Rather than return Ben's greeting, the driver said, "I'm embarrassed. I thought the car behind me was my family since they have a tan SUV." He continued to tell us that he'd assumed the blinking lights were a confirmation that it was his family. Finally, he asked for reimbursement of the entrance fee!

It is very useful to be able to distinguish our observations from our assumptions or interpretations. We have a natural tendency to believe that our assumptions are the "truth." However, in reality, we are often experiencing situations very differently from others around us. The first move in the OASIS Process is to develop the habit of noticing what you are observing. Next, you need to separate that from your own assumptions and reaction.

Identifying and Stating an Observation

If Chrissy had decided to talk to the man who was waving to us in the car in front of us, rather than making an immediate assumption that he was apologizing, she could have begun with her Observation—the O in OASIS Moves. "I noticed you were waving your hand back and forth as we were waiting to get into the Botanic Gardens." From her statement, the man would have known what Chrissy was referring to and he would have had some context for the conversation. He would have nodded in agreement that he had been waving his hand. Chrissy could also have said, "The attendant told us that our entrance fee had been paid by a car in front of us." Again, he would have readily agreed that he was aware of these observations. Starting with observation without judgment would have helped Chrissy and the other driver to begin to understand each other. That is a good beginning point for any conversation.

Brain Connection

Scientists have discovered that human brains are constantly making the kind of connections my family members made in their observation of the man waving in the car in front of them. In fact, our brains are connection machines. We are always developing associations and links between bits of information. As mentioned in an earlier chapter, our brains are a vast map of connections or neural pathways. The connections are comprised of long, narrow nerve cells (neurons) found in nerve tissue throughout the body and the brain's gray matter. Each neuron transmits electrical, chemical, and hormonal information from one end of the neuron to the other. A dendrite receives the information from one cell and the axon of the nerve transmits the information to the next neuron. A single neuron does not transmit information very far, but the neurons join to form neural paths or connections. Each time we have an experience or a new thought, neurons join together to form a path. Those paths reinforced through repeated use become stronger and more readily accessed. Those not reinforced are generally not very strong. Imagine a very complex map; then multiply it by many times. That multiplied version would represent the complex neural paths we each have of the world. We have hundreds of thousands of neural connections in our brains based on our past experiences.

As we make an observation, our neurons are firing automatically and we make instantaneous connections and assumptions. This happens so quickly that we often are not consciously aware of what we have just observed and are reacting to. The complexity grows because we develop multiple maps in our brains where we try to put together our various experiences related to a subject or an observation. In the example given, each of my family members associated the man's hand waving with a unique interpretation based on his or her own previous

OASIS Conversations / 48

experience. In addition, each person had many related maps of how people should treat each other and how to drive.

At any moment, we are each having different reactions to the same observation based on our past backgrounds, conditioning, and how our brains organize information. First, we take in information through our senses; then we compare it to our brain maps based on our backgrounds and try to make sense of what we are experiencing. You might want to think of yourself as a complex computer that has been programmed in unique ways without a clear manual! While it appears that we are seeing the same data that other people are seeing, we are each experiencing it differently. We assume that others see things or experience them the way we do. They often don't. Each of us has different internal maps and ways of responding. Also, often you are paying attention to different aspects of external, observable data than I might be. This makes it complex to communicate.

Identifying and distinguishing what is being observed from assumptions and judgments is a critical OASIS Move. First, we will highlight the benefits of identifying observations. Then we will practice using observable data and see how it fits in the OASIS process. Finally, I will give you some suggestions for making "identifying your observations" a habit.

Another Observation Scenario

In workshops, I ask participants to observe what I do for two minutes. Without further explanation, I walk out of the room, then back in. Then I look under participants' workbooks, I look behind doors, I clap, and I put my hands on my hips. I take off my shoe and put it back on. I throw a ball up in the air and take the caps off two markers and smell them. Then I ask participants, "What did you observe?"

Participants say: "You were unorganized." "You lost something." "You were frustrated." "You were nervous." "You were confused," or "You were rude." Some say, "You didn't know what you were doing." "You were upset." "Your behavior bothered me—it was irritating." These kinds of statements come quickly from participants. When I keep asking, "What did you observe?" they continue to state a wide range of their assumptions based on my behavior. Finally, a participant will state, "You left the room." Another might say, "You came in the back door," or "You threw the ball in the air."

Do you see the difference between an observation and an interpretation? Observations like "You left the room" or "You clapped your hands three times" are the facts—what a video camera would capture. They are the actions that occurred or the exact words that were said without the attachment of meaning. Nearly everyone present agreed to seeing and hearing the same observable data. However, most people immediately tried to make sense of what they observed. They paid very little attention to what was physically perceived with their senses.

We tend to jump to immediate conclusions about the meaning of actions. This process happens extremely quickly—so fast that often we are unaware of what we really observed—the actual data from which we make conclusions. Someone might say, for instance, that a person is lazy, disorganized, or confused and then believe the interpretation is really a fact.

Identifying Observations

The first move in the OASIS process is to identify your observation without making assumptions or judgments. This requires noting what information you take in through your five senses—what you are seeing, hearing, smelling, tasting, or touching. If you could capture what you see, as if with a video camera, you would report what you observed and heard. This step seems quite easy. For example, you could say, "I noticed you walked back in the room," or "I noticed you picked up the ball."

Our senses are the portals through which we collect raw data from the external environment. In interactions with people, we take in not only verbal data—the words others use, but we also assess non-verbal cues, such as "You frowned when you said that."

Scientists suggest that we take in over 30,000 bits of data at any moment. Our body systems cannot attend to all the data at once. We tend to organize around some observations and then others essentially become invisible to us. We selectively pay attention to certain data. You might visualize this as taking a flashlight and selecting something to spotlight. Much of this filtering process is unconscious and based on our experiences and past conditioning. For example, a movie expert might look at the same piece of art or film as a less trained person and have a very different interpretation. Each would believe she is seeing the same work, so her interpretations or assumptions are the "truth."

A trained architect will notice details about buildings that may be invisible to an untrained eye. An elevator technician told me that when he walks into buildings that are new to him, he notices the elevators first. He pays attention to the kinds of elevators and the dates they were inspected. He also assesses the safety of the elevators. In contrast, I rarely notice the date of the last elevator inspection. An experienced chef is likely to notice different ingredients and carefully observe food presentation techniques at a meal. Someone who considers food as fuel and often eats the same basic meal typically would not even notice ingredients or presentation. The more knowledgeable or educated we are about a topic, the more distinctions or variations we see that others without this experience just don't see. For example, a trained artist is likely to notice the type of brush stroke used in a painting and perhaps even be able to identify the artist. Others without this background will notice different things about a painting. Being trained in organization psychology and change management, I observe the challenges individuals and organizations face as they try to bring about change. I readily notice what is needed based on my experience and my training in cultural change, leadership, and change management.

Using OASIS Moves, we consciously slow down our process to notice what we are observing and separate the assumptions we make based on observations. I am not asking you to stop making assumptions. That is not possible or even productive. However, by slowing down the process, you will have the opportunity to examine your observations and assumptions. (We will explore more about awareness of assumptions in the next chapter.) In addition, by referencing observable data in your conversations, it is more likely that other people will understand what you are talking about. By stating what you observe (or don't observe), others will be able to follow your thinking and join you in the conversation.

In my workshops, I ask participants, "What made you think I was disorganized as I walked around the room for two minutes?" They usually say that when I looked under workbooks and under the table, they assumed I'd misplaced something, so they concluded I was disorganized. Another person observed the same actions and concluded I was confused. Neither conclusion was accurate from my perspective. So a helpful way to get to your observable data is to ask yourself, "How do I know...?" I know my friend is angry because she hit the table with her fist. When we quickly skip over the observable data, we lose the opportunity to catch the assumptions we make. We often believe our assumptions are the facts, so we get locked into that particular interpretation exclusively. We then are not aware of or open to other interpretations or options.

Notice What You're Noticing

As I write this, I look around my office and notice hundreds of objects. I notice, for instance, a piece of art by R.C. Gorman. I associate peace and expansiveness with the images of the women in his work. I also notice a framed postcard of a sculpture that impressed me at the Museum of Art in Cleveland. I discovered it when I was doing a post-graduate training program. The young girl depicted in the sculpture radiates with joy, which inspires me. I notice a navy-blue box with silk elephants on the side that was given to me by clients in Bangkok, which causes me to remember fondly my time with certain people there. I scan my bookshelves, and as I pass different titles, I remember what those books have meant to me. Some opened entirely new worlds.

Now I turn toward my window and look outside. I notice the expanse of Lake Michigan and I appreciate its ever-changing beauty. I hear the music of Kenny G playing saxophone, and I remember the first time I heard his stunning music. While tasting my licorice-flavored tea, I take in the beauty and enjoy the fragrance of fresh flowers. The aroma of flowers takes me back to when I graduated years ago. My room then, full of fresh flowers, felt celebratory, and I experienced a special sense of aliveness.

Now, I resume typing and feel the familiar keyboard beneath my fingers. I enjoy clicking away. I particularly love it when the words are flowing and my fingers have to race along to keep up. Overall, I experience relaxation and a sense of comfort in my office.

In just a few moments, my attention shifted among many pieces of "observable data" that I took in through my senses. With each observation that I see, touch, hear, or smell, I also have associations, assumptions, and emotions intertwined. My assumptions about a piece of art, music, or the lake are likely to be different from yours. You may find the artwork unattractive and the music may not move you. For example, fresh flowers may annoy a person with allergies. Yet even with our different backgrounds and assumptions, we are likely to agree that I have orange Tiger Lilies on my desk and that Lake Michigan can be seen from my window.

When communicating with others, focus on identifying some of the pieces of data you are observing, and then separate assumptions from the data. This separation is particularly important when differences of opinion are likely to arise.

How many times have you jumped to a conclusion based on an observation that made sense to you but was not the whole story? For example, a coworker arrives late for a scheduled lunch. You might evaluate his behavior as "rude." However, perhaps you or he got the appointment time wrong. I remember when I was disappointed in a colleague who did not call for a scheduled appointment. My evaluation was that our call was not important to him. When he called exactly an hour later, I realized my mistake. I had forgotten to account for the different time zones. If I had challenged him, scolding him for the missed scheduled call rather than commenting, "I thought our appointment was at 1:00 p.m.," I might have lost a client. With so many pieces of observable data to notice at any given moment, and so many ways to interpret the data based on our backgrounds and experiences, it's amazing that we ever communicate clearly, isn't it?

Make It a Habit to Notice

I think it is especially fun to develop the habit of identifying observations. One good way is to take a camera with you and pay close attention as you look for what would make interesting photos. Notice the pattern of rectangular windows in a high-rise building or the bright yellow and purple tulips in a garden. I enjoy taking images with my camera. I also take them in my mind when I don't have a camera. Sometimes, for example, I simply pay closer attention to what I see on my way to work. Even in my home, if I choose, I can become more aware of shapes, colors, or items that have drifted into the background of my awareness.

Pay attention to your other senses such as what you hear. For example, I can become more conscious of the sound of the computer keys as I type. I also notice that I quickly begin making meanings. I ask myself, "Am I typing quickly enough to capture my thoughts?" I'm also aware of the rhythmic tick of the clock on my desk and of music in the background.

I notice that when I smell brownies baking, I am reminded of when I was young and made them for friends. I remember, too, special times when I've made them with my daughter. I then notice that I have a warm feeling of appreciation for her and that experience together. I also consciously notice how the smooth granite tabletop feels as I knead bread dough for baking. I feel the dry, dustiness of the flour on my hands. Then I'm reminded of my father making sourdough bread and how delicious it was served warm at our big family meals. Sometimes, I notice the feel of my feet hitting the ground as I walk across the city. I notice the different sensations in the soles of my feet as I walk first on a sidewalk and then through a park.

Pay attention to your observations. Besides being aware of different sensations, you are also likely to notice the various memories, associations, and assumptions you make. This process happens continuously.

Observing is one of the key skills of being self-aware. Years ago, I was just like a "bobbing head." In my focus on being efficient, I was moving so fast that I was not aware of my sensations. I quickly made and acted on my assumptions. Many of the executives and others I work with currently are experiencing life the same way. By becoming aware of what you observe, you are more likely to remember that others notice different things and interpret situations differently. This is an important first step to communicating effectively with people who have different experiences than you do—which is everybody! I encourage you to notice and practice sharing your observations with your family members. I am forever amazed by how what appears obvious to me is not the same, for instance, as what my daughter is observing.

Why Is It Valuable to Identify Observations?

Benefits of identifying observations and then separating them from assumptions include:

1. You can catch yourself assuming and jumping to conclusions without a basis.
2. You know that both you and the person you are talking with are talking about the same thing.
3. You know how to begin a conversation without making the other person defensive.
4. When you use observable data in conversations, it increases understanding and creates more trust in your relationships.

5. The process of noticing supports you in being more present and mindful.

Catch Yourself Jumping to Conclusions

During your workday, take a moment to ask yourself, "What did I observe that is leading me to this assumption?" For example, if you conclude that a colleague is ignoring you, can you identify what you observed that made you think this? Perhaps you noticed your colleague talking to someone else at a meeting or you did not receive a call from him that you expected. You may consider multiple explanations for not receiving the call. Maybe the person called your office number rather than your cell phone. Perhaps you did not pick up your messages, the person left you an e-mail, or you did not get a message that someone was supposed to deliver. Were you clear about your expectations? Was the person anticipating that you would call him? Of course, the person could really be ignoring you…! Practice describing the observable data on which you are basing your assumptions.

Orient Others

Think of observations as if you are viewing a buffet. Many plates of different kinds of food are laid out in front of you. I may notice the dessert tray and comment on how delicious the food looks. You may think I'm referring to the banana cream pie, yet I'm really noticing the chocolate fudge brownies (I favor dark chocolate). Without my identifying the particular dessert, we could have a whole conversation about it where you are assuming I'm talking about the pie. By my mentioning the brownies, you know I'm interested in and referring to them. How many times have you had a conversation only to realize later you were each referring to different things, thinking you were talking about the same thing?

This situation happened to me a while ago. A family member wandered away from the meal we had together to take a phone call. I went into my home office to finish a report. I realized an hour had passed by. Earlier that evening, I asked my family member to help order a gift for someone on the Internet. When I returned, he seemed agitated, perhaps annoyed with me. I saw his red face. I noticed that I also felt frustrated with his absence. My observable data was that his face was red and that I had not seen him for over an hour. I said, "Your face is red." He said he was really frustrated with me and he felt he'd wasted his evening. I remained calm and asked whether he could be more specific. (I was looking for observable data.) He said he was upset that I was on the phone for more than an hour when he had wanted to show me a gift online to complete the gift-ordering task. I had not been on the phone.

When we went to the phone to investigate, we found that it had been accidentally left off the hook. His observable data was seeing a light signaling the phone was in use so he assumed I was chatting. Being courteous, he had waited for me to hang up. He finally gave up in frustration. While we were both frustrated, we saved ourselves from arguing about it by sharing our observations. Clearly, neither of us had been in the wrong. Although, I could have chosen to follow up with him earlier rather than assuming he was involved with others and would find me when he was ready.

Reduce Defensiveness

When you start a conversation with assumptions and judgments and act like they are facts, it causes defensiveness. If my family member had said, "You were rude and ruined my evening" without sharing his observable data first, I could have been defensive. I might have verbally attacked him for not being clear about his expectations or for his un-justified outburst.

In the workplace, if I observed that Marla, a staff member, did not volunteer to join a project committee, I might assume that she was not committed to the team. Marla might become defensive if I stated that. Then, she probably would be focused on protecting herself rather than being open to solving my concern and coming to an agreement. However, if I start the conversation by saying, "I notice that you did not volunteer to join the committee," Marla might offer that she is working on some other aspects of the project or give other evidence of her commitment.

By acting as if my assumption that "Marla is not committed" is a fact, I can easily gather support for my flawed viewpoint. Here's how: If I do not explore my perception and continue with my assumption that she is not committed, I will behave in ways that convey that perspective. Perhaps I will not inform Marla about other related meetings or information critical to the project's success. Since I assume Marla is not committed, I then act as if she is not. She may pick up on this attitude and decide to put her effort elsewhere. Then my assumption has become a self-fulfilling prophecy!

Increase Understanding and Trust: Get Specific!

When we have a misunderstanding with another person, it can lead to mistrust. For example, my colleague, Kathleen, and I agreed that we would have dinner at Tiparo's Thai restaurant down the street from our conference hotel. When I received a call from her on my cell phone as we were each going to our rooms, I said, "Okay, I'll meet you at 6:00." We had been meeting after our conference for the last few days in the hotel lobby. That evening when I waited in the lobby for her, Kathleen did not arrive. As I reflected on our confirming conversation, I realized we did not specify where we would meet. In fact, Kathleen was waiting for me at the restaurant! What seemed obvious to me—that we would meet in the lobby—was not to her. After I called her, I learned that she had assumed I might get delayed with another meeting. She had thought it best to go to the restaurant to be sure to get us a table. Oops!

By understanding what another person is observing and responding to, you are more likely to grasp his or her concern or issue. If a colleague tells me she is not satisfied with a report I submitted, I can only guess why. Was she expecting it to be longer, in a different style of writing, or to have additional items included or excluded? Was she concerned about minor typographical errors? Often, conversations occur where each person involved believes he or she knows what the other is talking about. Sometimes, it is not until later that you find out otherwise. Sometimes, you never find out!

A client could not understand why a colleague seemed so distant and angry. The two of them did not talk candidly, and working together was no longer fun. After learning the OASIS Moves, Rose said to her colleague, "I notice that you have not talked about your family lately." Her colleague told her how angry she was that Rose had moved a plant in the office. This was a plant her mother had given her, and since her mother passed away, she felt the action was disrespectful. Rose was shocked. She had moved the plant in the winter near a window to give the plant some additional sun. Her intention was to be thoughtful and extend the plant's life. If her colleague had identified her observation earlier and had a conversation, these teammates could have experienced a more positive work environment.

As you use OASIS Moves, you will ask people to share what they are observing, to clarify what they are referring to, or to ask whether they can be more specific. Even if individuals are not aware of the OASIS process, you can help them to be clearer about their concerns or perceptions by asking questions that help identify their observations.

This next example comes from a workshop I gave where Barbara, a professional in the organization, introduced me. I noticed that she was very abrupt in her introduction. She crossed her arms and seemed nervous. Later, I asked her how she was succeeding with her work. She revealed that she had just had her annual performance review. Her boss had said to her, "You are not management material." Barbara was quite upset since she was ambitious and had thought she would move up in the organization. I told her I had noticed she had given a short introduction for my workshop that day. She explained that she was trying to act like Sally, who had been recently promoted to manager. Barbara thought Sally's brusque style was what was required of managers in her company. Since her boss did not give her any observable data about what she considered management behavior or specifically share what her concerns were about Barbara's behavior, Barbara had to guess. Both would have benefited by being more specific with each other about what they thought constituted managerial behavior.

Be More Present

Another benefit of noticing observations is that you are more present to what is happening and more mindful. Many of us are thinking about the past or the future and are missing what is actually happening in the moment. A critical differentiator of excellent leaders is their ability to be focused and with people in the moment. Practicing noticing observable data will help build the neural pathways and ability to become present. People notice when someone is with them fully in the moment and when a person is not really available. The skill of being present is highly correlated with success and satisfaction. In fact, research by Harvard psychologists Matthew A. Killingsworth and Daniel T. Gilbert indicate that not living in the present is detrimental to well-being. They found that people spend 46.9 percent of their waking hours thinking about the past or future and that this lack of being aware in the moment typically has people report being unhappy.

Identifying Observations Invisible to Others

We have been primarily talking about external observations, such as noticing someone walking out of the room, car drivers waving, or external displays like the buffet, that others will notice when you point them out.

However, sometimes you are responding to observations that will not be so apparent. In these situations, too, share what you are noticing. For example, if you just watched a TV show about healthy eating, rather than simply not eating the celebratory dessert you usually share with a friend, you might say: "I just saw a show on healthy eating and a doctor explained the value of reducing sugar and fat. I'm going to follow his advice and eat fruit for dessert instead." This explanation helps your friend know what is going on with you. You don't need to share every such observation—only when it might clarify a situation. Otherwise, your friend might ask, "Why aren't you sharing and enjoying our usual guilty pleasure? I know it's your favorite dessert."

Sometimes, your observation will be an internal sensation. For example, "I have a headache, so I'll sit out this game of charades." Again, by simply sharing your observation, you assist others in understanding you. Then they can rely less on their assumptions, and they don't need to conclude that you don't like playing charades or you don't like being with them. These conclusions might have negative consequences for you the next time they are looking for someone to share some fun. It is useful to notice your internal sensations, such as your stomach tightening or your closed throat, and notice how you make sense of these observations. Ideally, you will become skilled at reporting what is happening within you, particularly in close relationships.

Also, if you point out an observation, "I notice you're frowning," the frowner may then report, "Yes, I am trying to figure out a problem and need a few moments of quiet." Sometimes, you may have an intuitive feeling but no observable data. You might say to Miriam, "I sense that we should review our plan again. I have a gut feeling we've left something important out." With this comment, Miriam will know what you are considering, even if she cannot see your experience.

Practice becoming more aware of your observations, both those fully available to others and your internal sensations. I've found that as I practice separating observations from assumptions, the process becomes more natural and enjoyable. Like any skill, it gets easier with practice. Eventually, it will become second nature.

Our Background Influences Our Observations

I was with a colleague on a business trip overseas. We went to a tailor so she could have a dress custom-made for her. When she received the dress, I thought it looked identical to the sample she had wanted the tailor to match. However, she immediately noticed that the stitches were much wider. She also detected that the button-holes were not made the way she liked. She caught other details that were essentially invisible to my uneducated eye. As she carefully identified these differences, I observed them, too. Most of us have not been trained to consider that we may be paying attention to different data than other people. In other words, multiple "realities" or "truths" exist.

In web, newspaper, and magazine articles, you will notice both observable data and assumptions. I once worked for a company where I followed developments in the United States Congress. I had the opportunity to sit in on some official hearings and then to read about the meetings in newspapers and other publications. I soon recognized that each piece took a different slant and reported differently on the same observable data. The reporters' backgrounds and their publications' perspectives greatly influenced how the hearings or meetings were covered in news stories. Since then, I know that no media presents the only "truth."

We saw the same experience during the vote whether to impeach President Clinton. All of the Congressional representatives vowed to listen to the data and vote based on the testimony, yet each person voted along his or her party lines. Their backgrounds and experiences influenced how they interpreted the data. Congressional Representatives, however, are likely to say they were being true to the observable data.

Brain Connection

Have you ever had the experience of thinking about purchasing a certain make of car, say a Prius, and then, suddenly, you notice how many cars of that make are on the road? Before, you may have hardly noticed the small hybrid cars, but when you seriously considered purchasing one, it seemed that the model you were interested in was everywhere. The Reticular Activating System (RAS) of our brain supports us in honing in on the Prius cars. Again, our interests, preferences, and experiences influence what we observe.

Practice Identifying Observable Data

While the concept of observable data is quite straightforward, it takes practice to separate our assumptions from our observations. Since most of us have a lifetime of believing our interpretations are the "truth," we need practice. For example, if I said, "Sid is not committed to the team," you do not know what observable data I am basing my assumption on. Just because I state it as fact—that he is "not committed"—is not sufficient information. If I include that he did not provide his section of the report on Monday as the others did, then you know what I am basing my conclusion on. That's a start. We have a grounded fact to begin our conversation.

Read the following statements and identify those that provide the observable data:

1. Yves did not ask me to share my report in today's staff meeting.
2. Rosie always talks too much.
3. I read in the attendance report that Jon took eight sick days this year.
4. Last week when I arrived late, you asked, "What's the matter? Can't you afford an alarm clock?"
5. Caleb did not write and distribute the press release within the time frame of two hours.
6. Beth is ignoring me.
7. Shawn has exceeded the budget the last three months in a row.
8. Sasha is overly emotional.
9. Alicia is not a team player.

Review the answers below.

Statement 1 (Yves did not ask me to share my report in today's staff meeting.) is observable data. All attending the meeting or seeing a video of the meeting would agree that Yves did not ask the speaker to share her report in the meeting. A specific time and situation is provided to direct the listener's attention to a specific place and time.

Statement 2 (Rosie always talks too much.) contains two general-izations: "always" and "too much." These statements reflect judgment. Observable data is factual. "Rosie spoke for thirty minutes at the for-ty-five-minute meeting when each attendee was allotted five minutes. Rosie also spoke for thirty-five minutes at the last meeting and forty minutes at the meeting before that. The last three meetings she ex-ceeded the five-minute speaking limit." Any time you make sweeping generalizations, using words like "always" or "too much," you are likely to excite resistance in other people. They are likely to identify immedi-ately times when the item in question did not occur. For example, Rosie might say, "I didn't talk at all in the July meeting when I was sick."

Statement 3 (I read in the attendance report that Jon took eight sick days this year.) is observable data without assumptions. The person is simply stating what he or she read in the report that day.

Statement 4 (Last week when I arrived late, you asked, "What's the matter? Can't you afford an alarm clock?") is tricky. The actual statement is observable data. The person speaking is quoting what he heard and his observation. The comment being quoted is sarcastic and contains judgment and is not observable data. Identifying direct quotes is a way of stating observable data.

Statement 5 (Caleb did not write and distribute the press release within the time frame of two hours.) is an observation since Caleb did not complete the press release in the time frame.

Statement 6 (Beth is ignoring me.) is an assumption that does not specify the observable data. This statement assumes Beth's motives. The observable data that leads the speaker to the conclusion may be something like, "When I walked by the meeting, Beth did not invite me in or say hello." Perhaps Beth did not see the speaker or did not feel comfortable commenting at the moment the person walked by. If you asked her, Beth probably wouldn't even know what circumstance the person is referencing!

Statement 7 (Shawn has exceeded the budget the last three months in a row.) provides observable data without assumptions regarding the budget.

Statement 8 (Sasha is overly emotional.) is a judgment: no observ-able data is provided. If the speaker said, "Sasha cried in my office every day this week," that could be an observation from which the person is drawing the conclusion. Another person may interpret the observable data in a different way. She might not consider it excessive given the circumstances. Again, it is useful to be aware of generalizations such as the use of the word "overly."

Statement 9 (Alicia is not a team player.) is a judgment without giving the observation it is based on. Again, it contains a generalization and does not refer to a specific action or actions.

State Your Observations

Begin your statements about an observation like this: "I notice that…" or "When I see, hear, taste…." While we are exploring each of the OASIS Moves in order, you can report your observations throughout a conversation.

Remember to:

- Describe what you are observing the way a camera would capture it, without interpretation or evaluation. Refrain from evaluative words such as, "Joe is lazy."
- Be specific about actions you observe and include what a person said or did. "On Friday morning, you said…."
- Do not include assumptions or evaluations of the person's motives, feelings, or thoughts: "I did not receive a call from you," rather than, "You are not a team player because you did not participate in the scheduled team call."
- Avoid generalizations such as *always, too much, never,* and *often.*
- Take responsibility for what you are noticing with the understanding that there may be much that you are not observing: "I did not see you at the conference," rather than, "You did not attend the conference." In this situation, the person may have been present and yet attended different sessions, so you did not see her.

Summary

By being aware of our observations and separating what we observe from how we judge it, we can raise our awareness of reality and be more open to others and their own motivations for doing things. As a result, we will be better communicators, and be better able to negotiate an oasis between us and others. Now that you understand about the importance of observation, I challenge you to practice it in your daily life. Here are some techniques for practicing it before we go on to the next OASIS Move, A for Awareness, in the next chapter.

Practice—Developing the Habit of Noticing Observations

- Take photographs, saying to yourself, "Observation" as you take a picture of a tree, a building, and a person. You can do this mentally, without a camera, and simply identify your observation and separate it from your assumptions. By making this a habit, you strengthen your ability to observe objectively.
- Simply note the sounds you hear such as that of a truck, a siren, or a bird, and say to yourself, "Observation."
- Explore your other sensations. Pay attention to the sensations in your feet or your breathing as you walk, and notice your observations and your assumptions.
- As you read an article on the web or elsewhere, notice which statements are actually observations and which are assumptions that are offered as facts.
- As you watch TV, notice what you are observing separate from your interpretation. "I notice the character is leaving the restaurant," etc.
- Look for patterns in your observations. For example, do you tend to notice people who need support, or do you routinely notice the time people enter a meeting?
- Pay attention to the observations that the people you are communicating with notice. Ask others to be more specific or to give an example when they make a generalization. Separate what they are observing from how they are making sense of it.

CHAPTER 5

A Is for Awareness

What Are Your Assumptions, Emotions, and Background?

"Awareness is not the same as thought. It lies beyond thinking, honoring its value and its power. Awareness is more like a vessel which can hold and contain our thinking, helping us to see and know our thoughts as thoughts rather than getting caught in them as reality."

— Jon Kabat-Zinn

OASIS Conversations

Have a clear intention, plan when possible, and build rapport.

O = Observation

A = Awareness (of assumptions, emotions, and background)

S = **Shift** (to being open)

= Importance

S = Solution

Awareness in a Conversation

Become aware and choose what to share—thoughts/emotions.
"I assume, believe, interpret…" and/or *"I feel…"*
Share your background experience, standards, expectations, or perceived impact.
"Because I…"

Cue for Remembering A for Awareness

The cue for remembering A—the Awareness move of the OASIS process—is to imagine a thought bubble, like those found in comic strips. This image will help you become aware of your thoughts. The sensory cue for emotions is to focus on your stomach, where your solar plexus center, the seat of emotion, resides. Remember how you felt "butterflies in your stomach" when you were excited as a child going for an amusement park ride or a pony ride? Identify your emotions by completing the sentence, "I feel…" with one word. For example, "I feel happy." It is also useful to say, "Something in me is feeling…." This focusing technique allows you to observe your emotion rather than be enveloped by it. The sensory cue for background is to picture or feel a "backpack" of your historical experiences, standards, or expectations, i.e., the emotional experience or "emotional baggage" hanging on your back.

As an executive coach, many clients call me for regular consultation. In these sessions, we focus on each leader's goals and how he or she can be more effective at work, as well as live an enjoyable life. Let me describe an experience I had to illustrate how OASIS works.

One day, I was expecting a 3:00 p.m. call from Ted, an executive I coach at a Fortune 100 company. I stopped what I was doing and began preparing for the phone meeting. I noticed at 3:10 p.m. that Ted had not called yet (observation). I experienced tightness in my stomach and a feeling of anxiety (emotions) and began to think that Ted could be late or may have forgotten the appointment (assumptions). I questioned whether he was finding enough value in our calls (assumption). I checked my calendar. Did I have the wrong date or time in mind? Ted had forgotten and missed a recent scheduled call (background). Could he have been delayed with another meeting (assumption)? This had happened before not only with Ted, but other corporate clients (background). Ted is a leader with a lot of responsibility and demands that require his focused attention (background). As time passed and it got closer to 3:20 p.m., I began to notice tightening in my chest and I felt frustrated (emotions). I had stopped working on a big project that had a pressing deadline to take Ted's call. I began to feel irritated for losing momentum on my project (emotions).

At 3:25 p.m., I checked my voicemail. At 2:55 p.m., Ted had left me a voicemail message. I must have missed his call when I stepped away to get a drink of water and my phone ringer was muted since I was working on a writing project that was due. He indicated in his message that he was calling a bit early and was looking forward to our conversation. He said that he understood if I had gotten tied up on another project and that he would be open to rescheduling. At the end, he asked me to return his call. I had not expected him to call before the scheduled time.

Each of my assumptions about Ted's behavior had been wrong! I was glad I had not reacted and expressed my frustration via a text message. I was able to call Ted and apologize for not calling earlier and continue with our coaching engagement.

To get better at becoming aware, regularly build in the practice of asking yourself:

Given my observation of: _____.

I assume...

I feel...

Because. . . (My background, standard, expectation, or perceived impact is...)

In this situation, my observation was that I did not hear the phone ring to receive the call from Ted scheduled for 3:00 p.m.

I assume(d)... that Ted was late for the call or had forgotten it, or perhaps I had gotten the date or time wrong.

I feel (felt)... frustrated about not using my time well and losing momentum on another project with a tight deadline.

...irritated with myself for stopping.

...disappointed in Ted for being late.

...worried that Ted may not value our work together.

Because: I have an expectation that people will honor their scheduled appointments. I have a standard or belief that if someone can't attend an appointment, he or she will call me or e-mail to let me know in advance. Also, I had some history with Ted forgetting about a scheduled call. The impact on me was that I lost valuable time I could have used on a project that had a tight deadline.

When you take a moment to become aware, you allow the observer part of you to notice what you are thinking and feeling and consider your background's influence. This observer steps outside of the current situation or drama and observes as if it were observing someone else or directing a movie. The more you build the skill of observing and becoming aware of yourself and others, the more quickly you can assess a situation and hold back from unconsciously reacting. You can ask yourself whether your assumption is "true." Most of the time, we realize it is probably not a fact and we could benefit from further exploration. Using this skill, you will be better equipped to understand yourself and eventually others.

Becoming Self-Aware

Examine your assumptions, emotions, and background before choosing what to share with others. Internally, we process what we observe, making sense of it, and then select an action or response. Sometimes, this process happens very quickly. We may feel we don't have a lot of choice about our actions, particularly when we have a strong emotional reaction. We will focus on successfully addressing these challenges in the next chapter.

The ability to observe ourselves and become self-aware is one of the key characteristics that makes us human. We have the capacity simultaneously to make assumptions about an observation, experience emotions, and also become aware of what is going on. It is as if we are in a theatre, shining a light on the actors and noticing their thoughts and feelings. When we notice our excitement, some part of us is feeling excited and another part is noticing this emotion. Becoming aware is a critical tool for managing and supporting ourselves to engage in valuable conversations. When we are aware, we are more free to make a choice about how we will respond and what we will share with others.

According to the *Harvard Business Review*, seventy-five members of Stanford Graduate School of Business' Advisory Council almost unanimously identified self-awareness as the most important ability for leaders to develop. Sadly, many leaders, especially those early in their careers, believe they are working so hard that they don't have much time for self-exploration. Other research on emotional intelligence identifies self-awareness as a key distinguishing factor in determining success in many areas. The simple process of asking yourself, *"based on what I am observing, I assume..., I feel..., Because..."* will support you in greatly increasing your awareness and leadership capacity.

The Challenge of Becoming Aware

One challenge is to remember that our emotions are influenced by our thoughts. Sometimes we fail to realize that our thoughts influence our perceptions, emotions, and experiences. For instance, when we are absorbed in watching a really good movie, we get so engaged that we feel like the experience is real. Our thoughts determine how we feel about a situation. If you think, "I am going to fail this assignment," you are likely to feel stressed and worried. However, if you think, "I am going to be successful," you are likely to feel energized. Sometimes, our first instinct is to try to blame external circumstances for how we are feeling. We seem to forget that our thoughts are influencing our emotions and perceptions.

Let's try a simple experiment. Imagine you are in an airplane and looking forward to arriving at your destination. You hear an announcement that due to heavy air traffic, your plane is going to be late (this is your observable data). How do you respond? You may think, "I hate flying. Why are there so many delays? This is unfair." You may notice your emotions of anger, frustration, and worry. Or you could think, "This delay gives me time to read a book, complete some work, finish a movie, do some thinking, or listen to my favorite music." Using this second approach, you may feel peaceful and appreciate the time to yourself. The observable data—the delay of the airplane—remains the same. Your thoughts and declarations about the situation, however, influence your subsequent emotions.

The Consortium for Research on Emotional Intelligence in Organizations demonstrates that those who are most aware of their thoughts and emotions are more successful than their peers.[6] In many studies, people say they prefer to work with leaders who are self-aware. In fact,

---

6 See www.eiconsortium.org for current research on emotional and social intelligence.

this kind of awareness, which is part of emotional intelligence, has been found to be a greater indicator of success than cognitive intelligence in study after study. When we notice our sensations and emotions, we are more at choice to examine our thoughts and reflect on how we want to respond.

Our thoughts and emotions are messengers that support us in taking action. Because thoughts and emotions occur so quickly, we often react and move directly to taking action based on our perceptions. If we make it a habit to check-in with ourselves and notice our thoughts and emotions, we will be more at choice about how we want to act and relate to others. Since most of us were not taught to pay attention to our thoughts, emotions, and background, it initially takes practice. However, once you get in the habit, it is not hard. Often, you will first notice your sensations or feelings; then you notice your emotions, and finally, you can review your thoughts.

Meditation or mindfulness is one way to practice regularly paying attention to our thoughts and emotions. A lot of research supports the health and wellbeing benefits of mindfulness. To experience the benefits requires noticing your breath and your thoughts and emotions and labeling them; then you will be more aware and better able to act from a place of choice.

Practice: Becoming Aware of Your Assumptions, Emotions, and Background

Scenario

You learn in a meeting that your company is acquiring another organization. There will be significant reorganization. Your boss displays a draft of the new organization chart. You see that your role has been downgraded and two layers now exist between you and your boss.

What is your reaction to reading this observable data?

Complete the following:

I assume...

I feel...

Because...

Remember that the "because" has to do with your background. What in your background (experience, standards, expectations, perceived impact) is a source for your assumptions?

Defining Assumptions

Assumptions are your thoughts, interpretations, or ideas about some observation. Assumptions are hypotheses about the meaning of something related to you, others, or the environment. Imagine a cartoon character with a thought bubble containing words that reflect thoughts. We will discuss judgments in detail in the next chapter. For now, note that when we are in judgment, we firmly believe we are right and cannot easily identify other possible assumptions. When we make an assumption, we can often generate other possible reasons for an observation, rather than just one.

After reading the scenario above about the reorganization (observation), you probably began to make some assumptions about what could be going on. It is natural for us, as humans, to try to make sense of events. A conversation may have begun inside of you. What are your thoughts or assumptions? Let yourself go. Make up a story. This is what we do when we make an assumption.

You might be asking yourself some of these questions: What actually happened? How were decisions made regarding the new organization structure? Will the new organization value me and my team and what we bring to the organization? Will my years of service be valued? Who are the winners and losers? Will my salary be decreased with the lower grade? If so, when will it happen? Will I lose face and prestige with this change? Who made the decisions? Did anyone go to bat for me? Perhaps I am not valued, and those from the new organization will be more valued. Do I need to look for another position?

Assumptions are our thoughts about observable data—what we see, hear, or learn about. We learned in the previous chapter how quickly we can make assumptions. Our survival depends on trying to make sense of things, and this helps us to feel more in control. Most likely, you made up a story after you read the observable data—even before I gave you questions to consider. This is how our minds work in response to data. Generally, the more relevant the data is to us, the more quickly we make assumptions. For example, you are more likely to jump to assumptions if you feel your job is threatened than if you hear a reorganization is occurring in a neighbor's company. The same would be true—you'd have a more neutral reaction—if you read about a merger in a news article.

When I share example observations with workshop participants, I ask them to share their assumptions. They typically generate a wide array of them about each situation. The assumptions vary depending on the participants' experiences.

In the reorganization scenario, some people might assume they will lose money and prestige. Others assume things will work out positively. Some focus on their failures to gain allegiance and support for their roles. Others immediately move to action and what they need to do to secure employment. Some become paralyzed and feel like victims. Some question the merger's purpose and how decisions are being made. We are usually quick to identify an assumption that makes sense to us. Remember: many possible assumptions can be made from an observation!

In my OASIS Conversation workshops, usually about 80 percent of assumptions given about a piece of observable data are negative. This is human nature. I hear the same negative assumptions throughout the world. Fundamental attribution error is the human condition of assuming negative motives about others' behavior. I am not alone in this observation. Social psychologists have found this phenomenon in their research across cultures. How does fundamental attribution error serve us? It positions us to respond to whatever may impact us. If we assume negative motives for another's behavior, we prepare ourselves to respond quickly to protect ourselves. If I assume that my client may not be committed, I am in a better position to address this issue and work more effectively with him. Alternatively, I may choose to work with a more committed client.

People commonly make the assumption that a bias exists when they don't understand a response. You might think, "I am being demoted because of my gender, my lack of education, or a devalued area of expertise in the company. Perhaps my manager did not like me enough to fight for me." Of course, real bias often does exist and a history of bias is likely to support this assumption.

Social psychology research shows that just as we err in making negative assumptions about another's motivations, if we are observing similar behavior in ourselves, we are likely to generate more positive assumptions. This is called positive attribution error. For example, we can easily rationalize that being a few minutes late for a business meeting is not a big deal, that we are typically on time, and that we work hard and deserve a pass. We are not generally so forgiving of others for the same behavior. Notice how quickly we develop stories about given situations. Our personal background strongly influences how we develop our assumptions (stories). If you have been through mergers and reorganizations where you felt you were negatively impacted, you may expect this again. If you have experienced the opposite, you may be expecting to find a positive benefit for your career with the new organization.

Sometimes we have what Robert Weiss refers to as a negative or positive sentiment override toward another person. For example, if you have a good relationship with your manager, you are more likely to assume she was taking action to protect you during the reorganization. With a negative sentiment override, you are more likely to assume your manager would hurt you if she had the chance. We need to be aware when we start believing that another person is selfish or primarily focused on his or her own needs. This perspective influences our assumptions and actions.

Since we all have a natural "negativity bias" that helps us prepare for potential danger and protect ourselves, we tend to assume things won't work and others will hurt us. Just knowing about this propensity allows us to examine our assumptions more closely. According to Daniel Kahneman, Nobel Prize winner and author of *Thinking, Fast and Slow*, we experience many unconscious errors in our reasoning and biases. He argues that we naturally are biased in what he calls our quick "System 1" thinking and that a second look enables us to slow things down and reflect again. Two different parts of our brain are used. System 1 uses association and metaphor to produce a quick and dirty snap shot of reality and is filled with biases. System 2 involves a more deliberate and rational assessment and takes more conscious attention and energy. It is slowing down and reflecting that enables us to notice our cognitive biases.

Benefits of Noticing Assumptions and Slowing Reactions

Slow yourself down a bit and notice the thoughts you're having. Try to catch yourself and recall that you make things up, and notice that your thoughts are based on your background and conditioning. Then, consider that you may not have all the facts and you may have a natural tendency for negativity bias. With this stance, you are likely to remain more curious and open. By remaining open, you are less likely to take action that you'll regret later, and you are more open to connecting with others.

Notice your thoughts and feelings and hold back from reacting until you learn more. In my late call situation with Ted, I was glad I did not respond in frustration and anger. In fact, it was my responsibility to check my voicemail for messages, and Ted may have had reason to be irritated with me. I benefited from slowing myself down and noticing my assumptions.

Notice your assumption that your boss did not support you, and manage how you respond to the draft organization chart. Rather than react, you will be better positioned to ask questions about the plans going forward and you will remember that the chart was only a draft with room for modifications and dialogue.

Noticing your main assumption and considering other assumptions will keep you open for dialogue. Since we are prone to think automatically that our assumption is the correct interpretation, instead, practice looking for a number of possible assumptions about a given situation.

Given our background, we often think our assumptions make sense, so it is not easy to generate other ideas. We may immediately think that the proposed organization chart is based on favoritism rather than merit. When you cannot generate other assumptions and you are certain you are "right," you are making a judgment.

I spend more time searching for possible interpretations when I am in a foreign land or faced with an important situation that may not immediately make sense. For example, when I can't understand why someone did not fulfill his or her promise, I may be more curious about possible options. It particularly pays to slow ourselves down in situations where the people involved have different backgrounds. Increasingly, you and your colleagues may come from different countries, have generational differences, or come from different fields of study or work. If you are in sales and your colleague is a lawyer, you are likely to see a situation differently.

How to Identify Assumptions

The way to build the muscle of noticing and identifying assumptions is to ask yourself habitually, "What are the thoughts, assumptions, or stories I make up about the observable data?" "Is my assumption true?"

Then ask, "What are other possible assumptions or stories?" Remember—it is human nature to develop a negative assumption, particularly about someone's motive. Practice considering other alternatives.

Begin the habit of noticing your assumptions. Start today, when you are interacting with people. You may want to keep a journal to record in writing and reflect upon some of your assumptions. You may discover interesting patterns based on your background. Notice especially when your assumptions are not accurate. Perhaps you assumed your spouse didn't want to go to a party when he or she did. What led you to that assumption? How will you know the next time? Do you notice a pattern of assumptions? Maybe you notice that you continually assume people won't follow through on their agreements with you.

Notice your patterns and how they influence your responses to situations. You may have a pattern of assuming people will let you down. Knowing this can help you to consider more closely whether your assumption is accurate and work to shift an habitual response.

Experiencing Emotions

Just as we generate assumptions based on observations, we also experience emotions. Emotions are sensations (feelings) we experience in our bodies and the labels we use to define them. Emotions are like waves of energy that pass through us and mobilize or demobilize us from taking action. An emotion is energy in motion. For instance, if you are excited about your partner's suggestion to go out dancing, you will experience a sensation in your body and have energy to get a babysitter, make arrangements, and go. Emotions are messengers giving us clues about what is important to us.

Emotions, like our assumptions, are impacted by our experiences. If you were raised to believe that people should be on time, then when someone is late, you are likely to experience sensations, such as tightness in your chest, throat, or stomach, and feel angry, upset, or disappointed. On the other hand, if you believe a scheduled time to meet is a target rather than a strict deadline, you are unlikely to experience the same emotions when someone arrives or calls a few minutes late. Our emotions are impacted by our thoughts about what's important to us. If we are scheduled to meet someone and we have a value that it is polite to honor our appointments, we are more likely to experience stress and anxiety about our partner being late. Alternatively, you may feel fine about your partner being late for a day at the beach that has no specific time constraints. However, if you are tired and become focused on how often your partner shows up late, you could experience a heaviness in your body. You might even become angry. That will definitely negatively impact having fun together at the beach!

Our assumptions and emotions are closely related—almost like the words and music of a song. Sometimes our thoughts are dominant while other times our emotions are. Also, some of us are more conscious of feelings than others. For instance, if you grew up in a home or culture where emotions are valued and easily demonstrated, you are more likely to notice your feelings and be comfortable in expressing them. If emotions were not emphasized in your family or culture, however, you may not be as fully aware of your feelings. For example, many of the executives I work with are not aware of their body sensations or emotions. They may have learned to override—ignore their feelings—because they learned somewhere that business professionals are expected to suppress their feelings.

Years ago when I worked with a Wall Street firm, I introduced the value of constructively expressing emotions at work. A man in the group said, "This is Wall Street; we don't have feelings." In fact, I had been hired to work as a consultant with the firm because it was experiencing high turnover of some of its best people. Its employee survey showed that people did not feel valued and respected by their managers and coworkers. Employees were spending their valuable energy fighting each other. They could have been working together on important projects instead. In this Fortune 100 company, the CEO and other leaders started using the OASIS Conversation process and sharing their emotions first with each other and then with their staff. Afterward, they saw marked improvements in employee engagement as well as in business results.

For a long time, I was not that aware of my own emotions. I remember going to a workshop where participants were asked how they felt after different exercises. I discovered I couldn't identify what I was feeling. I could easily report my thoughts, but my feelings were quite elusive to me. After that experience, I started paying attention to my emotions. At first, I noticed emotions at the movie theater—especially strong feelings like anger or sadness. Then I started becoming aware of more subtle feelings. I learned in time that emotions serve the purpose of notifying us to pay attention to something. For example, as I write this, I notice I feel a tightness in my chest and I feel worried. What am I worried about? I slow myself down and make an assessment. After thinking about it, I take it as a cue that I need to make reservations for a flight. I don't want to risk paying a higher fare or being unable to leave at my desired time. If we acknowledge our feelings as messengers, then we can learn from them and use them for support to move into action. After I made my flight reservations, I noticed I felt more relaxed. The energy of the emotion moved through me after I responded to the need. Emotions are waves that emerge, grow, stabilize, and then naturally decline. Sometimes, they seem to persist, and then they benefit from empathy and being acknowledged.

Our emotions have a sensation component where we may feel tightness in our chests or a pressure in our stomachs. If we slow down and pay attention, we may be able to identify a sensation and an accompanying feeling. The tightness in my stomach can be that I feel anxious, worried, concerned, or alarmed. Like learning any language, it gets easier to name feelings as you pay closer attention and notice them. Notice whether you feel comfortable with a sense of openness and energy to move toward something, uncomfortable with a feeling of constriction and energy to move away from something, or neutral without a feeling for movement.

At the other extreme of awareness are people who over-indulge in feelings and drama. Some people become overly sensitive to emotions, are easily hurt, and react strongly to emotions. They tend to use their emotions to influence others. If you have a tendency to over-react to emotions, you will also benefit from noticing your emotions and naming them.

Benefits of Noticing Your Emotions

Emotions alert us when to say yes or no to something. Feelings provide us with clues about where to pay attention and focus our energy and what actions to take. What differentiates successful leaders, professionals, teachers, and parents is not just their IQs, but also the ability to be aware of their own emotions as well as those of others and then know how to work with this awareness.

Many of us become so busy that we do not notice our feelings. If we listen to them, and actually feel them in our bodies, emotions serve us by calling our attention to things that help us to be more effective in the world. For example, if you are talking with someone and you begin to feel a bit tight in your chest, this can be a cue that you need to pay attention. Likewise, if you pause to experience gratitude, you're apt to feel more joy.

Our emotions give us energy to take action. If we get angry, we are more likely to say or do something. If we don't feel strongly about an issue, we are unlikely to respond. For example, if you experience feelings about a political candidate, you are more likely to support or fight against her campaign. The same thing happens in families and workplaces. If you are excited about an idea or new product, you are likely to mobilize your energy to plan a surprise party or develop a marketing plan.

If you do not pay attention to your emotions, you are likely to go directly from noticing some observable data to taking action or not taking action. When a person is late, you may immediately react, such as by reprimanding him, cutting the person off in mid-explanation, or complaining. When you shine the spotlight on your own assumptions and emotions, you can explore whether your assumptions are accurate or not. If you do yell and later find out that it was your mistake, however, you will need to apologize. You are also likely to have created some friction and mistrust between you and the other person.

Another benefit of noticing your emotions—if you acknowledge that you are upset by thinking or saying, "I feel angry"—is you can take action to cool yourself down. For example, you might take deep breaths or go for a short, brisk walk. In a high state of emotion, you won't have full access to your rational or creative brain so you can consider and explore alternatives.

When a young daughter was told she could not watch another television show, she became angry and began to yell and resist. In the heat of her anger, she said, "I don't like you," "You don't love me," "You always watch your show!" and "I never want to see you again." All of these words sprung from her anger in a few minutes after the television was turned off. Later, she apologized, saying, "I'm sorry; I guess I got carried away." This is what often happens to us when we are in strong emotion. The current of the emotion carries us away into reactions that are often not thought out. This current can be referred to as an "amygdala hijack"—leaving us with limited access to our rational capacity. Sometimes, we feel like we can't help ourselves. Learning to work with our emotions comes as we develop. Children at young ages are not expected to have this skill, but we expect adults to be aware of their emotions and manage them well.

Make a habit of noticing your emotions and realizing that they are temporary and part of a system aimed at protecting us. We need to appreciate and respect our emotions for the messages they bring. By practicing noticing our emotions, we can catch ourselves, allow the energy to move, and shift to a more creative state.

Managing Emotions

As discussed, when we are in the heat of a strong emotion, we do not have full rational capacity to solve a problem or consider options. Sometimes, the energy displayed when we show strong emotions isn't pretty. Unfortunately, the way we may try to manage strong emotions in ourselves and others is to cut them off. We tell ourselves or others to stop crying or stop being angry. Does this usually work? Not in my experience. If I am upset and someone tells me I shouldn't be, I don't feel understood and feel even more upset and repress the emotion.

Parents often tell their children to stop crying, or to "straighten up." I have discovered that as a parent, when I do this, I may be upset, too, and trying to manage my own emotions. It works best to observe and acknowledge our feelings. By simply noting, "I am angry" or "Some part of me is frustrated." I can begin to allow the energy to shift and hold myself back from the instinct to yell, strike out, or run out of the room. By acknowledging our strong emotion, we have more of our rational capacity available to address the situation. Somehow, we think if someone would just stop feeling angry, we could solve the problem. However, telling others that their feelings are wrong or bad only seems to strengthen the emotion's fury. What we resist tends to persist.

Instead, learn to experience an emotion, notice your sensation, and label it, and then the emotion can naturally shift. You are, in fact, giving yourself empathy.

One of my coaching clients, Mary, shared that sometimes her negative feelings last too long. An emotion usually lasts a short time— approximately seven seconds. However, if we do not acknowledge our feelings and keep revisiting a situation, they linger on. As we review our story over and over, our thoughts perpetuate our feelings. Once we appreciate feelings and consider what kind of message or service they are trying to offer, we often experience a shift. For another example, Allie was still experiencing a feeling of being burdened by something heavy, like a major exam was pending, months after she made a critical error in a report for a client. Once she identified the heavy sensations and feelings of embarrassment and worry about being viewed as incompetent, she acknowledged and appreciated how these feelings were trying to keep her safe and ensure she was diligent. After giving herself empathy, she was able to let the heaviness go. She received accolades on her next report. The process of naming our emotions, and accepting them without judgment, supports us in shifting to having access to more of our brain, the neocortex and being more at choice. It is useful to have an open mindset and welcome our sensations and emotions as bringing us messages.

Brain Connection

Brain research supports the value of identifying sensations and emotions. When you are interacting with others and experience certain feelings, you may choose to suppress or ignore them. Trying to do so takes a lot of energy. In addition, if we try to suppress emotions when we are with others, they tend to sense some incongruity. A good option is to allow the observer part of yourself to welcome and label your emotion. By doing so, your prefrontal cortex becomes activated and your limbic system arousal can be minimized. In his book *Your Brain at Work*, David Rock reviews scientific studies and proposes that emotions and the prefrontal cortex work like a seesaw. Strong emotions can reduce prefrontal ability to see options while labeling can reengage the prefrontal cortex and the ability to think and explore. A particularly useful approach is to identify a metaphor or symbol for your emotions. Having a long internal dialogue may only add fuel and further inflame your emotions.

Taking Responsibility for Emotions

What language do you use when you are talking about your emotions? We are prone to saying things like, "You made me angry!" and think others are responsible for our feelings. To be clear, we will have feelings about what others are doing or saying, based on our background beliefs, standards, expectations, and perceived impact. However, no one can "make" you feel angry. We are each experiencing different feelings in response to a given observation. I may be delighted that a friend stopped by to see me for a few minutes yesterday as she passed my office. On another day, I could be frustrated because I was preparing for a meeting and in a rush. If I had a major deadline looming and was not close to meeting my project goals, I could have felt annoyed and upset by the disruption.

One day, we can be upset with the heavy traffic as we drive to work while the next day, we may not notice the delay. We may even enjoy listening to the radio and having time alone. What our needs are at the moment and how we are interpreting the traffic based on our expectations affects us. We might remind ourselves that we knew there would be traffic, but it is worth it to live in a town we enjoy and to have interesting work in the city. Based on my background, I might recall that the thirty-minute commute I am now experiencing is easy compared to the two-hour commute I used to have! In summary, I'll react to the same behavior or situation on different days based on what is going on for me at the time. Of course, this adds to the complexity of living and working with others since we can't know or always predict what is going on for them.

Moods

In addition to experiencing emotions related to specific observable data, we each tend to experience moods, which are more prolonged feelings. We might wait to see what our boss's mood is before asking for a raise or a vacation. We assess our partner's mood to identify the best time to make a request. Our moods can be based on how we are physically feeling, the weather, or specific events. We can feel relaxed and energetic during a holiday when the sun is shining and the weather warm, or we can feel stressed and worried when working on taxes. Some people are optimistic while others are more pessimistic. Our backgrounds and experiences influence our moods. Often our moods reflect what our inner voices are saying. For example, when I continue to repeat to myself, "I have so much to do and will never get it completed!" I experience pressure and worry rather than peace and joy. The more I declare this to myself and hold my body in a worried posture (body contracted and shallow breathing), the more I experience the prolonged emotion (mood) of worry. Over time, we may think our moods are the way things are. We fail to realize we can change our posture (stand taller and become more grounded and breathe more fully) and our thoughts ("I am grateful for this day and all that I have.") and impact our moods.

Whether we express them or not, emotions exist in our bodies. Many research studies have demonstrated the hazards of not dealing with our feelings. After analyzing hundreds of studies, Howard Friedman, Ph.D., a professor at the University of California, demonstrated that being chronically irritated, pessimistic, depressed, anxious, and cynical doubles the risk of contracting a major disease. He reported that disease occurs because links exist between the brain's emotional centers and the immune and cardiovascular systems. Chronic feelings then communicate themselves to our systems, affecting their ability to function properly.

Identifying Emotions

Like assumptions, it only takes having the intention and giving focused attention—shining the light of awareness—on feelings to begin to notice them. Scan your body and notice the sensations you are experiencing. Start with your head and simply notice any tightness or other sensations. Kathy became aware of tightness in her throat when she went to meetings with new people. She felt herself being more reserved than usual and labeled her emotion as "I feel nervous" (when I meet new people). To protect herself, she held herself back from speaking freely. This action may serve her or not. By being aware of her emotions, she can be more at choice about how she will respond. Holding herself back may have served Kathy at an earlier life stage, but it may not be her best option now. Just acknowledging her usual pattern may free her to try another option.

A way to differentiate emotions from thoughts is simply to notice and say "I feel ____," using one feeling word. "I feel like you are not committed" is not a feeling. This is a thought disguised as a feeling. If you can answer with one word: "I feel disappointed, happy, angry, hurt, excited, or concerned," then you have probably identified an emotion.

Remember, emotions are like waves that go through your body. Like waves, feelings will shift from moment to moment. Your feelings should not be judged and do not make you good or bad. They are natural, based on your interpretation of observable data, which, in turn, is based on your background conditioning. When Kathy noticed that she was feeling nervous, her immediate response was to be mad at herself. When she was able simply to notice and appreciate the message from her body, she realized she had succeeded with meetings similar to this one before. She relaxed.

Whether we express or repress our emotions, being aware of them will serve us well. For example, Shelly was very disappointed in her close friend's decision to move to another town for a better professional opportunity. Shelly had several options. She could be unaware of her feelings and act on them by not calling her friend for days. She could react by yelling at her friend and creating an argument, in which they got mad at each other and did not speak. If she did become aware of them, she could choose to express her feelings and tell her friend how disappointed and sad she was about her plans to move away. Shelly could also choose to wait to share her disappointment at another time and let her friend enjoy her anticipation and excitement about the new situation. The act of being aware of her feelings would support Shelly in having more choices.

Practice Noticing Your Emotions

Imagine you are on a beach. Notice the sand warming your feet and the sunny blue sky and billowy clouds. Check in with yourself and scan your body. How do you feel as you imagine this scene? Perhaps you notice your stomach and shoulders relaxing; you then take a deep breath and notice that you feel refreshed and joyful. You may recall walking or playing on the beach previously. Perhaps you remember the uncomfortable feeling of leftover sand in your shoes and finding the beach too hot. You may notice you have some energy to act—such as taking off your shoes, walking along the surf, or snapping a photograph.

Now imagine that you hear a woman screaming, "Help! Help!" Scan your body. How do you feel now? Do you notice your throat or arms tensing? Do you get up and run toward the woman? Do you feel excited? Afraid? Worried? Do you think about another time that you heard a call for help?

The scene changes. Now you observe the woman fiercely hugging and scolding her young son, who had evidently waded too far into the water. Again, scan your body; notice any sensations and feelings. Describe them. "I feel...(use a word expressing a feeling: relieved, satisfied, upset, pleased). How was it for you to notice your sensations and feelings? Do you see the relationship between your feelings and movement toward action?

More Practice

- Make an intention to notice your sensations and feelings. Label your feelings using one word. For instance, as I scan my body at this moment, I notice tension in my back. "I feel concerned." Or I feel tightness in my stomach. "Something in me is worried." (I'm thinking: Will I get this report done on time?)
- Notice when you are in interactions, when you are watching television or a movie, and when you read what you are feeling.
- Share your sensations and emotions with a friend. Agree that each of you will take turns noticing and reporting your sensations and emotions. Notice how your feelings change as you pay attention to different things.
- Review a list of feelings. Start noticing nuances of your feelings. For instance, are you happy, excited, optimistic, thrilled, joyful, or ecstatic?
- Remember to breathe and allow yourself to notice your feelings. Remind yourself that it is natural for humans to experience emotions.
- You may want to journal about your emotions. Look back at what you wrote on different days and notice how you were feeling. How did your emotions relate to your actions?
- Make it a ritual to share an event of your day and your emotional reaction with someone close to you. For example, "I had lunch at Dao with my college friend, Nina, today. I felt happy to see her and excited to hear her news about her new job." Sharing our emotions with others supports connection and builds trust.

When to Share Our Awareness of Assumptions, Emotions, and Background

In interactions with others, after becoming aware of our emotions, we need to decide what to share with another person. Sometimes, we will conclude that being aware of an emotion is enough for us. We won't need to share it. In other situations, it will be useful to share our assumptions, emotions, and background. Ask yourself, "Will sharing my assumptions, emotions, and background help or hurt the relationship at this point?" If sharing our assumptions will hurt, by making the other person defensive, it may be best not to share them at that time. For example, you may assume that your colleague did not attend a meeting because he doesn't care about the team's project. You are angry because you have a rule in your background that team players should attend all regular meetings. You may decide not to share because you know he's been told to attend the meetings by his manager. However, if he repeatedly misses meetings, and it's damaging the team's efforts, it may be appropriate to share your anger and get his attention.

Each situation is different and "it depends" on whether sharing will serve the relationship or not. Communicating is more of an art than a science. When we do not share our assumptions, feelings, or background with another, then often that person will assume or guess them. Sometimes, the person may guess wrong. When we can share our assumptions, emotions, and background, we make ourselves more vulnerable and reduce the need for another person to guess or assume.

Finally, strive to be authentic. If you are upset and say nothing's wrong, the other person is likely to feel the incongruence and doubt your honesty.

Identifying Your Background

Our background can be defined as our previous experience or history that impacts how we interpret our observations. Our standards or expectations about how things should be are included. Our background includes the context of cultural, work, and family experiences and our conditioning.

Let's return to the situation where you learned that your organization was merging with another company and you will now be two levels below your current role on the organization chart. When you initially read this observable data, you made assumptions and had feelings based on your background. If you have been through company mergers, you are likely to be more confident and realize that draft organization charts are likely to shift and should not be considered permanent at an early stage of the process. If you have a friend whose career was negatively impacted after a corporate merger, you are likely to be more alarmed. If you are relatively new to the organization, you could be worried about having enough support to secure a senior role. If you were considering retiring and starting your own business, you are likely to be more relaxed and positively anticipate an exit package. As you see, your reaction will depend on your background experience and current situation.

We evaluate differently depending on our past experiences, our expectations, and our standards for how things should be done.

A leader I coach was devastated when she saw her name several levels and grades below her current post on a draft organization chart after a corporate merger. She became sick to her stomach and began to make immediate plans to find another job. She found it hard not to cry after she had worked so hard for the organization for more than two decades. She felt devalued and hurt that she would lose her status. A few weeks later, she learned that, in fact, she was getting a promotion and taking over some additional areas! Her boss made a mistake in not telling people that the chart he shared was a draft.

Background Conditioning

How deeply rooted are some of our assumptions and judgments? Let's perform a couple of exercises that will illustrate the power of our background conditioning.

Exercise A

What is this? **VII**

Most of my workshop participants, answer, "The Roman numeral seven."

How can VII be turned into an eight with just one line?

You most likely responded with something like, "Draw a straight line down after the last two lines, which creates the Roman numeral "VIII."

Now, what is this? **IX**

You probably responded, "The Roman numeral nine."

How can this be changed into six with just one line?

* Please think about this before you look at the answer below. Most workshop participants are stumped by this question.

Exercise B

Fill in the missing number in the following sequence and identify the pattern that determines this sequence:

8 5 4 9 1 7 6 __ 0

After giving it some thought, read the answer on the next page.

Most people in my workshops find these exercises challenging. Usually, the person who figures them out was not paying attention when I put them on the flip chart, or else demonstrates the ability to stop, step back, shift, be curious, and see other perspectives.

Each of the exercises conditioned you to think about the problem from one perspective. In the first task, you learned within a few seconds to think about Roman numerals when I told you that most participants responded that VII was the Roman numeral seven. In fact, in my workshops, I say nothing, yet observe that participants quickly conclude that VII is a Roman numeral.

In the next few seconds, you were conditioned to think in straight lines, since VII can be transformed into a Roman numeral eight with the addition of a single straight line. When I asked you how to change IX into a six with "just one line," you most likely assumed I meant a straight line.

This earlier, simple conditioning made it likely that solving the problem was more difficult. You operated from the perspective or paradigm of Roman numerals and straight lines. When it came to solving the problem, you relied on your background experience to search for clues. Instead, the successful solution to the problem relied on a different viewpoint—an alphabet perspective. To shift from the Roman numeral and straight-line perspective into which you were "locked in," you must step back and relax to tackle the problem with a fresh perspective.

The answer is: Put a curved line, or an "S," before the other characters to make SIX.

Consider the impact of the few seconds of conditioning in the

Roman numeral exercise. Then imagine the impact of our lifetime of conditioning based on upbringing, education, and a multitude of experiences! Neuroscience research shows that we each have unique neural paths based on our experiences.

In Exercise B, you could probably determine fairly quickly that 3 and 2 are the only single-digit numbers missing in the series. However, your earlier training most likely conditioned you to think in terms of a mathematical mindset to pinpoint a pattern to the numbers. But if you tried to add, subtract, or use other calculations, you were unable to find a pattern. Once again, this exercise requires a different perspective— the alphabet paradigm.

If you spell out the numbers, you will quickly recognize that they are in alphabetical order: eight, five, four, nine, one, seven, six, three, two, and zero. Many adults are stumped by this exercise. Since they are not yet stuck in the paradigm of solving mathematical equations, children often have an easier time finding a correct answer. The next numbers in the series are 3 and then 2 because they come after six in alphabetical order.

Two people may look at the same observable data and insist that they see an entirely different picture than the other person. Similarly, scientists sometimes look at the same data from experiments and arrive at different conclusions based on their paradigms, perspectives, backgrounds, conditioning, worldviews, and history.

When we understand that everyone thinks he or she is right, it is easier to see the value in noticing and developing the ability to suspend judgments, while becoming open to other perspectives and mindsets.

Benefits of Being Aware of Your Background

Because some of our beliefs and expectations may be deep inside of us, we may not be clearly aware of why we're making certain assumptions and experiencing certain emotions about a situation. Our reactions may happen so fast that we just believe our view is the way it is! Having worked with multicultural audiences throughout the world, I have had the opportunity to witness the impact of backgrounds firsthand on many occasions.

For example, business people make different assumptions and have different emotions about someone arriving late for a meeting depending on the person's background. A person from Germany may be more upset about tardiness and consider the person to be unprofessional while a person from Brazil will probably be less concerned. In Brazil, the culture focuses less on clock time—events are allowed to run their natural course. Family and personality differences also impact how we respond to someone being late for a meeting. Someone who grew up in a military family, where dinner is on the table at six o'clock sharp each night, is more likely to expect others to arrive at a designated time. If you were taught to call ahead or let your caregivers know whether you were running late, you may expect the same from your colleagues at work. They may not have learned this courtesy or may think it would be "bothersome" for a manager to receive such an "unimportant" call. Different backgrounds and rules about how to behave should be considered.

Peter, a workshop participant from the former Soviet Union, was horrified when a colleague asked him to help identify who had taken something personal from his desk and shared it with others. No one had confessed. Peter was deeply offended by his friend's request. He abruptly ended their relationship outside of work and avoided his colleague as much as possible. It took some digging for him to realize that he related the request to former KGB interrogations. Peter was offended that his friend would think he would snoop for information and tell on others. Once Peter understood his own background and reaction, he had energy for reinstituting his friendship.

Understanding and being aware of your own background will help you clarify your expectations of others. You may share your expectation and ask whether others support your view or perhaps would like to suggest another alternative. Believing our way is "right" may lead to being angry or disappointed with others.

It is valuable to remember that we are all having different experiences based on our history and perceptions. Even words have different meanings and interpretations. When one person hears of a "high performing team," he may think this means sharing information, while another interprets it as each member doing his or her unique part to support a goal and having few meetings. If we remember that everyone is having a different experience, we will be more open to learning another's perspective and working to find common ground. We can shift from being judgmental to being open to learning more about another's perception and be in a position to co-create.

A Challenge Related to Identifying Background

Many of our expectations slip into the background so we are not fully aware of them until they are disrupted or violated. To be efficient, many of our behaviors become habits; the way we do things. For example, if I learned and now believe that people should return calls within a day, I will have judgments when people do not follow that rule. If I can manage myself and be aware of my expectation, I may decide to share it, and after discussing it with my colleagues, determine whether that time frame or a different one makes more sense. Sometimes our habitual patterns are no longer needed, so being interrupted gives us the opportunity to question them and adopt more suitable behavior.

Brain Connection

Our expectations influence the information we notice in the world. So many possibilities exist of what to notice that we cannot possibly take in all the available data. For instance, if we expect people not to support us, we will filter data and find verification for our expectations. We will ignore obvious examples of support and consider them exceptions. Remind yourself of what you want to look for in your home and work environments. You will be better positioned to notice moments of support, if that's what you seek.

At other times, you may slip into an inner dialogue based on your expectations and miss what is present in the moment. For example, if you expect things to go badly at a picnic, you could be mentally looking for negative circumstances and miss what is actually happening! Build the habit of checking in with yourself, noting your expectations, and being open for more data that may confirm or not confirm your expectations.

Another reality: many of our memories are unconscious. We can, therefore, experience reactions based on our past experiences without being fully aware of why we are responding in a certain way. Research on memory identifies two kinds of memories—explicit and implicit. Explicit memories are those that can be recalled. Implicit memories are not so easy to recall, yet they influence us. Explicit memories are encoded in the hippocampus part of the brain while implicit memories are more dispersed.

Our implicit memories color our experience in the present even though we are not consciously recalling them. We are all biased by our past, even when we are not aware of how our memories are influencing our perceptions of the present moment. For example, if as a child, you were scolded for speaking up about something you achieved and told not to brag, you may respond negatively when someone asks you to introduce yourself to a group or share a successful project. Our memories are stored as neural pathways (circuits), and when these circuits are aroused, they channel chemicals and electricity along a specific pathway. We then respond in the same way as the past. You may not know why you feel anxious about introducing yourself. The more you face similar experiences, the more the circuit is developed and the more easily it is triggered. People are influenced by their background experiences—whether or not they are conscious of it.

Human brain scans have identified spindle cells responsible for processing emotional experiences. When we were very young, our brains had few spindle cells and could easily become overwhelmed. Without full capacity to process our emotions, many of us elected not to experience our feelings fully. We chose ways to deal with issues such as not getting attention. We incorporated memories from our early years that served us then, such as "Don't ask for attention; you don't deserve it." These memories, which now may be unconscious, may have been useful in our youth; however, they may not serve us as adults. As we mature, our brains have a lot more spindle cells and a greater capacity to process feelings. However, many of us continue with our habitual patterns, so we may walk around with a lot of unresolved emotions from our background that still influence us. The more you notice these emotions and trust that you have the capacity to move through them, the more you will! Just the act of acknowledging your responses enables your growth.

Practice Noticing Your Background

- How does your background impact your expectations? Let's begin simply. Ask yourself, "What is behind my assumption?" "What in my culture, family, school, previous job, or experience is impacting my assumption?" For instance, ask, "Why did I feel irritated at my boss for not including me in the decision?" An answer might be: "I have the expectation that those involved will be included in the decision-making process and will have real input." After reflecting further, you might think, "I have this expectation because of my experiences with my parents where I was included as an active contributor. As the oldest child in a large family, I participated actively in discussions and decision-making. Lastly, my training in management shows that people have more commitment when they have input into a decision-making process, so it's good business practice."

- With friends or family, when you notice different perceptions, ask each person what in his or her background could have influenced his or her perception. For example, one man sees a beagle dog and is sad because it reminds him of a long lost, beloved pet. Another person may be worried or fearful because it reminds her of the time she was bitten by a dog. Notice how varied our assumptions and feelings are and how much they correlate with our backgrounds.

- Be curious about the backgrounds of those around you. When you understand someone's history, you can be empathetic, and you are more likely to find common ground. If you haven't already, ask those in your life some specifics about their backgrounds. Ask: Where did you grow up? What were some of the rules in your home? What was important to your caregivers? What do you believe are the key things a manager (or a parent) should do? How should parents and children relate? Who in your perspective is a real leader? How have you been influenced by a leader? What are some of the challenges you face with your manager? Pay close attention to people's stories and what is important to them and how they have been influenced. You'll learn a lot about why they act the way they do.

The Benefit of Sharing Background

After becoming aware of your own background, determine whether it's beneficial to share it—experiences, values, or expectations. Each situation is different; however, it may be useful to ask yourself: "Will it help or hurt the relationship to share my background or expectations in this situation?" Much will depend on your history with the person, the timing, her style, and your understanding of her background. The benefit of sharing background is that the other person has a clearer understanding of where you are coming from. She doesn't have to guess and operate from her guesses or assumptions. By sharing this information, we make ourselves a bit more vulnerable and open to others. Being vulnerable creates connection and understanding. I believe it is important for today's leaders to focus on being more vulnerable and thus creating more trust.

Often when we understand someone else's background, we can be more responsive and less defensive. We may not have to interpret the person's actions as being mean-spirited and directed against us. Understanding another person's background sheds light on a situation so it can be viewed more clearly. You don't need to agree with the person's perspective—just try to understand it.

How A—Awareness of Assumptions, Emotions, and Background Fits in the OASIS Conversation Process

So far, we have focused on becoming aware of your own assumptions, emotions, and background in an interaction. In challenging interactions with others, the first step is self-awareness. In fact, in those situations where time is available, you may want to plan for the entire OASIS Conversation before an interaction.

You can figure out your observation (O) and be aware of your assumptions, emotions, and background (A). You can also anticipate or guess what each move is likely to be for the other person. It is useful to be curious about others' assumptions, emotions, and background. Preparing will make you ready to have a meaningful conversation. However, in typical everyday interactions, you may not have time to prepare. Part of the art of having an OASIS Conversation is choosing what you will share of your assumptions, emotions, and background and when.

For example, if a person doesn't meet a report deadline, you can say, "I notice that the report is not complete as scheduled." Then wait for the person's response. He will undoubtedly make assumptions by your tone and demeanor about whether you are angry, upset, or curious. He may assume you are angry and become defensive. Instead, you may be concerned and surprised since it is unlike his usual behavior.

By sharing your emotions and assumptions, he is less likely to make negative assumptions.

On the other hand, if you are angry, you will need to determine whether it will help or hurt to share "I'm angry." When you express anger, some people will give you their immediate attention while others will become defensive. You need to guess whether sharing your assumptions, emotions, and background will be supportive. Also, remember that in an interaction, you will have a number of chances to share them as well as learn about the other person's. You may find it useful to visualize that you and the other person are operating out of different assumptions, feelings, and backgrounds. After that, focus your intentions on making sure you understand each other and can find common ground for agreement.

Summary

In this chapter, we defined and showed the importance of becoming aware of our assumptions, emotions, and background related to our observations. Next, we discussed the need to determine whether it will help or hurt an interaction to share our assumptions, emotions, and background. Being vulnerable—allowing the other to understand where we are coming from—and trying not to incite defensive behavior are guidelines to determine when and what to share. This decision depends on various aspects of your relationship with the other person and the situation.

Keep yourself open to an interaction by suspending judgment and shifting to being open and curious. To learn more about the shifting process, turn to the next chapter, which is about the S of OASIS Moves—shift to being open.

Practice

- Make it a practice to ask yourself, "What are my thoughts? What are my emotions? What sensations am I feeling in my body?"
- Regularly ask yourself, "What are my background, history, expectations, and standards in this situation?" Ask your colleague, partner, or friend the same.
- Slow down and notice your thoughts and emotions before taking action.

CHAPTER 6

S Is for Shift

How Do You Step Back from Reacting and Shift to Being Open to Possibilities?

"In times of change, those who are prepared to learn will inherit the land, while those who think they already know will find themselves wonderfully equipped to face a world that no longer exists."

— Eric Hoffer

"The true journey of discovery does not consist in searching for new territories but in having new eyes."

— Marcel Proust

OASIS Conversations

Have a clear intention, plan when possible, and build rapport.

O = **Observation**

A = **Awareness** (of assumptions, emotions, and background)

S = Shift (to being open)

⌇ = Importance

S = Solution

Shift (to being open) in a Conversation

Notice your judgment signal, stop, step back, and shift to being open and curious. Check your intention to be open.

"Do I understand?" "How do you see the situation?" "It's my intention…(to understand your view, to work together, achieve goals together, etc.)."

Cue for Remembering S—The Shift (to being open) Move of the OASIS Process

Usually, you notice when you are making a judgment and experience tightness in your chest or other areas and may hear yourself saying, "I'm right and he's wrong." Catch yourself before you speak and realize you are making a judgment. Visualize a bright red STOP sign with the T on the sign in the shape of a judge's gavel. This image may serve you as a reminder to stop, step back from the situation, and shift to being open and curious. Another useful image: picture yourself standing up with your hand held up to signify "STOP." Hang up and suspend your judgment on a hook, as if you are hanging up a judge's robes. Visualize yourself stepping back and shifting—literally opening your hands—to signify your openness to understanding the other person's perspective.

It is helpful then to remind yourself of your intention to be open-minded. Is it your intention to work together, achieve goals together, understand one another, and experience harmony (an oasis) together? Your openness to understanding another will show primarily through your body language and emotional stance of openness and curiosity. Ask questions to clarify, such as "Do I understand?" or "How do you see the situation?" You may also share your intention. For example, "I want to understand your perspective," or "It's my intention for us to work well together."

The Shift OASIS Move is critical for engaging in successful interactions. Noticing when you are closed/contracted or open/expansive will enable you to shift to create an environment where different perspectives can be explored. This chapter will demystify the move of shifting from contracting and reacting to being open and creating an environment for exploring possibilities. The key is to notice your reactions and to honor your intention of being open-minded. Although the steps of shifting may happen quickly (even in seconds!), we will identify each one. You truly need to understand this important OASIS Move to be a leader who can make a difference.

1. ***Notice your judgment signal.***

2. ***Stop, step back, and suspend judgment.*** Recall your intention to be open and assume positive intent. Cool down—if needed. (Suggestions for cooling down are given later in this chapter.)

3. ***Shift to being open and curious.*** Ask yourself and trusted others what other perspectives are possible.

At our core, we are concerned with survival. The natural, built-in fight, flight, freeze, or appease response to protect ourselves is universal. Each of us, however, reacts to perceived threats in unique physiological and emotional ways.

Let's look at each step in detail so you can incorporate it into your own shifting process when necessary:

1. Notice Your Judgment Signal.

For our purposes, a judgment is a state of feeling "right" and that another person or situation is "wrong." Judging includes being closed to different perspectives, information, and possibilities. In other words, "case closed." Being judgmental usually consists of thoughts such as "He has no right…" or "How dare he…" and physical sensations such as a tightness in the chest and strong emotions such as fear or anger (which serve as cues).

Become aware of your physiological and emotional responses when you find situations threatening or you are closed to possibilities. Consider this situation. Gary, a distribution and logistics manager, was urgently supporting a country's people in need after civil unrest. He received a truckload of desperately needed supplies, but to his dismay, he found that most of them were destroyed in shipping. The heavy items had been packed on top and had crushed the lighter ones on the bottom. This was the second shipment he'd received with most of the products damaged! Gary's face turned beat red. He seemed to grow taller and bigger. The usually calm and affable Gary transformed into a fire-breathing monster. He was furious!

"What the (blank!) did those guys do!" he bellowed. "Not again!" His heart beat faster, his chest felt tight, and he had trouble breathing. He couldn't believe he'd received damaged cargo again! He had complained with tact and given the specifics about the problems with the first truckload when it arrived damaged. How could this happen again! "Those packers need to be fired. How can I tolerate such incompetence?" he yelled.

These moments are where the choices lie. We can react immediately from our place of judgment and sense of rightness, which may result in other costs we may come to regret. Or we can choose another option. We can respond by becoming open and curious to learn more.

Becoming open involves managing your reactions to perceived threats and the sense that you are "right." Learn to recognize your internal responses, which signal that you are judging. Each of us has one or more predominant and recurring signals. Usually, the stronger the judgment, the more likely we are to notice the physiological symptoms. Begin to notice your reaction when you believe you are right and another person is wrong. Where do you feel your judging reaction? Does your throat constrict, head throb, stomach churn, or heart beat faster?

In addition to a physiological response to perceived danger, you are also likely to hear an internal voice that makes comments and judgments. Most of us recognize our voice of judgment. It's the adamant voice inside us that makes disparaging comments about others, situations we encounter, and even about ourselves.

Closed/Open Continuum

In the OASIS Moves process, assumptions are at one end of a continuum. You are able to consider a number of possible explanations for an observation and you are more open-minded. At the other end are judgments where there is no room for options. You are locked into thinking you are "right." For example, if you are expecting Emile to get some information to you and you have not received it, you can make a number of assumptions. He forgot, he became busy, he decided not to share information, or perhaps he e-mailed it rather than giving you a paper copy. These are possible assumptions. As long as you are open to explore a number of possible explanations, you are considering assumptions. If, however, you "know" he did not send the information because he is purposely trying to make you look bad and you see no other possible explanations, then you are making a judgment and are essentially closed to new information.

We need to be aware of both our assumptions and our judgments. The key way to work with our judgments is to notice our physiological signals. When we are in judgment or closed, we naturally constrict and experience stress in our body. We seem to have several predominant signals, such as tightening of the chest, increased heart rate, a tightened throat, or clenched fists. In addition, we usually have an inner voice saying such things as "Something or someone is wrong."

When we are judging, we are essentially closed and reacting to a sense of fear and threat. Our amygdala is activated. Our hearts beat faster and our cortisol levels may elevate. In a closed state, we don't have full access to our neo-cortex. We lose our capacity to think clearly and see other perspectives and solutions. "Being right" shoots adrenaline through our bodies and has an addictive quality. Most of us like "being right," and we do not consider the costs of being closed to additional input.

The most critical element of the OASIS Conversation pathway involves shifting your perspective by stopping, stepping back, suspending judgment, and being open to building productive and satisfying relationships. When you shift, you are activating a different part of your brain that supports you in seeing possibilities and being more creative. You experience a sense of flow, oxytocin levels may increase, and you may experience a greater sense of trust and creativity.

Closed/Judgment <-------Assumptions ------------> Open/Curious

Here's an example of how shifting your perspective to being open can help you. A client, Tom, an executive at a major consulting firm, called me and was furious. "I need to find a new job now! I can't continue to work in a firm where people are snakes!" Tom's voice was loud and stressed, so I could tell he was very upset. "You sound really angry," I said. "I'm more than angry," he replied. "My chest is tight; I can hardly breathe—I want out!"

How would you react in Tom's situation? Imagine that, like Tom, you are working on a critical project with a new client. You notice your boss and a colleague, Steve, who are both deeply involved with the project, talking in a conference room. As you walk by, their voices grow quieter. You could make many assumptions. Could they be discussing a part of the current project that doesn't involve you? Perhaps they are talking about another project. Maybe they are discussing a personal matter, like one of their sons flunking out of college. Could they be discussing one of a million other things?

If you are in an open state, and you assume they could be talking about a range of topics, you are making assumptions. However, if like my client, Tom, you "know" your colleague and the boss are talking about the current project and excluding you, you are making a judgment. Perhaps you have had coworkers take credit or undermine you in the past. This is what happened to Tom. Another colleague, with a previous employer, had taken most of the credit when they'd worked on a complex project together. This man had even gotten a promotion that Tom felt was undeserved. Tom was furious and positive that Steve had excluded him like his previous colleague. He was not going to be badly treated again! As I empathized, Tom relaxed. When we further explored what had happened, it became clear that he was basing his judgment on his past hurtful experience.

As Tom calmed down, then tried to be more open and curious, he considered different possibilities. Afterward, he talked with Steve in person and was able to be open and genuinely interested and respectful. He started by saying that he'd noticed Steve and their boss talking together in the conference room (observation). Steve told Tom that they'd been talking about an employee performance challenge he was facing. They were evaluating how he and their boss could best approach it. Steve confided that he'd even told the boss how well Tom was leading the project! Tom was relieved to know his judgment—that Steve was taking all the credit—was not accurate. He learned about the power of being open and curious even when he'd initially been sure he was "right."

Tom was pleased that he had caught himself and was able to refrain from acting on his first impulses. If he had, the relationship might have been hurt. Instead, Tom built a strong working relationship with Steve. Also, Tom eventually did get the promotion.

When we lock into the sense that we are "right," we may not even question ourselves. The sensation of being right can be addictive. The dopamine surge is satisfying. We may react so automatically, falling into our habitual patterns of reaction, that we don't even know we have other options. Overcoming this sense of being "right" is a challenge. We fall into our habitual patterns of reacting based on our backgrounds.

For instance, Tom fell into his old pattern of action—getting angry, feeling like a victim, and leaving.

If you interact with others in a state of openness with genuine curiosity and wonder, amazing results can occur. We rarely get this kind of focused attention, and it supports other people in becoming more open, too. You will be amazed by how much easier things are. For example, as my clients get more curious and reflective, they are in a better position to be creative. I notice that when I am open as a coach, my clients and I can examine reactions and assumptions together without fear or defensiveness. Interestingly, just paying attention to another person's experience without judgment often causes a change to happen and new possibilities to emerge.

Research in a number of fields is also demonstrating that emotions are contagious. Elaine Hatfield and colleagues, authors of *Emotional Contagion*, identify the strong influence of both positive and negative emotions on others. When we sense that someone is open or closed, we tend to react in a similar way. Your openness can spread to others and influence the climate.

Brain Connection

When judging, we are experiencing the classic fight, flight, freeze, or appease adrenaline reaction to a perceived threat. Our older brain structure and limbic system, which are the emotional parts of the human brain, immediately react to potential danger. This happens even before the neocortex, or thinking part of the brain, can register the perceived danger and provide rational input. Our response happens so quickly that it appears automatic, so we may not be immediately aware of it. That's why it is useful to get to know our predominant signals and understand that we are closed to new information.

On a physical level, the brainstem reacts to potential danger where rapid mobilization of energy is needed. The brainstem reacts in a fight, flight, freeze, or appease response to ensure our survival in the face of potential danger, an attack, or a harmful event. This reaction served humans well when sensing danger was a literal matter of life and death. Walter Bradford Cannon observed that animals react to perceived threats with a discharge of the sympathetic nervous system, which primes the animal for a stress response. Humans also react and the adrenal medulla produces hormones that affect the response. In a perceived effort to control a situation, some people naturally react in a fight mode and may yell or get angry. Others react more predominantly in a flight manner with fear, which may involve leaving the scene. The freeze response involves pausing like a deer in headlights, almost waiting for the danger to pass. Others may react by actually moving forward to appease others, to address issues, or take care of others as a learned response for safety. We are wired with this basic survival response. While we are likely to experience each of these types of reaction, it is common to have one type of reaction dominate our patterns. The limbic part of the brain creates emotions that guide us to move toward or away from something.

When we become aware, the cortex of the brain allows us to think about a situation and essentially supersede the limbic reaction. We can calm down amygdala-based fear reactions by secreting a neurotransmitter called GABA (for gamma-aminobutyric acid) that inhibits subcortical firing. We can then experience more balance and a greater sense of ease. The secretion of the hormone oxytocin, sometimes known as the "cuddle hormone," creates feelings of wellbeing (as does a mother's hug to babies).

When we are experiencing the basic survival response of fight, flight, freeze, or appease, we are responding automatically and reactively. We need to catch ourselves in this emergency response and shift to an open, receptive state when we are not actually in danger. Most often, we are not in physical danger. We can connect with our natural state of wellbeing.

When we are able to stop and step back from a judgment, we are using the power of the middle prefrontal region of the brain to put some space between input and our reaction. This ability to pause before taking action is a critical component of emotional and social intelligence. We can then become mindful of what is happening, refrain from responding, and manage our impulses as we consider our options and feel more at choice about how we will respond.

The exciting news is that research in recent years verifies the neuroplasticity of our brains. This means that how we focus our attention shapes our brain's actual structure. The more we focus on shifting from judgment or being closed and constricted to becoming open and expansive, the more we are shaping our brains to be more resilient and experience wellbeing. Research supports that you will not only experience more positive interactions but better overall health. You can actually be enhancing your health and sense of wellbeing as you focus on being more open to different perspectives and different people. We have many opportunities to practice this skill as we interact with myriad people and situations. You don't have to sit and meditate. However, doing so will also support your ability to shift more quickly into the state of openness and non-judgment.

To be truly open-minded toward others, we also need to take a supportive and compassionate stance toward ourselves. We all have critical internal voices, so we also need to learn to be open and empathetic toward these parts of ourselves. Our critical voices were formed to serve us and help us survive and manage in our environments. As we mature, these critical voices may not be serving us anymore. By appreciating how they have served us and giving them empathy, we may be able to shift our relationships with them.

Notice Your Signals

Shifting requires more than the intention to be open. It helps to notice your physiological signals of being contracted or closed. You may also decide to work with a friend and remind each other to check in and notice your signals. As you practice, you will gain expertise. Soon, you will be able to check in with yourself and notice your signals of bodily sensations and inner talk.

Body language reveals a lot. Children are particularly effective in picking up signs of judgment. For example, Taylor, age eight, can tell when her mother is ready to leave a place and is not happy. Her mother's face becomes red and her walking pace quickens. A coaching client, Claudia, who worked in a not-for-profit organization, said she was not sure she even made judgments or had signals! Her staff members were present and they couldn't help themselves. They laughed. Immediately, her back got stiff. That was the physical signal that her staff had come to recognize, and that's why they laughed. Claudia was startled (and a little embarrassed) by her own lack of awareness. Becoming aware of this signal did help her to manage her responses, though.

Claudia's situation of not having any awareness of her signal isn't unusual. In our fast-paced environments, we have learned to desensitize ourselves to the point where we are often unaware of what we are feeling in our bodies. Another client, Jake, learned to override his feelings and ignore his body's response to judgment and stress. For many, this behavior became a habit in childhood. By slowing down and paying attention, Jake discovered that he felt tension in his shoulders before he exploded in anger. Some of us shut off our feelings because we didn't feel safe and didn't want to feel badly. This is a useful response for some of us in childhood, when our lives are more controlled by parents and others. However, this response often doesn't serve us as adults.

Research reviewed by Tom Stone[7] shows that as adults mature, we have a much greater capacity to process our feelings. We will develop more than seven times as many brain spindle cells as we had as infants! (Spindle cells are activated with increased blood flow in experiments where subjects are given emotional stimuli. They help us grow our ability to process a wider range of emotions and to be more self-aware and better able to manage our emotions.) Unfortunately, some of us have not exercised this capacity.

2. Stop, Step Back, and Suspend Your Judgment. Recall your intention to be open and assume positive intent. Cool down if needed.

You can train yourself to use your internal signal as a trigger to shift into the physiological state of openness. Every time you notice your stomach tighten, your face flush, or your inner voice say, "I'm right and he's wrong," visualize the following.

Imagine a large red stop sign in front of you. The stop sign image is your cue literally to stop, step back, shift, and become open to listening. Visualize the "T" in the stop sign in the shape of a judge's gavel. Recognize that you are making a judgment. Imagine yourself taking off your judge's robe and hanging it on a coat rack nearby. When a neural circuit (wire) is activated and poised for a response, the neural pathway is responsive to change. It is like the neural pathway is hot or in a liquid, flexible state and can be modified.

Practice stopping and shifting into an open state when you notice your physical signals of being closed and in judgment. By stopping and

---

7 Stone, T. *Pure Awareness*. Carlsbad, CA: Great Life Technologies, 2007.

being open, for minutes, hours, or more, you create the opportunity to gather additional information. You can reclaim your cloak of judgment and act from your judgments later if you decide to do that. Remember that at any given time, each of us experiences only one view: ours! We may be stuck in our perspective based on our background conditioning—remember the Roman numeral exercise from an earlier chapter? Our conditioning may limit the observable data we notice and our ability to entertain other perspectives. Even if we are consciously trying to see all sides, we may miss an obvious or alternative perspective.

Relax your hold on the judgment (at least temporarily). Brain research confirms that this is a useful process. Recall the contagious nature of emotions and your goal of creating an oasis with others. Neuroscientists say, "Neurons that fire together wire together." (The axiom was first coined by Donald Hebb in 1949.) When brain cells communicate frequently, the connection path strengthens. The more you practice being open-minded, the quicker and easier it will become.

Make it your intention to be open. Remind yourself: "I don't know what I don't know." More satisfying and productive interactions are possible if you are open to others. You are rarely in life-threatening danger. Hold the vision of experiencing an oasis within yourself and with other people. Life will be more engaging. Wouldn't you rather have peace and health than be "right"? Choose the statement that best applies to you in a given situation. "I would rather be _____ (successful, happy, etc.) than be "right."

Scan your body and notice how you feel. Take a few deep breaths and allow yourself to relax. Hold the intention of being open in a dialogue with someone. Remember that emotions are contagious, so coming to a conversation in an open stance supports others in being open.

Practice

Do you remember a time when you did not agree with another person? Or a time when you made a strong judgment about a situation? As you imagine either of these, what do you notice in your body? What are your prominent signals?

Imagine Scenario: Not Chosen
You hear that you have not been selected to be on a

team that you really wanted to join. You believe you are
well-qualified and should have been selected.

Notice your immediate reaction. Did you make a judgment about the person selecting team members, the situation, yourself, or all three? Do you feel open or constricted and closed?

If you made a judgment, do you notice a shift in your body? Where is it? What does it feel like? Is there constriction or heaviness? What are you thinking or assuming? Is the feeling familiar?

Katie, an OASIS Conversation workshop participant, responded with a feeling of heaviness in her chest and heard her internal voice say, "I can't depend on Dimitris to make good decisions; he is not reliable or competent; he must not like me" (judgment). The voice continued: "I have supported Dimitris in the past, so I expected him to advocate for me" (background expectations).

Another person in my workshops reported that one of his signals in times of threat or stress is to smile, even if he believes it's inappropriate. His brother has the same response. Upon further reflection, he realized his mother also smiles when she feels threatened. This response landed him in a number of troubling situations in his youth. Now that he's aware of it and has experienced how it is interpreted, he's changing it.

Listening to Our Signals

Learn to trust the OASIS process, knowing that you can always choose judgment as an option later. Check inside yourself regularly to notice whether you have shifted from being judgmental, as if in an arid desert, to being peaceful, as if in an oasis state.

While intellectually, we can agree it is valuable to suspend judgment, in the heat of the moment, it is often quite difficult. This is especially true if we feel strongly that another person is not behaving appropriately or seeing things clearly. The more our emotions are engaged, the more difficult it is for our intellect or rational mind to be available to new information. Gary, the manager with the damaged shipment, eventually recognized his internal signals and used them as a cue to stop, step back, and suspend his response to judgment. He calmed himself down. He became open and curious. When he was ready, Gary talked with the packers. Initially, they *had* packed the heavy items on the bottom and the light items on top. Later, when the quality control representative inspected the truck, he confirmed this. Continuing to be curious, Gary eventually learned that the crane that had lifted the truck car from a train to the truck had flipped over the car! This had crushed the supplies. Because of his inquiries, Gary gained added understanding and the problem was corrected. If Gary had not questioned further, some of the packers may have lost their jobs, although they'd done nothing wrong.

Research on emotional intelligence shows that people who pay close attention (have heightened awareness) to themselves and others are more successful and fulfilled. Remember that feelings are transient. By acknowledging them, we can move through them. I've learned another really interesting fact. In addition to noticing my feelings and sensations, I find it useful to remind myself that brain research, reviewed in Michael Shermer's[8] work, suggests that we each have an "internal spin doctor." This voice tries to protect us by making up a story that puts us in the judge's seat and makes us look good (at least to ourselves). Knowing this tendency always makes me question my judgment or story.

Once you have noticed your signal in a situation and have stopped, stepped back, and suspended judgment, you need to become more aware of the judgment itself. It consists of the assumptions and emotions you have about the observable data you have selected. Therefore, this S (the shift move of the OASIS process) is an opportunity to review the "O" (Observable Data) and acknowledge "A" (Assumptions, Emotions, and Background).

When we move into judgment extremely rapidly, we may not even be conscious of the perceived danger. We may not be aware of a whole set of assumptions we have made about the observable data. Often we notice our signal first and must work backward to identify the O and A. Now that we have noticed our signal and temporarily suspended judgment, it is time to ask ourselves, "What am I responding to?" It is time to inquire, "What is my observable data?" "What am I assuming?" "What am I feeling?" "What is my background, my expectations, my rules, or my history?"

Practice

---

8 Shermer, M. *The Believing Brain: From Ghosts and Gods to Politics and Conspiracies—How We Construct Beliefs and Reinforce Them as Truths*. New York: Times Books, Henry Holt and Company, 2011.

In the following case, practice noticing when you are closed and judging, and then note your observable data, assumptions, emotions, and background.

> *You have been paired for a project with a coworker who has a very different working style than yours. You are detail-oriented, diligent, and like to turn in projects calmly before deadlines. Your coworker is much looser in style, less focused on details, and usually just makes deadlines or misses them slightly, causing you a lot of stress and anxiety.*

Are you open or closed? Notice your signal (in your body and/or voice).

Visualize the stop sign and stop, step back (breathe). Suspend acting on your judgment and shift to be more open.

What is your Observable Data?

Are you Aware of your assumptions and emotions?

What is your related background (expectations, rules about how things should be, or past experience)?

Cool Down

Before responding to a person with whom you are experiencing a difference in perspective, check your emotional temperature. You may find it useful to give yourself a score from 1–10 on your level of judgment: 10 reflects being in an open or cooled-down state, and 1 reflects being closed, boiling, and very upset. Most of us are not at our best when we have not cooled down. When we are boiling, we are operating primarily from the emotional, rather than the rational, part of our brains. The more contracted we are, the less interest we have in understanding another person's perspective. Fewer resources are available to listen. Instead, our real need is for the other person to understand us. We often want to do more than simply tell the other person what is on our mind. We might want to make sure that person experiences our pain. (Does this sound familiar to you?)

Unfortunately, when we react without awareness or control, we lose some of our power and ability to influence. When we are angry or boiling, the other people in the interaction are likely to observe or sense this and become defensive. This does not lead to positive outcomes. Cooling down can take a few seconds or longer, depending on the situation and your state of mind, but clearly it is worth whatever time it takes. When couples are angry with each other and lose their rational capacity, research conducted by relationship expert John Gottman[9] demonstrates that a fifteen-minute break supports the parties in cooling down and coming back to the conversation with more options and more focus on creating win-win solutions.

I have coached quite a few managers who were known for "blowing their lids." Jack, a CFO of a Fortune 100 company, had jumped from corporation to corporation, attaining higher and higher positions. He soon reached the top of the corporate ladder—very early in his career. He was extremely bright and known for outworking most people. However, he had the terrible flaw of becoming irritated and blowing up at staff, his peers, and vendors. He had little patience for people who did not understand complex problems. He would become very upset when he found even a minor mistake or when someone did not deliver adequately on a request. His sarcastic tirades did not endear him to others. Naturally, people responded defensively. Many began to resent him. Some even flatly refused to work with him.

Eventually, the CEO told Jack that despite his intelligence and skills in finance, he would need to leave the organization unless he learned to manage his emotions. Until this point in his career, Jack's intelligence and ability to see and address problems had propelled him to success. However, his management role required more than just his intellect. The company's culture required people to be respectful of one another. Jack was asked to engage in coaching and had six months to demonstrate new behavior. He accepted the challenge and I became his coach.

After Jack was introduced to the OASIS Conversation pathway or the OASIS Moves, he identified his first signal: his pulse rate. As he received reports that did not meet his standards, his heart would begin to pound quickly. Jack also noticed he had an internal voice that started to berate people. It would say: "No, you have it wrong. You idiot! That's not what I wanted! Why can't you do it right?" As he learned to use his signals as a cue to stop, Jack also noticed his anger and frustration. When problems and solutions seemed so obvious to him, he couldn't believe that other people didn't view them in the same way.

---

9 Gottman, J.M. *The Science of Trust: Emotional Attunement for Couples.* New York: W.W. Norton Company, 2011.

Jack practiced the OASIS Conversation process. For example, the observable data was that a staff member had brought him what he viewed as an incomplete report. His assumptions, emotions, and background were that he felt angry and that people should always supply all of the required information. If they didn't, he assumed they were incompetent.

Jack usually rated himself a 1 or 2 on the low end of the closed-open scale. He recognized he was usually boiling emotionally. He became aware that he got quite upset—even if someone disappointed him on a small matter. With effort, Jack began to employ strategies to cool down and become open. He took a deep breath, got a drink of water, or looked for humor in various situations that would have upset him before. He created an image of his personal oasis: hiking in the mountains. He had a good sense of wit and found that being open to humor really helped calm him. After a relatively short while, Jack had reaped tremendous benefits from practicing the OASIS Moves. When I talked to some of his peers and associates, they said, "Jack's become a new person!" Today, they enjoy working with him and appreciate his intellect more.

The most dramatic change occurred in Jack's family life. Since he was quick to anger and be critical at home, his marriage was troubled, as were his relationships with his children. As Jack used the OASIS Conversation process, these important personal relationships improved as well. Jack's eleven-year-old daughter confided in me how much fun her father is now. She also added how much she loves him.

Some of us boil much more quietly than Jack, but with equally detrimental effects. Victor, an information technology professional at a manufacturing company, often got irritated when people did not do things his way. He would become agitated, internalize his anxiety, and say nothing or even leave the scene. Because he did not have the skills to express his feelings and needs openly, he inadvertently acted them out. While he said nothing, colleagues could feel his hardening and coldness. Sometimes when a coworker asked, "Is something wrong?" Victor would reply, "No." Some learned to go away and wait until he got into a better mood. However, this dance of avoidance and retreat increased their frustration with him and added extra time to transactions.

After becoming aware of his signals (tightening in his neck and shoulders), Victor learned how to cool down. He took a few deep breaths. His personal oasis image was being in a quiet forest of pine trees. With time and coaching, Victor became less defensive and more open to dialogue. He wasted less energy in being anxious. When he calmed down, he was more interested in learning what his coworkers had to say. He practiced and became more effective in communicating. Those around him could not believe Victor's transformation after he had completed an OASIS Conversation workshop. A winning result was that Victor and his colleagues became significantly more efficient at getting the work done.

Brain Connection

Research by neuroscientists such as Angelika Dimoka, using fMRI (functional magnetic resonance), supports that two separate areas of the brain are activated when we are in the judgmental/reactive, "desert," state and when we are in the open-minded/creative, "oasis," state. When we feel threatened because someone has a different view of reality, our protective, fear-based neural network, located in the lower area of the brain, is activated. Our hearts beat faster, and we tend to experience constriction because we are often holding our breath.

When we are particularly threatened and experience an amygdala hijacking, we lose access to our rational prefrontal cortex. The limbic area of the brain that stores past memories exacerbates the experience of threat as we recall negative past memories and experience them as recurring. Our stress increases, causing our cortisol hormone levels to rise. Then we are more prone to negativity and distrust.

When the prefrontal cortex neural network, located in the higher part of the brain, is activated, we are more relaxed and comfortable with others. We become more open and we experience coherence. The release of the chemicals oxytocin, serotonin, and dopamine allows us to feel more trusting and positive. With prefrontal cortex activation, we have access to creative thinking, empathy, and possibilities.

Cooling down enables us to calm our fear-based neural network. Research shows that the human brain has the natural capacity to experience a state of connection and wellbeing. While we've discussed that we are wired to protect ourselves, that is not enough for our survival. We also need cooperation and sharing to help us survive. An added benefit: when we are open and take action that supports others, we are rewarded with a wave of chemicals that create a pleasurable response.

We cannot be in this open, peaceful state (oasis) and also in the reactive stress response we experience in judgment (desert).

The brain's plasticity allows you to build new circuits. The more you build the neural pathways for openness, the more you will have ready access to them. This state is also ideal for innovation and creativity. The neuroscientist, Antonio Damasio, finds this state of openness to be optimal for collaboration and effective functioning. We are healthy and at our best when we are open and experiencing an oasis.

Ways to Cool Down

Each of us needs to identify the calming strategies that work best for us. I suggest writing a list of personal strategies and keeping it handy. Then when you need to cool down, you can consult your list and pick one. Because we are drenched in adrenaline when we are in judgment and stressed, it is useful to have a ready list to consult. We know that our rational brain is incapacitated!

Sometimes cooling down will be easier than at other times, depending on the circumstances and your state of health and wellbeing. Cooling down will be harder when you have had a string of challenges and stressors within a short time. For instance, it may be particularly difficult after weeks of little sleep, your spouse being out of town, your child sick, and what you perceive as your boss's unreasonable demand that you work late on a last-minute project. In these circumstances, you will want to reference your cooling-down strategies list. Here are a few strategies that work for me and others I coach.

Assume Positive Intent

It is natural to expect the worst. We quickly jump to blaming and assuming that others are against us. I have worked in many organizations where people don't feel included and the culture has become "every man for himself," because people have not learned to have mindful conversations and create a positive atmosphere. One of the quickest ways to begin to change such environments in teams is to agree on the norm of "assuming positive intent" from others. You will recall from our chapter on respect that everyone has different ways of behaving and a different definition of respect. When we can make a habit of assuming positive intentions, we can cool down and be more curious about others' actions. I have encouraged leaders of large organizations to emphasize the mindset of "assuming positive intent." This perspective has made a huge difference. I encourage you to make it your mantra and notice how quickly you can cool down and interact effectively with others. You might want to apply it to yourself too. Many of us are quite brutal in judging ourselves. What would happen if you assumed positive intent and you were doing the best you know how at the moment? We can all learn and do so more quickly when we are less defensive and more self-compassionate.

Breathe!

One great way to cool down is to breathe fully. When you make a judgment, your body constricts—you may hold your breath and de-oxygenate. By breathing deeply, you can bring oxygen back into your body.

Many of us concentrate our breathing in our chest rather than in the center of our body. Breathing primarily in our chest can indicate that the fight, flight, freeze, or appease mechanism is activated. We are likely to experience more anxiety and stress when our breath is primarily in the upper part of our body. With focused practice, you can begin to take deeper breaths in your belly where most of the blood circulation occurs, and experience greater relaxation and openness.

Try a few slow deep breaths now, and see what you notice. As you breathe in, allow your belly to expand like a balloon. Then, exhale fully, allowing the air to leave you. As you exhale, notice the relaxation in your body. You will then naturally breathe in. Repeat this a few times. How do you feel? Can you experience yourself calming down?

Here's another exercise you may find useful. Sit on the edge of a chair or stand, and as you round your back, allow the air to leave your belly. Next, arch your back, look at the ceiling, and allow your lungs to fill with air. Breathe through your nose. Repeat the rounding of your back, and allow your breath to be released from your belly. Continue this practice for a few minutes several times throughout the day. Become familiar with the relaxed feeling of breathing fully.

Breathing deeply sounds so simple that you may underemphasize how important it is. For much of my life, I thought I understood breathing and would automatically agree when told of its importance.

However, when I finally practiced it regularly, I noticed that I really did feel more present and alive.

Imagine an Oasis

Another useful technique is to imagine a place that you find beautiful and enjoy. Take yourself there for an internal oasis. One of my mental destinations of choice is the island of Santorini, Greece. I experienced a beautiful few days there and recall the most incredibly blue sky I have ever seen against the white clay homes with blue rooftops. Brilliant pink flowers overflowed the window-boxes. The ocean water was a transparent blue-green that stretched for miles. When I swam in a pool on a volcano's edge, I felt so refreshed and alive. I smiled just to know I was alive! By returning to this place in my imagination, I feel calmer, happier, and have a greater sense of wellbeing.

Shake Things Up

When we lock into judgment, we also may freeze our bodies in position. Move your body to shake up your static perception. Sitting with your arms locked and chin down, you perceive a situation one way. If you stand up, move around, open your arms, and look up, you are likely to shift and have more options. Moving around can shift your perspective. Try maintaining your judgment, "I am right; he should not have postponed our meeting" as you skip around the room and try different body positions. Simply notice what happens. Experiment with different tones of voice (with your office door closed, of course…)!

Take a Time-Out

Some people find that following their mother's advice to count to ten before saying anything in anger works well. (A workshop participant told me privately that his mother told him to count to 100! That worked for him and for her.) You may decide to take a walk to enjoy some space and oxygen. Some people go get a drink of water or take a restroom break as their way of taking a few minutes to cool down. You will want to pay attention to the type of situation you're in to determine whether a time-out is appropriate.

Take a Different Perspective

Finding a different perspective is often useful for cooling down. My finance client, Regina, found it worthwhile to take a walk to a cemetery near her office. She would imagine how she would feel about a given situation at her death (or even within a couple of months or a year). Looking at her problems from this longer-term perspective, she could see that the worries she had were less critical or even unfounded. Without going anywhere, you can ask yourself, "How will I feel about this two days, a month, or one year from now?" Notice how the different time frames allow you to experience the situation somewhat differently.

Another way to identify different perspectives is to ask how others would experience a similar situation. Ask yourself, "How would my brother look at this situation? How would my favorite hero perceive it? How would a particular author or comedian view it? How would my teacher see it? How would a person in a hospital or nursing home perceive it?" The idea is to generate several perspectives.

Other questions are "What's a more positive way to look at this? What could be other explanations for a person's behavior?" The more you can put yourself in the other person's shoes and formulate his or her perspective, the more you are likely to cool down. I was disappointed when a friend did not call much. I thought, somewhat sadly, that she only called me if she needed something. When I considered her situation more carefully, I could see that she had a very full life—a busy job, a challenging commute, and a husband, children, and extended family. Later, when I had my own child, I understood even better how little time she had available for friends.

Seek Out Empathy

One of the most effective methods of cooling down is to have another person understand our feelings—give us empathy. Many of us naturally call a friend when we are having strong feelings. We may say, "Can you believe what my boss did? I am so hurt; how could he do this?" A person who cares and has good listening skills can provide empathy by responding, "I can hear that you are really upset." Feeling heard and understood by another helps us calm down.

You can even give yourself some empathy. I imagine that I have two parts. I stand in one position and talk about my strong feelings. Then I move to the other position and allow another part of me to give empathy. Once when I was in Africa facilitating a workshop with a group of managers, I was upset about how a colleague handled a situation with the group. Before talking with her, I wanted to be sure that I was calm and open for the dialogue. Given the time difference, it was not easy for me to call a friend for empathy. Instead, I allowed one part of me to say, "You are really upset with what your colleague said to the group." Then, I moved to another chair and allowed a different part of me to respond to the empathy. "Yes, I don't think her comment helped the group and I am disappointed." I continued to shift chairs, allowing one part of me to give another part empathy, and after a few minutes, I cooled down and was ready for the conversation with my colleague about the meeting and our plans for the next day.

Get a Second Opinion

When we are locked into a negative judgment, it can be useful to brainstorm other possible interpretations with a friend who can also provide empathy. For example, Jane walked by a conference room and noticed that several of her peers were meeting. Since she had raised questions about their plan of action on a proposed project, she immediately thought they were proceeding on the project without her. She felt hurt and upset. Using OASIS Moves, she cooled down by brainstorming other possible interpretations with a colleague. Jane later found out what they had been doing. They had been planning a surprise party for her birthday! When you believe something is true, it is useful to explore how it may also not be true.

See Your "Opponent" With New Eyes

Since it is easy to let yourself see the person you are judging as "the enemy," remind yourself of what you like about the other person—his or her strengths and contributions. You can also recall the common goals or vision you share. Basically, you can remember that you really are on the same side (even though you may have strong negative feelings about him or her at the moment). Remember fundamental attribution error—our natural tendency to assume negative motives of others. It is very useful to "assume positive intent" of the other person.

You may find assuming positive intent to be an especially valuable approach in your committed relationships. For example, can you remember why you married your partner? Think back. You can recall that you had shared goals and a positive commitment to each other.

Appreciating others is quite useful. What do you appreciate about the person?

Consider Your Contribution

Make it a practice to consider your own contribution to a misunderstanding. Each person involved contributes some part. Gary, the manager described earlier who received damaged goods, realized that he did not fully investigate the problem the first time it happened. Working in a country that he'd never been in before, he was not fluent in the language. In retrospect, he regretted not exploring the problem more fully the first time the supplies arrived damaged. If he had, he could have done a better job describing and communicating the problem.

Have Compassion

Remember: no one is perfect. We all make mistakes. I've certainly made my share. It helps me to remember that people get locked into their perspectives and really can't see alternatives. If you are feeling threatened and not respected, remember specific instances in which the other person has been respectful to you. Sometimes it helps me to consider how the other person might be threatened and so is responding from that place. This helps me to see the person as vulnerable rather than intentionally trying to thwart or hurt me.

Consider What You Can Learn—Be Curious

Think about your interactions and determine what you can learn from interactions that haven't gone well. For instance, I might want to set clearer rules for my daughter about doing her homework. In retrospect, I can see why she expected she could skip her homework the time she asked to—because I did not emphasize the importance of her completing it the week when we had guests. She didn't understand that I had made a special exception for that circumstance.

Be Grateful

Take time to reflect on what about the person and situation makes you grateful. Recall how appreciative you are for all that you have. Take an optimistic perspective and focus on trusting that things will work out even when it is not clear how. Recall your resilience.

Write It Out

Write a letter to the person you're having difficulty with, stating your feelings and perspective. You don't actually have to send it to experience the benefit of expressing your feelings. You may move to another place emotionally as a result of writing it out. If you try this strategy for cooling down and think you may decide to send the letter, wait until the next day. One of my clients, Fred, pushed the "send" button after writing an e-mail for this purpose. While he felt better immediately, a while later he knew that the communication did not support coming to agreement with his colleague. He regretted having sent it.

Divert Yourself

If you listen to your favorite music, do yoga or other stretching exercises, take a bath or shower, exercise at the gym, or just walk outside, these activities may help you cool down. For some, the process of meditation or any kind of quiet contemplation supports restoring calm. Remember how you feel when you are more relaxed and move into that place. Singing, like laughter, requires taking in more oxygen and is uplifting. Other diversions such as art, gardening, woodworking, or knitting may be used. Even reading may help because it puts your thoughts elsewhere, so it distracts you.

Remind yourself that the purpose of cooling down is to have satisfying and productive interactions, rather than just getting your grievances aired. After all, you are likely to have ongoing relationships with your colleagues.

Practice

Think of a recent time when you were closed and boiling emotionally. Perhaps you were upset with a colleague or your spouse. Then note on the closed-open scale of 1–10 your level of judgment. Were you at the low end, closed and overflowing with emotion and judgment? Or were you closer to the high end of being open and non-judgmental? What supported you in calming down?

Review the list of possible strategies and consider how effective each is for you. Identify at least three effective calming strategies for yourself. List them on a card or in your calendar or phone, which you can keep nearby. When you need to calm down, try one of the strategies. Don't stop there. Experiment with additional strategies, and revise the list as you discover what works best for you.

Suggestions for Cooling Down

- Breathe.
- Imagine and experience an oasis.
- Get empathy from a friend.
- Give empathy to yourself.
- Exercise.
- Take a walk.
- Drink some water.
- Connect with your sense of wellbeing.
- Write a letter stating your feelings, but don't mail it.
- Take a short break.
- Visualize a time when you were calmer.
- Imagine that you are in the future and have worked through your differences.
- Ask how you would consider the issue you're upset about on your deathbed? At five years from now? At three months?
- Listen to music.
- Find humor and laugh.
- Engage in an activity or hobby that calms you, such as art, music, gardening, or woodworking.
- Sing.
- Brainstorm other possible perceptions of a situation with a friend.

- Read or recite a favorite poem.
- Remind yourself of what you like about the other person and his or her strengths.
- Remind yourself of the common goals or vision you share with the other person.
- Consider and define what your contribution is to the misunderstanding or challenge.
- Remind yourself, "I don't know what I don't know."
- Remind yourself that people are not perfect and we all make mistakes.
- Assume positive intent by the other.
- Remember times when the other person has been respectful to you.
- If all else fails, eat chocolate!

3. Shift to Being Open and Curious

Once you have noticed your judgment signal and you have then stopped, stepped back, and cooled down, you can shift to being open and curious. When we can shift into the emotions and mindset of openness and curiosity, we can enjoy a relaxed body state, too. An open mindset—including wonder or curiosity, appreciation, compassion, optimism, and non-judgment—supports us in finding an inner oasis. The energy created can be used for finding an oasis with others.

Pam, another client, experienced a sense of judgment when she joined a company that maintained a very different culture from her previous fast-paced financial company. She had learned to be quite direct and address potential problems in staff meetings. Now, in a more polite environment, an insurance company, she judged that staff members were not direct enough. They also needed to act more swiftly according to her. In this unfamiliar territory, Pam did not know the rules and felt out of control. She had moved her family across the country and had taken what she considered to be a big risk to join the new company. To her, it seemed obvious that her team needed to make changes—that was why she thought she had been hired. However, each time she offered reasonable suggestions, she encountered resistance. "We've tried that before. That won't work here." She reacted by becoming closed, judgmental, and quite critical. She knew she was "right." Because her colleagues sensed this attitude, they alienated her even more.

In this situation, Pam's judgment, the tightness in her chest, and her internal voice saying, "They are wrong" were cues that she needed to cool down. At first, she ignored the cues, reacted in a fight or flight manner, closed down, and stopped being open to new data. However, when this behavior did not get results, she caught herself and worked to cool down and shift to a more open stance. She allowed herself to be grateful for the experience, recognize her staff's talent, and shift to being open and curious about their views. In response, team members relaxed and began to trust her; soon, Pam and her team developed a shared picture of where they were and a new vision of success. Eventually, with more OASIS Conversations, the team became quite successful and respected Pam's leadership.

By noticing her judgment and stopping herself (even though she believed she was "right"), Pam was able to calm herself down and become open. Stress dumps cortisol in our blood and weakens our immune systems. By slowing down our reaction-based quick judgment, we conserve energy for more productive, positive thoughts and tasks.

We each experience different states depending on the part of the brain most activated by the neural paths being excited. When in fear and judgment, the older part of the brain is more dominantly activated. When the neocortical brain is dominant, emotions balance and you have a sense of wellbeing and greater access to your rational and creative brain. It is like being in an "oasis."

Visualize the following:

Imagine yourself stretching your arms wide-open—the way you might to welcome a young child after you've come back from a trip. Next, imagine a nice warm shower of acceptance flowing from you to the other person. Let your body relax and be open to learning more and coming to agreement. Imagine that you and the person you are conversing with are relaxed and moving together on the path toward an oasis.

We gauge body language, tone of voice, and other verbal and nonverbal cues to determine someone's openness. Although we may not be correct in our assessment, we do assess, consciously or unconsciously, how open someone is to us. We react accordingly. We close ourselves in self-protection when we sense that somebody is not open.

Whether consciously or not, we sense when someone is open to us, and then we are likely to be more open in return. In fact, we experience a sense of resonance when we are open and the person or group we are with is also open.

It is helpful to show genuine interest. If you have your arms crossed over your chest during a conversation, the other person is likely to interpret your posture as a signal that you are opposed to his or her perception. In the same way, crossing your legs and drawing your knees toward your body may signal a lack of openness. To change this, relax your body and sit with your arms by your side, your legs slightly apart, and your body leaning a bit forward—toward the other person. This conveys openness and supports trust. A smile indicates you are approachable.

When we are open and connected to another person, our body language may mirror each other's. When we are in rapport, we tend to mimic each other unconsciously. You might have noticed that when you are having a meaningful conversation with someone, you both have your legs positioned at a similar angle, or you have your arms in a similar position. Consider checking body posture occasionally as a test of your rapport. However, the most important thing is to be open-minded and curious about possibilities.

Practice Being Open

Think of a person you distrust or dislike. Notice how you feel when you are with this person or you think about him or her. Notice your chest, head, and stomach. What are you thinking? What do you notice about your body? What are you feeling? Does an image come to mind? When Jamie did this exercise, she noticed a sense of caution in her body. Her chest and stomach felt tight. She didn't think she could trust the other person, so she felt anxious and guarded. She chose having a shield in front of her as an image. The shield would defend her and separate her from the other.

Now, think of a person you trust and whose company you enjoy. Notice how you feel when you are with him or her. How does your chest feel? How does your stomach feel? What are you thinking? What do you notice about your body? What sensations do you experience? Is there a color or words associated with this feeling? Does an image come to mind?

As I do this exercise, I notice feeling a sense of warmth in my heart and chest. My shoulders and back are straight and confident. I feel relaxed and sense that my eyes and face are soft. I imagine myself opening my arms to this person. Remember how you feel—physically and emotionally—in this open state. You will want to recall it to get your body in this place when you most need it.

Another useful exercise is to remember a time you made a judgment about someone that you later found to be inaccurate. What did you learn that shifted your perspective? What can you learn from this experience?

Creating an Inner Oasis of Openness

In this state, you are open to discovery and learning, and your mind is alert and relaxed. You are in the present moment. We can choose to foster this state of openness rather than waiting for it to happen.

To help you create this personal inner oasis of openness, imagine yourself in a past situation that felt open as if it were happening now. Consider asking a friend to coach you in identifying the specific sensory and visual elements of your image. Ask yourself (or have your friend ask you): What are you feeling? What do you see, hear, taste, or smell? What sensations do you notice in your body and where? Is there a sound, a color, a metaphor, or a memory that stands out? Keep these sensations close at hand, for they will help you to recreate this sense of openness at will.

To reconnect with my sense of an open oasis, I envision a playground, hear laughter, and imagine a sense of liveliness and space. I feel a sense of expansiveness and expectation. Others have different images that work for them. Jason pictures a pool of crystal clear water that is soothing and rejuvenating. Joan, a coaching client, uses the image of a forest and a treehouse as a place where she experiences being open. Another client, Andres revisits a favorite spot from childhood. He sits on top of a boulder on a hill looking out. His entire hometown is displayed in front of him. He says when he envisions the panoramic view, he experiences a sense of openness to others. He also feels an eagerness to learn and an optimistic sense that he will be okay. Jim conjures up an image of his favorite stretch of sand on the ocean. A place in the desert in New Mexico is where Carlos pictures himself, while Marie remembers a beautiful church in France where she sat in silence, feeling reverent and open.

You may also want to keep an object that will help you to reconnect with your sense of openness. Mike experiences an oasis when he is windsailing, and he displays a photo of himself windsailing on his desk to remind him to be open in his interactions. Ellen keeps a picture of her best friend to remind herself to be open to others as she is to her friend.

As you use your cue—be it a sound, a color, an image, or a sensation—to recreate this sense of presence, begin to rehearse being in this space of openness. With practice, you will be able to step into this place at will. You can also train yourself to be open by pairing the experience with other habits. For example, you may focus on being open as you commute to work on the bus or as you walk. You may ask yourself: "What would it be like if I were open now?" and listen for a moment as you shift into it.

Summary

This chapter delineates the OASIS Move of shifting from judgment to being open to creating possibilities with others. In it, we learned to notice our judgment signal; to stop, step back, and suspend judgment; to recall our intention to be open and assume positive intent; and to cool down—if needed—and be open to possibilities.

Now that you have shifted (S) to being open and curious, in the next chapter, we will explore how to identify what is important (I) to those involved in a conversation and focus on exploring different perspectives to find common ground.

Practice

Imagine how someone you admire would be open in a situation like yours. For example, you might ask yourself: How would Gandhi, Mother Teresa, or Buddha respond in this situation? Or, to use a popular phrase, "What would Jesus do?" Call upon the image of this person during situations when you find it challenging to be open.

I Is for Importance

What Is Important and How Can You Create an OASIS of Understanding Together?

"The ability to listen, in its broadest sense, is at the heart of engagement....
Engagement is expressing oneself and listening to the expression of others....
Engagement is thinking, inquiring, and exploring possibility."

— Michael D. McMaster

OASIS Conversations

Have a clear intention, plan when possible, and build rapport.

O = Observation

A = Awareness (of assumptions, emotions, and background)

S = Shift (to being open)

🌴 = Importance

S = Solution

Cue for Remembering

The sensory cue for the importance (I) component of the OASIS Moves process is:

1. To visualize or feel yourself pointing at your own heart: What is important to me?

2. To visualize or feel the other person's heart: What is important to you?

3. To recognize the space that connects the two of you: What do we share that is important?

Importance in a Conversation

In a conversation, you will ask others, "What is important to you? What do you need?" You will also ask yourself and share, "What is important to me?" You will ask "What is our common ground or shared interests; what is important to both of us?" The key is to listen for understanding before jumping to solutions. The act of listening and understanding takes place before identifying solutions and agreements.

On the Path Toward an Oasis

The act of understanding what is important to others, sharing what is important to us, and noticing the common ground enables us to experience connection.

When we are in a state of judgment, we are primarily acting from the reactive reptilian-brain stem and limbic parts of our brain. We are moving fast to protect ourselves. We limit the information we take in and focus on action using our limited repertoire: fight, flight, freeze, or appease. As we stop, step back, suspend our judgment, and shift to being open, we essentially move from relying on our reactive brain to activating our rational, open, and reflective learning brain. Using it, we are better positioned to understand and begin to consider alternatives. As we shift and become present and open to learn, our open stance can be contagious. In return, others are more likely to tap into the creative and reflective learning sides of their brains. Understanding what is important to those involved before taking action supports our experience of creating an oasis together.

Identifying Importance

To explore the importance component of the OASIS Moves process, let's study a work situation between Rita and Indru. We will look at the value of identifying what is important and finding common ground. The process builds and deepens the experience of trust, which facilitates successful interactions. In the next chapter, we will examine listening skills for creating understanding about what is important.

One of the goals of the importance phase of the OASIS Conversation process is creating a climate of openness for learning and dialogue. Our aim in this process is to be open to listen and learn and to support the other parties in opening up.

Case Study: Manager and Staff Member Communication Breakdown

Rita, a manager of information technology in a large multicultural organization, complained, "Indru does not open his e-mail on a regular basis. As a result, I have to worry about whether he is getting back to clients. Then I have to send him more e-mails or call to remind him. I'm tired of hounding him to get the work done." Rita reminded Indru, who reported to her, that she expected him to read his e-mail, quickly respond to the clients he'd been assigned, and report back when the problems were resolved. She said, "I've tried everything, but nothing works; he doesn't read his e-mail. He just doesn't care. I don't think he should be on my team."

Rita was a participant in one of my workshops. She decided to use the OASIS Conversation process with Indru. The first thing she did was to notice her signals and the judgment she was making. A sense of overall stress and a tightening in her stomach were the signals she identified. I also noticed that she was tightening her jaw and her fists as she spoke. Being a results-oriented person, Rita recognized her tense stomach as a familiar response. Rita judged that Indru didn't care about his work. No other explanations were possible. She "knew" that she was "right" and Indru was "wrong." Rita was stuck in judgment.

I gave Rita empathy by saying, "It sounds like you are really tired of following up with Indru." She readily agreed. I said, "So, you are really tired of this worry." She replied, "Yes. I need to try another strategy." As she received empathy, I could see her shift her physical position—her shoulders dropped, her voice became calmer, and she stopped clenching her jaw and fists. I asked her about the quality of Indru's work. "Clients say positive things about him," she said. "They say he does a good job fixing their computer problems. I wonder how he sees this situation?" she concluded.

Next, I asked Rita to identify her observable data. Her first response was, "He never reads his e-mail." I asked, "Never?" She described her observation (O): "Indru did not respond to my e-mails on two occasions regarding the Stetsen project this week. Also, I did not know how to respond to Lois, Indru's client, when she asked me about the status of her project this week. I had not received an update from Indru." Both of Rita's observations were factual. They would be good points to use to begin the discussion with Indru. Rita admitted that she does not usually provide observable data to Indru. When she had previously approached him, she just directed him to read his e-mail and indicated her frustration with him by the tone of her voice. After that, she had walked away and not given him a chance to respond.

Next, Rita became aware of her assumptions, emotions, and background (A). Rita assumed that Indru did not read his e-mail and did not care; she felt frustrated and angry. Her background was that she was focused on results. She responded quickly to customer requests and expected the same from those who worked with her. A year earlier, Rita worked with someone who did not meet client needs. She initiated disciplinary action, which consumed considerable time. She found it quite unpleasant. She didn't want to experience that drain of her time and emotions again.

Next, I coached Rita to stop, step back, and suspend acting on her judgment and shift to being open. While not her natural response, she did. She made the choice to move (shift) from her judgmental perspective to becoming open and curious. She visualized the stop sign and taking off her robe of judgment. Rita was open to understanding what was important to Indru, sharing what was important to her, and seeing what they both agreed was needed (I). She appreciated the value of first trying to understand the situation without jumping to action.

Rita began her conversation with Indru with some rapport-building comments about the weather. She noted that the weather was getting warmer and she asked about his upcoming vacation plans. After a few minutes of friendly conversation, both Indru and Rita relaxed. Rita opened by stating her observation (O). "Indru, I noticed that you did not respond to my e-mails regarding the Stetson project on two occasions this week. Also, when I was asked by Lois about the status of her project on Wednesday, I didn't know how to respond since I did not see an update from you."

Rita made a choice about what she would share regarding her Awareness of her assumptions, emotions, and background (A).

She began by stating her assumption:

Rita said, "I assume you are not reading your e-mail on a regular basis."

Then her emotions:

"I am frustrated and feel disappointed."

And background:

"I expect you to manage requests and respond to client needs quickly. I don't think I should need to follow-up with you so much." Rita said this matter-of-factly rather than harshly.

Stop, Step Back, Suspend Judgment, and Shift to Being Open (S)

Rita focused on stopping, stepping back, and being open and curious to Indru's perspective (S). She wanted to find out what was important to him (I). She took a deep breath and was calm and open.

Importance (I)

Rita asked, "What is important to you here?" Indru replied, "I think I have demonstrated my strong commitment to meeting our clients' needs. I work hard and always try to solve their problems. I don't like to waste time when I am working with them on the problems." Rita listened and used the skills of paraphrasing and giving him her full attention. "So it's important to you to do a good job on the client requests." Indru nodded his head "Yes" emphatically. Rita offered, "You get a lot of positive comments from the clients. Many of them request that you work with them." Rita could see Indru relax as he saw that she understood he valued excellence and that he worked hard. Rita asked, "What else besides responding to clients efficiently and working hard is important to you?" Indru replied, "I want the clients to feel they are a priority and that I am responsive." Rita paraphrased and gave empathy, "So it's important to you that clients respect you and see that you are committed to meeting their needs." Indru smiled and nodded.

He then asked her, "What else do you need from me?" He was

genuinely curious now. Rita felt that he was paying attention and was really interested in what she had to say. This was something she had not noticed in the past. Rita agreed with Indru, "I am glad you want the clients to have their needs met. That, of course, is a high priority for me, too. I also have a need to be informed. I don't like feeling like I have to follow up with you. I need assurance that clients are being served. I feel embarrassed when I don't know the status of a project and can't tell a client who asks me."

Indru apologized for this. "I did send an e-mail to Lois and I talked with her assistant. I guess she didn't see my e-mail telling her that I fixed the problem. I need to do a better job of keeping you informed. I didn't expect her to go to you." Rita mentioned that they had happened to be in a meeting together and that Lois had asked casually. Indru confirmed that he usually communicated directly with the clients. He had thought that putting a results summary in the monthly report was enough for Rita. "I didn't realize that you wanted to be kept up-to-date on individual projects. I read your e-mails making assignments and get to them as soon as I can. Sometimes some projects take longer than expected. Often, past clients find me and want me to work on their emergency situations. I try to fit them in." Rita had not realized that Indru had been receiving a lot of informal requests.

"I like having some independence and confidence placed in me," Indru said. Rita, paraphrased and gave empathy. "So you are saying you have felt like you are doing a good job and reporting adequately in the monthly report? You expected me to understand that you have been working hard and are being responsive to our clients?" Indru said, "I don't know what to do with your e-mails. Sometimes, there are duplicates and I am already responding to the client. That's what happened with the Stetson case. I was already working on the project and working on the Jake project, too. I find it hard to stay current on the e-mails."

Rita said she could understand Indru's perspective. "I'm not looking to add more to your workload. I can see we need a better process for communicating about the projects." Then she added a reframing question, which is useful for determining strategies and actions. "Given that we both want to serve our clients in an efficient manner, we know it's important that you have your independence to be responsive to client requests, and finally, that it's important for me to be kept informed; let's explore our options."

Solution (S)

After being understood by the other, Rita and Indru were ready to brainstorm options and then agree on a strategy and actions. Since Indru was often away from his desk, Rita suggested that he use a smartphone to update her. He could send messages to her directly about the status of his projects. Indru suggested providing weekly reports rather than monthly updates. Rita suggested more staff meetings. For each option, they discussed how the action would support what was most important to each of them as well as their joint goals. After discussion, they decided to create an online project report that could be accessed by both of them and by peers. Inside the file, each team member would fill out a form with the date of the request, the project, the status, and expected completion date. Indru would fill out this form daily—within four hours of working on a project. Rita could log on to check the project's status. Rita agreed to minimize her e-mails so Indru didn't get bogged down. Indru and Rita's conversation ended with both feeling like they were heard and understood. Their relationship, trust level, communication process, and the work product were enhanced.

What Is Important?

First use the three questions to identify: 1) what is important to you, 2) to me, and 3) for us. Then, you must be open to learning the other's perspective and to sharing your own. Since it is our nature to rush to action, we have to train ourselves to consider the three questions so we don't actually solve the "wrong" problem! Alternatively, you may say or take actions that aren't in your or the other person's best interests. For instance, I remember once when I wished I had not been so quick to criticize a staff member's report. When the person became upset, I had to address that, too! If I had slowed down, I would have seen that the research I had asked for had been collected. I hadn't focused on how I wanted the report presented when I had initially made the assignment. The two of us had contributed to the misunderstanding. I apologized and asked that she ask for clarification from me if I failed to explain clearly what was needed in the future.

To remind myself of the benefit of understanding, I often say to myself, "I need to slow down in order to speed up." I have the confidence that by managing my desire to move to action and by being open to understand and engage in dialogue, we will create a better solution. When

I say, "Identify what is important," I am talking about becoming aware of the priorities of those in a conversation. This involves understanding different perspectives, which includes different views, needs, wants, intentions, goals, visions, values, beliefs, and interests.

Benefit of Understanding What's Important

By clarifying what is important, you will have a greater chance of satisfying those needs. When Rita focused on what was most important to Indru, he was able to focus on what was important to her. What they agreed on satisfied both. Identifying what is important helps you to sort through priorities.

People may say they want something without reflecting on what is really most important to them. For example, Dirk, a manager of a small firm, told his employees that he wanted them to work late. He would come in and check the employee time-log to see who had worked longer hours. When I questioned him, he realized that what he really wanted was to know that his employees cared about the business. He wanted evidence that they would do what was required to meet customer needs. This might include working past the 5:00 p.m. official closing time.

After gaining clarity, Dirk talked with his employees and conveyed his needs. They showed him many examples of when they had gone the extra mile and how satisfied customers were. They were eager to show their true commitment to the firm. Before the discussion about what was really important, the staff members felt devalued. They considered being asked to work late as a punishment, especially when there was no need! Ask yourself: What is behind a need or a request? When you get closer to the essence of what is important, you may discover several ways to satisfy it.

A challenge in interactions is learning what needs are strongest at a given time. For example, Rita, profiled in the earlier case study, had several needs. She needed to make sure clients were being served efficiently. She needed not to waste her time and energy following up with Indru. She needed to be informed. She also needed to work effectively with a colleague (Indru). Finally, she needed to be respected in her role. By focusing on her needs, Rita could be more intentional about making agreements with Indru to satisfy what was most critical to her. In addition, this knowledge helped her understand and manage her propensity to blame Indru and others.

Before she gained clarity, it was a lot easier for Rita to feel like a victim. She blamed Indru and spent energy in a non-productive way. We can stop this pattern by slowing down, recognizing what we need, and becoming more creative in looking for ways to satisfy what is important to us.

Most of us share similar basic needs. For example, we need to be nourished and to be safe; we have a need for fairness and respect; we have a need for creativity. We each have a need for independence to make our own choices. We have a need for a sense of belonging and connection with others. We need to be understood and valued. While we all have a need for accomplishing tasks and having relationships, our priorities and the importance we place on these vary.

People have noticed over the centuries that others have different priorities, interests, and styles. Many attempts have been made to categorize people to help us remember that other people are different from us. Some of our needs are related to personality differences. Other differences are learned from our culture, upbringing, organizations, and experiences.

It is useful to understand some of the dimensions where people have different priorities around various needs. Differences are what make people interesting, and they serve us in achieving goals. A person who is organized and strong with detail can support someone with an exciting idea to execute. Be aware of some of the priorities of people you interact with often. For example, I know that being on time is a high priority for my colleague. Since I am aware of this, I can be responsive and work to meet this need.

However, to make things even more complicated, you may notice that you and others are not stagnant. Sometimes, you will place a greater importance on building relationships. Sometimes, you will be more interested in achieving a task or having fun. Sometimes, you will need space to focus, and other times, you will prefer being with people. We may have similar needs, yet we may express them in different ways. I may satisfy my need for creative expression by writing, and you may enjoy sharing a story in an intimate conversation instead.

Besides our needs, we are each influenced by our experiences, beliefs, and values. I am strongly motivated internally to make a difference while my colleague is highly motivated by having fun interactions with others as he achieves work goals.

Given our past histories, our life experiences, and who we are as individuals, we come to each interaction with different intentions and goals. These differences create the potential for misunderstandings, lack of trust, and just plain old confusion.

The goal of the I (Importance) move of OASIS is simply to have a two-way dialogue to understand what is important to those involved. If we can keep our stance of openness and lack of judgment, we make it okay for each person to share openly his or her needs, intentions, and goals. With the spirit of understanding and dialogue, we will learn where there is a shared importance. Clearly Rita and Indru both want to serve their clients efficiently. Given their shared intention and agreement about what is important, they could identify common ground and agree on some actions.

Brain Connection

Brain scans have identified the area of the brain where, when activated, we experience emotional balance, relationship harmony, and connection with others and ourselves. While workplaces and many cultures seem to value thoughts and intellect over emotions, we are continuously learning more about the critical nature of emotions and needs. Through your emotions, you determine what is most important so you can make decisions that allow you to get these needs met.

Your limbic brain sorts through your thoughts, emotions, conscious and unconscious memories, expectations, experiences, and bodily sensations. Then it moves on to assess and prioritize what is most important to you at a given moment. Next, your limbic brain provides an emotion or message to your neocortex. Your brain let's you evaluate how important something is based on the message's strength.

Pay close attention and listen to your and others' emotions. At times, you may become highly stressed and feel overwhelmed by emotions. You may disassociate from them and use your thinking process to over-analyze what is important. When you become comfortable checking in with yourself and naming your feelings, you become skilled at identifying what is most important to you and others.

We used to think that humans acted as independent systems. Now, with the help of brain imaging instruments, scientists can see that we are wired to connect with each other. The brain scans show that circuits form when we interact with other people. That neural bridge allows us to sense what others are experiencing—and they can sense what we are experiencing. During our interactions, neural pathways or circuits are firing and we experience a range of feelings that impact our own and others' brains and their experience of emotions. So, if you tune in, you are likely to understand more about what is important to others than you thought possible.

Each conversation involves an exchange of energy and information. We need to pay attention to the content of words and also the emotions we convey. Positive psychology research supports that we feel more creative and have more energy for action when we experience positive emotions in interactions. Negative emotions create a downward spiral where we fail to understand one another and trust is reduced. Positive emotions ignite an upward spiral where we are open to new ideas and trust is enhanced.

Dan Siegel[10], a respected interpersonal neurobiologist, supports that each conversation is a connection of minds between conversation partners. Our minds regulate patterns of energy and information flow, which create our experiences and understandings and influence our actions. In a conversation, we are co-creating a shared understanding. Our words, non-verbal behavior, and attention influence the interaction.

To be an effective leader, you must sense what is most important to those you are influencing and whose support you need and create positive emotions. Positive relationships have a beneficial impact on our health and success.

How Do We Know What Is Important to Others?

Take a learning stance where you remain open and curious so you can observe and listen fully. You may not be clear about what you need or what is most important. Some of us still need to learn to reflect on what is most important to us. In some cultures, it is even considered impolite to express needs.

First, you can simply pay attention. You can notice a person's behavior and then inquire to see whether you have correctly identified

---

10   Siegel, D.J. *The Developing Mind: How Relationships and the Brain Interact to Shape Who We Are.* 2nd Ed. NewYork: Guilford Press, 2012.

what is important to him or her. For example, Rita could have noticed that Indru submitted a full report each month on the status of his projects and he identified his successes. He even included client comments. She could have said, "I see from your monthly reports that you are completing some challenging projects. I assume you want to make sure our clients are served efficiently." This kind of statement could have helped Indru to feel understood and may have clarified for him what was important for him and them both.

In addition, you can ask questions like, "What is most important to you?" Next, actively listen and help the other person discover and clarify what he needs, what his intention is, and what he values in a given situation. Remaining open, suspending judgment, shifting, and being curious to learn is much more important than the actual questions you ask. In the space of this kind of inquiry, everyone is safe to learn and reflect. This is something we don't experience enough.

Note how a person responds to suggestions and ideas. If Rita had suggested Indru try another position outside of her team, she would have seen his disappointment. If she had suggested he work on a particularly difficult client problem, she would have noticed his excitement about the new challenge.

With time, you will learn what is most crucial to specific people. For example, I know that paying attention to time is very important for my colleague, Robert. When we are working together, I can meet his needs by informing him about the length of different segments in a workshop I am facilitating. I also offer specific directions to participants so the exact timing for exercises is clear to all. I learned about Robert's need from observing him and asking him what is most important. I also noticed that as he has become comfortable with the material, he has become somewhat flexible regarding timing. So while people change, often some of their most important needs remain fairly constant.

Some areas that are likely to be important to people include being respected, being appreciated, being a part of something, and achieving. Each person, however, will want these areas demonstrated with observable data in different ways.

Clarify What Is Important to You

You can use the same process of reflecting to become clear about what is most important to you at a given time. You can ask yourself what is most important regarding your relationship with a colleague. Perhaps you are focused on achieving a tight deadline since you have a few other challenging projects. The more transparent you can be, the more likely others will feel they understand you. If you are not transparent, people will feel compelled to make assumptions about your motives and behavior.

Sudip, an introvert, tended not to share much. His colleagues assumed he did not care about a project and was withholding information. Not long after, Sudip had a conversation with his colleagues and said that he had just needed time to reflect. His colleagues came to understand his approach. Sudip would say, "I'm going to sleep on this. I'll let you know my thoughts in the morning." His colleagues appreciated having a timetable, and less energy was spent guessing about Sudip's intentions and mistrusting him.

Practice

List what's most important to you—those things that you value. For example, for me, it is very important to work toward results. I like to make a difference and influence others. I also value connecting with people. When I coach clients, I help them identify what is most important to them—their core values. I ask them to identify some moments when life felt good for them. For example, I taught a leadership program in Asia, Africa, and South America. I enjoyed traveling and supporting people with concepts that could influence them and others. I loved the diversity—the group included participants from all over the world. From this memory, I can confirm that the following are important to me: making a difference, travel, diversity of perspective, connecting with others, and having fun through learning. (My family joined me for a few days during a program, which made my experience even better.) The more that I have these elements in my life, the better I feel.

You will be in a better position to support those around you when you know what is most important to them. Ask and notice, rather than assume, what others value most. You may be surprised.

Besides knowing what is generally important to you, it is useful to know what is important to you in the moment and what is important as you move forward with your relationships.

Find What Is Mutually Important

Clarify what is mutually important between those you interact with and yourself. This clarification includes common goals, needs, interests, and intentions. When we experience a joint goal, we feel more connected and can relax more. Building rapport and finding common ground are important. We naturally feel more connected and safe when we realize we share things in common with others.

When you identify what is mutually important, this common ground essentially draws you and the other person or people into the same circle. As humans, we unconsciously divide people into groups of "Us" versus "Them." When you start talking about "us," you have drawn an invisible fence around you and the person you are interacting with—us. You are no longer potential adversaries. Instead, you are a team working together to understand what will be best.

Identify what is jointly important in the moment and in the future. For example, you and a work colleague may both agree that you need to figure out how to complete a report that is due. You will also want to make sure you figure out how to work well together so you can avoid future misunderstandings. Every interaction, including disagreements, offers fodder for the relationship's future. In the case we studied, Rita gained understanding about the status of Indru's current projects and felt confident that clients were being satisfied. The OASIS Conversation with Indru also set the groundwork for their future relationship. Working through difficult situations successfully with others creates confidence in relationships and may strengthen them—especially when people feel understood.

Summary

This chapter examined a specific case study to demonstrate the need to explore the three questions: What is important to you? What is important to me? What is important to us? It is useful to understand what is important before jumping to solutions. The next chapter will review the critical skills needed to listen and co-create shared understanding.

CHAPTER 8

Continuing with I for Importance

Listening Skills for Fostering Understanding

"To listen well is as powerful a means of influence as to talk well, and it is as essential to all true conversation."

— Chinese Proverb

OASIS Conversations

Have a clear intention, plan when possible, and build rapport.

O = **Observation**

A = **Awareness** (of assumptions, emotions, and background)

S = **Shift** (to being open)

 = **Importance**

S = **Solution**

I've shown different ways for you to become open in the previous chapters. However, the people you are living or working with may not have read this book or learned the OASIS Moves, so how do you support them in being open? First, pay attention and observe whether they are open. As we've learned, if they are boiling in emotion, it is unlikely they will have access to the full capacities of their rational brains and be open to possibilities. They won't be available to identify what is important and find solutions with you.

Your job is to keep checking to make sure you stay open and to determine whether the person you are speaking with is also open. How do you do this? You pay attention. Ask yourself, "Am I open? Are we experiencing an oasis?" Notice when you move to judgment; then catch yourself and take steps to regain being open and curious. Airline attendants direct you, in the event of an emergency, to put on your oxygen mask first, even before helping young children with their masks. To support others in being open, first we need to be. Then it can become contagious because, as recent brain research[11] shows, we possess mirror neurons that reflect others' emotions. You've probably had the experience of being upset or stressed, but then you calm down when another person seems calm and confident.

Even before focusing on someone else's words, notice the person's posture, body language, and tone. Does she seem open to possibilities? Be open-minded yourself and then carefully listen to her. When people's feelings are acknowledged, they are more likely to shift and move to an open state. When you listen, you give the person an "oxygen mask" by reducing the focus on your own needs and focusing on his or hers. This may not be easy for you at first.

Many of us do not experience people fully listening to us. Something special happens when another person listens to us. When we hear ourselves, we can relax and become more open. Throughout a conversation, you and your partner are likely to experience a number of shifts. Stay aware as you notice your coworker, family member, or neighbor shift from being open to closed or defensive. Then simply stop sharing your perspective. Instead, focus on fully listening to the other person. Your goal is to listen and support the other person in feeling safe and becoming open again.

A teacher once told me that I had two ears and only one mouth, so I should listen twice as much as I talked! This is useful advice. Most of

---

11 Iacoboni, M. *Grasping the Intentions of Others with One's Own Mirror Neuron System.* PLOS, Biology, February 22, 2005.

us think we are better listeners than we are. I find that many leaders and managers tend to talk more than listen. When they start listening, they learn a lot and are much more effective. When I work with teams, I help people learn how to listen and demonstrate understanding of one another. During these workshops, people are often amazed by the benefits of simply listening and letting each other know they have heard one another. The teams often report that by simply listening with the intention of using these skills, they experience more understanding, can identify common ground, and create better solutions. The more we practice listening skills, the more they become a part of us; we become unconsciously competent at using them. Having both the intention and skills for listening will help you to experience life like you are living in an oasis.

Mirroring, Empathizing, asking Empowering questions and Tracking the type of interaction are critical skills. You may want to remember the acronym "MEET" as a reminder to use them. While listening skillfully will help identify what is important, you will use it throughout your conversations and through all phases of the OASIS Conversation process. Let's review each of these skills.

Mirroring—MEET 1

Mirroring is the first important skill of the MEET acronym. Mirroring is the process of letting your conversation partner know you are listening and then reflecting back what you hear the person say. First, attend to the other person and show interest, which encourages the person to speak. Physically lean forward and pay attention. The more we can act like a mirror and reflect what we hear without input, the more useful this process is. In many cultures, mirroring includes maintaining eye contact and using encouragers such as "yes," "I see," "really," and "hmm." By your body language and being fully present, you demonstrate your interest. This attention helps people clarify what they are thinking and feeling.

For example, in the earlier case study, Rita gave Indru her full attention. She stopped working and looked directly at him. She uncrossed her arms when she began to listen to him. This was new behavior for her. She would usually be reading memos or working on her computer when she spoke with him. She also refrained from giving her opinion and first tried to hear his perspective. She trusted she would have time to share her view.

In addition to giving attention, mirroring involves demonstrating to the person that you are hearing what he or she is saying by summarizing or repeating it in your own words (paraphrasing). In the case study, Rita might have said, "You're trying to meet the deadline," and "You left project updates for our client, Lois, through her assistant and on e-mail." These responses often evoke further elaboration and clarification by the person speaking. Sometimes, people use parroting—mechanically repeating word for word what the other said. Be careful with this, though, because it can be annoying. In addition, remember that mirroring does not mean you necessarily agree with what's being said.

Some common ways to introduce paraphrasing are:

"It sounds like..."

"If I hear what you are saying..."

"It seems like..."

"So what you are saying is..."

Rita summarized what she heard Indru say. "So what you are saying is that you are focused on satisfying the customers' needs. You don't feel comfortable taking time to respond to e-mail when you are with clients. Is that right?" In response, Indru clarified and added new information. "Yes, I tend to go directly from one project to another to be efficient. Therefore, it is difficult for me to respond to lots of e-mails."

Sometimes a person speaks without many pauses. It is useful and okay to interrupt if you want to make sure you are following his or her story. You might say something like, "Wait, let me see if I am following you..." or "I want to make sure I'm with you..." or "I'm not clear about...."

Some common ends to paraphrasing are:

"...is that right?"

"...is that what you meant?"

"...am I following?"

"...did I understand you?"

Use your own words. Let's say a coworker says, "I have so many things to do. I need to get the report done, and it needs to be done well. I also need to help the kids with their homework, which is due tomorrow. Besides that, I need to call my aunt, who is in the hospital." In response, you might mirror by leaning forward, giving eye contact, and nodding your head to demonstrate understanding as you say, "It sounds like you have a lot on your plate today, including getting the report done, helping with homework, and touching base with your aunt." Your coworker might add more details. You might be able to ask her how you could help her get the report done more quickly or volunteer to help in another way, if that's appropriate. Just by reviewing the list out loud with you, she may decide to ask her spouse to help with homework that night or call a relative to see whether someone else will be visiting her aunt so she could call her on another day.

Listening means managing the spotlight of attention. Effective listeners have learned to stay focused on the other person for long enough to understand what is important to them.

Be careful not to grab the spotlight and get caught in the "Me, too!" syndrome. Have you had the experience of telling another person about your need for a medical procedure, only to have her immediately start talking about her own medical experiences? Or maybe you started sharing about your Hawaiian holiday when the other person started talking about his vacation there and the spotlight dims on you? Don't be that person to others; instead, you can briefly mention, "I was in Hawaii last year," so the person knows you've had a common experience and doesn't feel the need to explain all the details to you. Then return your attention to the other person. Don't take the spotlight for a prolonged time when you are trying to understand the other person. Keep your attention focused on the individual until he or she feels understood and open to developing solutions.

Mirroring supports us in understanding a person's story, situation, and thoughts about it. Also, through our listening, the other person is likely to become more clear about his or her own thoughts and perspective.

Empathy—MEET 2

Empathy is the second critical skill of the MEET acronym. While mirroring is reflecting back what a person is saying, empathy is identifying and acknowledging a person's emotions. We are trying to understand how a person may be feeling. Of course, given our different backgrounds, people experience different emotions regarding situations. While one person may be excited about starting a new project, someone else may be afraid or angry. We each have the need for empathy, and it is vitally important for creating an oasis with others. In an earlier chapter, we identified compassion as a way of offsetting judgment. Similarly, empathy helps us "be in the shoes" of another and sense that person's emotions.

Emotions are waves of sensations and feelings that move through the body. I think of it as e-motion—energy in motion. The waves of emotion are often present whether we acknowledge them or not. There is value in identifying an emotion. First, the other person can tell that you are trying to understand, and often you do understand. This creates a connection between you and the other person, allowing him or her to feel safer. Second, it supports people in understanding themselves and it prevents them from being stuck in their responses. The possibility of shifting emotions is created. Just as it is useful to identify and name your own feeling, when you identify another's feeling, he or she can shift from the emotional limbic response (of the desert) to being more rational and creative (in the oasis) as the prefrontal cortex activates.

Providing empathy to yourself and others is critical for successful relationships. You have to experience empathy to appreciate its power. Often, leaders are shocked by the impact that experiencing genuine empathy has upon influencing others and being influenced themselves. I strongly encourage you to invest in learning how to give empathy.

In my workshops and teambuilding sessions in organizations, I support people in giving empathy to others. Following are effective ways of giving empathy:

Name the Feeling

First, you can simply name how you guess someone feels. You base the guess on what the person has told you and how he looks. Rita could have said to Indru, "I imagine you feel frustrated when you receive multiple e-mails from me related to the same project." Then she should be silent or "zip it up." This gives Indru a moment to pause, go inside himself, and reflect about whether he is frustrated or not. He might say, "I'm not frustrated; I'm disappointed." Or he might agree that he is frustrated or continue to name other feelings he is having. Once Indru identifies and has his feelings acknowledged, often the emotion is free to shift. Without the acknowledgment, Indru may be stuck with his emotions. You may notice he is still in the emotion of frustration when you see his red face and furrowed brows. He may continue to tell you how hard he is working and how his efforts are thwarted.

When you name a feeling, such as "You seem angry," you are essentially putting a stake in the ground. Then the other person can stop, reflect, and pick up the stake or name a new feeling. Either way, the process of suggesting a feeling supports the person in clarifying his emotion. In the West, we are generally comfortable in naming specific emotions. We can use one feeling word, such as "You must be: tired, upset, confused, worried, angry, etc." To differentiate feelings from thoughts, use this simple phrase: "I imagine you feel _____," or "I'm wondering whether you feel ____." "If I were you, I would be or feel ___." (To help you identify feelings, you can find a list of emotions at www.OASISConversations.com.) Of course, we can never fully imagine how someone else feels, but the process of trying lets the other person know we care and are attempting to understand.

We may mistakenly identify a thought. For instance, "You feel that I should have been on time." Since this is really a thought, it will not have the powerful impact of identifying an emotion. It is more useful to say, "I imagine you feel disappointed."

Often, people experience a number of feelings, so after one is identified, another may then become clear and you can identify that emotion, too. You might say, "So you are both tired and upset."

Show You Can Relate

Often when we experience strong emotions, we feel like we are the only ones going through the storm. It helps to be reminded that we are not alone. If it is true, it is useful to share, "I can relate. I once had one of my team members leave in the middle of a project." If someone expresses worry about a pending presentation, you might say, "I can relate. I was afraid the first time I gave a talk to that group. My knees shook." No need to go into too much detail—you'll take the spotlight away. If the person asks for more details, tell briefly about your experience and put the attention back on her.

Give Non-Verbal Empathy

In the West, where we are often comfortable with naming a feeling, another option is to "try on" how you believe a person feels. By doing so, you will demonstrate it non-verbally. People will interpret from your facial expressions and body language that you are feeling their pain or joy or another emotion. In the East and other parts of the world, people are more attuned to reading these signals. Reading your feelings supports others in acknowledging their own. People, especially from the East, are likely to feel embarrassed or that they have lost "face" if you directly name their emotions. For example, saying, "You seem tired" or "You are angry" could be embarrassing. Pay attention to the person you are talking with and notice his or her responses. In any case, it is valuable to attune to the other person's emotions. The person you are listening to will notice your internal alignment and sense your empathy. Your compassion and understanding will be reflected by your demeanor, which will impact how the other person perceives you.

Identify a Need

People, particularly those from cultures and environments that are less supportive of naming emotion, will respond better to an expression of understanding their needs or the situation. For example, if a colleague says, "My promotion finally came through," you could show your understanding by saying, "Recognition for your excellent performance is important." Your colleague is likely to agree and feel understood, which is the goal of giving empathy. In one of my workshops, a participant from China felt most understood when the situation he was experiencing was acknowledged. He told about the poor service he received from a waiter in a local restaurant. When I gave him empathy about it, he felt a bit embarrassed. However, when I focused on the situation instead and said, "A waiter should be responsive to you, the customer," he felt understood and supported. For him, the statement regarding his need and identifying the situation was more supportive. He did not want to lose face.

If someone shares that an important committee accepted her proposal, you can guess at the underlying need and situation. "It helps to know that the committee is listening to suggestions and responding." In this circumstance, the attention is more on the underlying need and the situation. Pay attention to the person you are conversing with and notice her response. You can then adjust your response to reflect that you understand her situation in the way she needs to hear it.

Responses That Are Not Useful

Often people will say to others, "I understand," or "I know how you feel." This may be useful if the other person knows you well or has a similar background. If not, a response to this kind of statement, whether said aloud or not, may be, "No you don't!" or "How could you? You haven't lived my life!"

Sometimes, people give responses like "It will work out" or "Don't worry" or "Time heals everything." While the intentions may be positive, without addressing and honoring the emotions, people will remain stuck with their feelings. Also, these platitudes are a form of offering solutions. Be sure to give empathy before suggesting a solution.

In my workshops, I have participants practice listening without offering solutions. Many people find this quite difficult since their first instinct is to offer solutions. When we rush to offer a solution before giving empathy, we are likely to miss supporting the other person in calming down. We may offer a solution that will not satisfy the real need. In our anxiety over someone else's feelings, it is easy to think solutions will take care of things. Give empathy first and then you both will be in a position to identify possible actions. Make sure you have identified what is important before looking for solutions.

I recall a time when Alysa, a coaching client, had her computer crash. She lost an important report she had been working on for several weeks. Unfortunately, Alysa had not printed a paper copy of the report and could not retrieve a backup copy. When she told coworkers her horror story, she received a range of responses. Most of them were not empathetic. Instead, they offered possible solutions or admonitions like: "Why don't you call IT and see if they can retrieve a previous version?" "You should always back up." "You shouldn't ever trust this system." "I always print a paper version of my drafts." Alysa's stomach was in a knot and she was very upset. For days, she felt more and more upset as she received such responses. Finally, someone said to her, "How frustrating! That must be so upsetting. I can relate; I once lost my term paper and it was the entire grade." Alysa sensed the person understanding her and agreed she was upset. She felt the fist in her stomach relax and her shoulders drop. Her tone of voice shifted and she even had a wry smile on her face. "I guess I have learned my lesson about computer backup."

Beware of Sympathy

Again, often with good intentions, people say things like, "I feel sorry for you," or "I pity you." Sometimes such statements support people in feeling small, which is not healthy. Again, it depends on the relationship, the circumstance, and the tone of voice. Just be aware of your comments and remember that empathy is about acknowledging emotions and understanding how a person feels.

Brain Connection

We've talked about mirror neurons and our special ability to tune into how others are feeling because of them. Researcher Marco Iacoboni and his team at the University of Parma, Italy learned about these important neurons when working with monkeys.[12] Studies show that even monkeys have empathy and recognize pain in other monkeys. For example, some monkeys would forgo pressing a lever for big rewards of food when they realized other monkeys would be penalized. Some were even willing to starve to ensure others were not suffering.

Iacoboni observed that people and monkeys are able to feel what others experience as if it were happening to them. When studying macaque monkey brains, he noticed that when a researcher brought a peanut to his own mouth, the monkey's brain fired as if the monkey were grabbing and bringing the peanut to its own mouth, even though the monkey did not move.

If we check in with ourselves, we are likely to sense how another person is feeling. In our brains, spindle cells support empathy. These neurons have a body size about four times that of other brain cells with an extra long branch to make connecting to other cells easier. Transmitting thoughts and feelings to them happens quickly. This quick connection to others' emotions helps guide us in understanding them.

When we give a person our attention, and he senses that we are safe (and he is not experiencing an "error-detection" response that we are judging him), he is more likely to calm down and feel more relaxed and less stressed. When people are feeling strong emotions, they do not have full access to their creative capacity. When we give them our attention and empathy, by naming the emotions they are experiencing, or feeling their emotions, arousal of the prefrontal cortex is heightened. Then they relax and are relieved from their strong emotions. They

---

12 Iacoboni, M. *Grasping the Intentions of Others with One's Own Mirror Neuron System.* PLOS Biology, February 22, 2005.

experience resonance with us, receive our empathy, and are better positioned to see possibilities.

As a person receives empathy, he shifts from one neural pathway to another, and you can sense this as he relaxes. You will notice he can access more of his creative and rational brain. This is what I refer to as the OASIS state. The limbic system and neocortex act like a seesaw. Empathy and understanding enable a person to shift from emotional states to accessing the neocortex, the more rational part of the brain.

The Benefit of Empathy

The value of empathy cannot be overstated. Empathy is the secret sauce that builds meaningful relationships and a sense of trust. We are drawn toward those who work to understand us. It is critical to be intentionally empathetic and understanding toward those you work with, your family members, and neighbors. In the previous case study, Rita was upset and embarrassed about being unable to respond to a colleague about her project's status. In the midst of her strong emotions, Rita jumped to accusing Indru and even questioned his future employment. She did not have full rational capacity when she was initially angry. By Indru giving her empathy, "I can see you are upset about not having the information," she felt understood, identified her emotions, and was able to breathe and calm down. As she relaxed, she became open; then she was capable of seeing the situation more clearly and considering potential options.

I have seen many workplaces transform after people gave each other empathy and understanding. Energy could then be devoted to developing innovative solutions.

Be Silent (Zip It Up!)

Silence is important when listening and particularly when giving empathy. After you have identified a possible feeling the other person may be experiencing, it is important to state it, "You're feeling upset," and then "*zip it up*"—refrain from talking. The silence allows a person to reflect and determine what he or she is feeling and then either confirm your guess or otherwise identify how he or she is feeling. We may give empathy, but then not create enough space for the other to take in what we say or to reflect. Instead, we may move on to another topic or issue and leave the person with whom we are talking feeling misunderstood. When we rush on like this, the empathy is not heard.

After we identify a person's feelings, it is valuable to give the person a moment to reflect and experience his or her emotions. For example, as Mary moved to a different department and left two staff people behind without clearly defined roles, she felt frustrated and also sad to leave them. When identifying feelings, simply provide empathy, "You're upset about leaving," or "You are sad," and then don't continue to talk. Be in the silence. You might sense how the other person must be feeling. Let the other person receive the empathy and then break the silence by agreeing or clarifying. Often, you will notice that in this process the other person will move his eyes from direct contact to a less focused look. He is checking in to identify how he is actually feeling. This may be the first time he has really looked inside to understand his own feelings about the issue. Empathy is a gift; let the person experience it.

Feelings Shift Like Waves

If feelings are denied or unacknowledged, people often act them out. For example, an angry person may fail to share important information or may leave a meeting early. When emotions are acknowledged by empathy, they are free to shift. If you acknowledge that a coworker "must be disappointed" not to have received positive feedback on a presentation he worked hard on, the coworker feels understood. He can acknowledge his disappointment. He may then relax rather than unconsciously acting out his disappointment by being brusque with coworkers.

It's a human need to be understood. There is value and a sense of connection in just knowing that another person understands our feeling—even when nothing can be done. It helps just to feel less alone. After receiving empathy and acknowledgment, it is easier to be open to hearing other perspectives and exploring options.

The shift in the OASIS Conversation between Rita and Indru came when Rita gave him empathy. She stated, "You must feel stressed when you are moving from emergency to emergency, and then when you check your e-mails, it is not clear which ones are new and which ones are duplicate reminders from me." Indru did begin to relax then. He realized that Rita was trying to understand his experience. Before, Rita had focused on her own needs and did not consider his. As Indru felt understood by Rita, he became calmer and more interested in her perspective and needs.

How Much Empathy Is Needed?

Look for visible signs that the person to whom you are giving empathy receives it. After Alysa received empathy about her computer crash and the loss of her report, her demeanor visibly shifted. Alysa took a deep breath, her shoulders dropped, and she relaxed into a rueful smile. Next, she shifted the conversation to what she could learn from the experience. When people receive empathy and feel acknowledged they may say something like, "What can we do?" Once they feel acknowledged, they will feel ready to move on to considering next steps. People who receive empathy report feeling relaxed and open. Interestingly, once people receive empathy, they often stop fighting to express their viewpoint. They become interested in the person who gave them empathy. Notice if this is your experience.

Offering empathy typically doesn't take as much time as you would guess. Most people don't get enough empathy, but a little goes a long way. Yes, when people have not received empathy for a long time, they may need a lot. In these situations, you may want to spread it over a few meetings.

Empathy: Acknowledgment (Not Agreement)

You may be reluctant to give empathy because you don't agree that the person should be feeling the way he or she does. You may think that you personally would not be feeling the same way. Remember that emotions just are—there is no right or wrong. Would you tell a person she is wrong about being hot? People have different bodily responses to the temperature. Yes, you might be cold and you might be surprised that the other person is hot, but that is her experience. It doesn't serve you to say, "You shouldn't be hot," or "I'm not hot."

I had a similar experience on a scenic train ride in the mountains in Argentina. A woman on the twenty-minute ride complained that the seats were not comfortable, the train car was cold, and there was no restroom on the train. She was angry. She criticized the train, her husband for booking the trip, and even the scenery. She clearly was not having a good day and needed some empathy. People didn't want to give her empathy because they were having a different experience. They were enjoying their view of nature just outside their windows. Also, her harsh tone did not endear her to those around her. I said, "You're disappointed and upset about the experience." With one sentence of empathy, she took a breath, relaxed, and said, "Yes, I expected something else." Shortly, she cooled down and became more pleasant. We even had a conversation about her life. The result was that the brief ride was better for everyone in the train car.

Later, I asked the friend who was with me why he didn't give the woman empathy. He said it was because he didn't like her behavior and didn't agree with her assessment. He was satisfied with the train ride. Empathy does not mean you agree; it is just acknowledging how the other person is feeling. If you are concerned, you can say you are having a different experience, but you can appreciate how difficult it is for the person.

If you refrain from giving empathy to people who seem particularly angry, harsh, or needy, they may continue to be angry. The challenge is that without empathy, it is difficult for the person with strong emotions to shift. She may feel alone. In some situations, she actually is. Many managers have written to me after workshops to say they have been shocked at the power of giving empathy to some "difficult" people. One manager gave empathy to his boss whom he viewed as unavailable and uninterested in him. After some genuine empathy, she relaxed and turned to him to find out what was important to him. They forged a new, better, and more successful relationship.

Another manager complained about one of his staff members throughout a week-long workshop. He got some empathy about the challenging staff member. When he returned to the office, he acknowledged her emotions. He said that he knew some of the work conditions were frustrating, so he understood they made her angry. He could not change the work conditions very much, but the empathy supported his staff member. After that, they worked together to create a more positive environment.

Remember, giving empathy does not mean you necessarily agree, so don't allow that concern to hold you back. Try to find compassion for others. Recognize that they are experiencing things based on their past histories and conditioning. You are very unlikely to know what their experiences are.

Our interpretation and labeling of emotions is influenced by our backgrounds. If we have a history of being abandoned and feeling lonely, we may interpret our friend leaving for another job in another state with feelings of loneliness. Another person may feel happy to have some added time for herself or time for other friends. Because we each have different backgrounds and histories, we automatically experience different feelings for a similar situation. For example, a person with perfectionist tendencies is likely to feel upset when a supervisor questions a section of a report. Someone with a different background experience may feel pleased to receive feedback from the boss and interpret it as support. A third person may expect the feedback and be disappointed about not receiving more direction from the boss earlier.

Because we continually have emotions triggered based on our assumptions and backgrounds, it is hard for us to remember that people have very different feelings stirred by the same or a similar event. We need to remember that we habitually move into our automatic thoughts and feelings and others do the same. We need to be kind to each other, and ourselves, realizing that we never know the whole background triggered for others.

A Challenge to Giving Empathy

Also, give empathy when a person is angry or upset with you. Imagine your coworker angrily stating that you didn't show up as you had promised at 4:00 p.m. While it's natural for you to become defensive in these types of situations and to protect yourself with an excuse ("The traffic was bad") or blame ("No, you're the one! You had the time wrong!"), such times are perfect for giving empathy. Notice your coworker or spouse in strong emotion. Attend to the person and give him or her empathy, even though it may seem counterintuitive. Remind yourself that you will have a chance to share your perspective later. You might say, "I see that you are really angry," or "I know I'd be mad if I'd had to wait this long." Next, you need to "*zip it up*" before offering explanations or solutions. Let the other person notice what he or she is feeling and express frustration, disappointment, or embarrassment. Then you may notice the person relax, take a deep breath, and be more open to hearing your story.

I realize that I am asking you do to something that is not easy—to suspend your natural reaction, suspend your judgment, and first attend to the other person to give empathy. This will get easier for you with practice.

Remember that you do not have to guess correctly how a person feels; you only need to have the intention to understand. With this goal, you will start noticing the clues in what people are saying and in their body language.

Our goal is not to evaluate the validity of the person's feelings, but simply to understand those feelings. Certainly, it is not easy to give empathy to someone when we don't agree with her reaction. But after you give empathy, the person is more likely to become open to hearing your perspective.

Often, we want someone first to hear our point of view. (If he did, he would see why it makes so much sense!) Yet, we need to remember to "seek first to understand, then to be understood" as Stephen Covey emphasized in his best-selling book *The Seven Habits of Highly Effective People*. Since you are the one reading this book, and you are interested in gaining the skills in using the OASIS Moves, you may want to take responsibility for being the first to listen. If you are worried that your conversation partner may not give you equal time, you may want to start with an agreement. "I will listen to what you have to say, and then I would like you to hear my perspective. Will you do that?" If he agrees, you may need to check in with him later, asking, "Have I understood? Anything else?" If he says he feels understood, then you can offer him your perspective. You may even remind him of his agreement to listen to you.

You can take steps to have others give you empathy before an interaction to support yourself in being open to listen. When needed, I talk to an understanding friend or give myself some empathy before a difficult interaction. This supports me to listen first.

Empowering Questions—MEET 3

So far, we have looked at the MEET acronym's Mirroring and Empathizing. The next skill for listening is asking Empowering questions. An empowering question is one that opens another person to share and listen. Ideally, an empowering question helps the person to learn and reflect. While a closed question can be answered with a short yes, no, or factual information, empowering questions are open-ended and invite dialogue.

In the process of understanding what is important to a coworker, whom we'll call Nila for this example, it is useful to ask empowering questions to get a clearer sense of her perspective and increase understanding of an issue. Empowering questions are clarifying and open the speaker up rather than interrogating or closing her down. These kinds of questions demonstrate respect for the speaker and come from a place of genuine openness and curiosity to learn. Empowering questions will allow Nila to learn and clarify her viewpoint in order to find what is mutually important. Empowering questions continue to shine a spotlight on the other person with the intention of really understanding what she is trying to communicate.

People have a natural tendency to answer a question or to search for an answer. For example, if I ask you, "What's important in your life?", most likely you will begin to answer the question internally almost immediately. Perhaps family comes to mind, or making a difference somehow, or completing the big project in front of you.

Our questions can be quite powerful in the way they direct attention. We begin searching for a response when someone asks a question. A question can direct attention to the past or the future, to mistakes or possibilities. Questions directed at whom to blame and what's wrong will direct Nila down one path, while empowering questions about what is possible and options for addressing the issue direct attention to a more positive avenue.

Questions Support Learning

Research by David Cooperrider and others in the area of appreciative inquiry reinforce the value of asking questions that direct people's attention positively and toward solutions. The research demonstrates that asking questions about problems directs attention to what is not going well and can lead to people losing energy for action. Conversely, if you ask questions to discover what contributes to a work group's level of high performance and success, the focus moves to learning about cooperation and success rather than what is not working. In other words, your questions can direct attention to two different avenues of exploration. One is likely to be more positive and helpful toward developing solutions than the other. The more conscious and curious you are, the more you will shine a light and direct attention toward possibilities. So you need to be aware of the impact of asking empowering questions.

Empowering questions support the responder in learning. When you ask empowering questions from a place of openness and curiosity and with a growth mindset, it supports Nila in being open to learning also. We can become more conscious about the kinds of questions we ask others. Our purpose should be to keep Nila open and to allow her to explore her perspective and what is most important to her. Such clarity will support you and Nila in finding common ground and shared purpose.

We fail to ask empowering questions when we believe we know what is going on—that we have things figured out, or that Nila is wrong. If we are not indeed curious, our questions are likely to be flat and directive, reflecting only our perspective or agenda. If we are suspending judgment and truly curious, we will be learning with Nila, and we will be open to what is expressed. We sense when a questioner is genuinely curious and interested rather than trying to lead us down a prescribed path or script. We tend to resist questions coming from the closed or judgmental place.

Many of us learned in school that there are right and wrong answers. However, when we come from a place of being curious and suspending judgment, we are open to learn about the world from the other's perspective. We can ask Nila questions to learn more about her observable data, assumptions, feelings, background, and needs.

Empowering questions should be clarifying—the goal being to understand more. Once I was talking to a colleague about an important issue that concerned me. After I spoke, she asked me an unrelated question, "How does your family like Chicago?" We had moved to Chicago a short time before. It was a perfectly fine question; however, it did not clarify what I was talking about. In fact, for me, it was jarring because it seemed unrelated to the concern I was expressing. Make sure your questions are related to the topic at hand, and if not, clarify how you believe the question is relevant. I became less interested in talking to my peer after her question. It did not open me up to learn more or help me to experience her focus. By comparison, empowering questions focus on the other person and demonstrate respect for him or her. When I ask an empowering question, I am telling Nila that I respect her, believe she knows the answer, and is capable of learning.

Empowering Questions Are Open-Ended

It is important to ask open-ended questions that allow the speaker to elaborate and explore. Closed-ended questions can be answered by a yes, no, or a single phrase. For example, "Are you tired of the project?" is a leading question that can be answered by a yes or a no. However, a question like, "What do you like about the project?" is open-ended and encourages a response that elaborates. Notice that leading questions imply the expected answer and suggest there may be a right and a wrong response. By being curious, we are more likely to create a better understanding of where the other person is coming from and what the person needs.

Sometimes the simplest questions can be the most effective and powerful. For example:

"What else?"

"What do you need?"

"What else is important to you?"

"Where do you want to go from here?"

"What's working now?"

"What do you want to see more of or less of?"

What or How Instead of Why

Notice that I have refrained from questions employing "Why? or "Why not?" The word "why" often sends an alarm to our systems, making us become a bit defensive. People from all over the world have confirmed such a reaction to "why." Of course, some of it is the tone and the way the word "why" is delivered. I think it stems back to days when an adult would ask, "Why haven't you done your homework?" or "Why haven't you taken the trash out?" Generally, the person asking was not really looking for an explanation. Instead, it was a judgment or a reprimand. My sense is that we internally respond to "why" with a sense of accusation, and then we move naturally into defending ourselves or justifying rather than exploring and learning.

Michelle, a senior manager in a Fortune 100 company, is responsible for quality and related initiatives in her large organization. She asked people "why" everywhere she went—"Why is productivity so low?" "Why is it costing so much?" "Why are the results not forthcoming?" However, she informed me that the change in her experience was dramatic as she moved from asking "why" questions to "how" and "what" questions. She now asks, "What do you make of the productivity results?" "How can productivity be enhanced?" "What's working well in your operation?" Once Michelle made this transition, employees started responding to her in a very different way. People became less defensive with her new line of questioning and more excited talking about quality enhancement projects.

Don't Jump to Questions Too Quickly

As valuable as questions are, I encourage you to make sure you do not jump right to questions in your interactions. It is useful to make sure you have spent some time mirroring and giving empathy first. It is beneficial to give the other person eye contact and your full attention. Check out whether you understand what the person is saying (mirroring) and reflect the person's feelings (empathizing). Most of us quickly jump to questions without letting the other person know what we have heard regarding his or her thoughts and feelings. I have noticed that when people jump too quickly to questions, sometimes the other person becomes frustrated or defensive. By first reflecting back what the person already said, it is easier to develop rapport.

Look at the Questions You Ask Yourself

It is also useful to pay attention to the questions you ask yourself. We are constantly asking ourselves questions about people and situations. Make sure your questions are coming from your open and curious oasis perspective rather than a judgmental place. Rather than internally asking, "Who is to blame?" "What's wrong here?" "Why is he a failure?" "Why do I always mess things up?" or "How can I prove I'm right?", try questions such as, "What is this?" "What can I learn?" and "How can I create a win-win environment and agreement?"

Track the Type of Interaction—MEET 4

The final critical listening skill that makes up the MEET acronym is to Track the type of interaction. I've broken types of interaction into three modes: 1) telling, 2) selling, and 3) gelling. Each mode benefits from the previous skills identified, and reflects a different goal, level of energy in a conversation, and level of trust. Let's look at each mode in detail.

Telling is simply a transaction where information is being exchanged. One party is "telling" and the other is listening. We engage in this mode when we ask about data and learn information from others. When we schedule a meeting, we are listening to identify a date and time for the conversation. When we ask about factual issues, such as the weather, the budget allotment, or understanding a concept, we are engaging in a transactional and factual manner. Through the sharing of information and facts, others are influenced. It is valuable to listen actively and to paraphrase back what you are hearing. We engage in telling or receiving information often, so this kind of communication is essential. Notice when you are engaging in a transaction where you or another person is "telling." In such situations, you may want to provide more empathy and ask more empowering questions to initiate a transactional conversation where you convey or learn information.

Selling is when you are engaged in a conversation where one or both parties are working to influence one another to take action or change a belief or behavior. In this conversational mode, a person builds the case for his or her position. Again, influencing others to adopt our ideas or to buy our services is an important conversation. In organizations and in families, we are often trying to get our view across and to influence others to take action. To enhance these interactions, it helps to be attentive, provide empathy, and ask empowering questions. A win-win perspective will support you in demonstrating respect. Influencing others and selling our ideas has become increasingly critical since many are less disposed to respond to us based on positional power alone.

Gelling is more of a generative mode where there is less focus on someone winning and people are in an open, oasis-state, focused on creating something new together. In this conversational mode, there is energy for possibilities, co-creation, and partnership. The parties are listening to one another, and a sense of excitement may exist about creating something new. When you are in this space with others, you know you are in the oasis flow. You have an open mindset where you welcome what "is" and what is possible. You are open-minded, open-hearted, and open to taking joint action. You see possibilities and move toward them together. You are now thinking as "we" and have moved beyond compromise and even win-win. Be on the lookout for these kinds of listening moments so you can create more. Again, these transformational interactions take all of the skills of attending, empathizing, asking empowering questions, and being aware of the moment. In this mode, you will understand another person's perspective and be open to creating something new. There is a high level of trust in this mode.

I find it useful to track the kind of conversation I am engaged in; then, by being open and vulnerable and creating more transparency, I can often shift the conversation to be more in the "gel" mode. I do this by stating that I want us both to be open to our co-creation possibilities, and I listen to others, providing empathy and creating a trusting respectful environment. I find it particularly valuable to create the "gel" environment with teams. For example, I often work with teams being formed after an organizational merger. The team is much more effective in the "gel" mode. Of course, the other modes are needed for clarification and understanding of the different cultures.

When we are aware, we have a choice of which mode we operate from. I can tell my daughter to clean her room, try to sell her on the benefits of doing so, or have a gel-type conversation where I am open to being influenced and am curious about her views. Trust is likely to be enhanced in the gel mode. Likewise, Arun tried telling business leaders that they would need to adapt to a new technology. They resisted his direction even though he was in the role of Chief Technology Officer. With some coaching, he tried the sell mode where he had a clear agenda and focused on influencing his colleagues. With more attentive listening, trust increased. When he embraced the gel mode, trust was greatly enhanced, and in fact, he and his colleagues developed a better solution than the one he initially proposed that met his and the business' needs, and he experienced more positive and trusting relationships. It is useful to assess each situation to determine the most appropriate mode. The sell and gel modes will require more time, yet they will create more trust and less resistance. I often say, "You need to slow down to hurry up." Sometimes, an investment of time and listening can speed up results in the long run. On the other hand, you will want to tell people to leave a house in the case of a fire. By being aware, we can better choose which mode is most appropriate.

Taking Another's Perspective

All of the listening skills support you in taking the other's perspective, which involves trying to put yourself in an other's shoes, even though it is not really possible to do so. Your aim is to understand how the person makes sense of the world given his or her background and experiences. Again, this does not mean that you agree or have a similar sense of reality, only that you understand the other person's viewpoint and experience given his or her background.

To build this skill, it is valuable to pay attention and be interested in learning about other people's perspectives. It helps to read, watch movies, and ask people about their views of life and various topics. Notice when you hear different perspectives. Catch yourself from jumping to the conclusion that the other person is wrong, and instead, try to learn more. What makes the person see it in such a different way? Try listening to the news on a channel with a different political perspective than your own. Read articles that reflect different perspectives. In our polarized world, we have many opportunities to pay attention to different perspectives and build our listening and learning muscles.

To try on the other's perspective, it is useful to understand the person's background experience. So much makes sense, even if we don't agree, when we learn more. People's behavior follows a thread of logic, even if it doesn't make sense to us at first. When Rita understood that Indru didn't feel competent doing multiple tasks at once and felt uncomfortable checking his e-mail at client locations, she could understand why he chose not to check his e-mail more often. When she understood that he thought he was choosing the best action to serve his customers, it made sense to her. Again, she would not do it the same way Indru did, but she could validate that his actions made sense from his perspective. Rita could say, "I can understand how you didn't want to take time away from clients to respond to multiple e-mails." Such validation, not necessarily agreement, supports our conversation partner in feeling understood, and then the other person can relax from trying to convince you that he or she is "right."

We might paraphrase how we hear the person's logic. "Given that you waited two hours for me to finish the report and, therefore, missed another meeting, it makes sense that you are furious and frustrated. You believe you wasted your time waiting." Such validation allows the person to know that you can understand his thinking. It does not mean that you agree with his interpretation, but that you understand it is his truth and how he makes meaning of events based on his background and logic. By being curious and really trying to see the world from the other's perspective, we can gain a lot of insight and be closer to identifying what's important to him or her so we can find common ground.

Refrain from Offering Solutions

I have separated the Importance (I) move from the Solution (S) move in the OASIS process to emphasize the importance of holding back from jumping to solutions. Ironically, when you learn to be comfortable without jumping to a solution and focus on understanding the other person, she becomes much more interested in understanding your perspective, and then viable solutions tend to emerge easily—almost without effort.

An important part of taking the other's perspective is learning how to manage our natural impulse to offer solutions. Given our natural propensity for safety, we can find it uncomfortable when people have different views, different needs, or unresolved issues. In order to reduce our internal tension, our natural reactive mode is to get things "tidied up." We may do this by getting the other person to see that we are right, to get him to change, or to make her wrong. Often we want to tell others what they "should" do. A critical skill is to manage our internal tension and refrain from immediately offering solutions before we have fully understood the other person. People are rarely open to being told what to do or moving to solutions before they have felt heard.

When Rita learned that Indru would prefer not to interrupt work with clients to check his e-mail, she naturally felt some discomfort in this dilemma. Rita's response in the past had been to jump in and solve "the problem" by telling Indru what to do. Rita, like many of us, had the natural inclination to offer solutions quickly.

It's human nature to become uncomfortable when a person has an unsolved problem or concern. We immediately want to resolve it because it can incite tension in us. By offering a solution, we begin to alleviate our tension, and often, we think it will alleviate the other person's tension. However, when someone else gives us an answer, we often reject it. Most of us have played the "Yes, but..." game. "Yes, but that won't work for me," or "Yes, but I tried that already."

If we can learn to manage our own tension and trust that the person we are talking to will find the best answer for him- or herself when given some space, our interactions will be more effective. This kind of thinking allows us to stay curious and open for inquiry with the other person.

The belief that others can find the best solutions for themselves is quite a paradigm shift. Early in my consulting career, I would conduct interviews, focus groups, and surveys in organizations and then provide a report to senior management or the Board of Directors. As part of my thick reports, I would offer suggestions for how the organization could take actions to improve its culture and productivity. In my role as an expert on leadership and organizational culture, I provided creative solutions to companies. I can be a quick study, and I usually find it easy to identify solutions for others. In fact, as soon as clients start talking about their challenges, I notice I immediately identify some options. However, when I noticed that clients did not always follow my advice, I learned not to offer solutions immediately, and I now spend more time in dialogue about the issues; then, solutions begin to emerge easily from the organization's members. In fact, a commitment to take action on their solutions comes readily. When clients experience being heard, they identify creative solutions, are committed, and experience greater results.

This paradigm shift has made a huge difference for me personally. I have learned to manage my internal tension and become comfortable with the process of giving people time to be heard and then to consider their own options. I find it fun to watch people come up with their own solutions. Ironically, clients value me more, even though they are doing more of the work. Because people know their situations and develop their own solutions, they invariably are more committed and follow through more often.

I believe people really have their own solutions, but they need us to listen to them so they can focus on what's best for them. In addition, as we listen to people, they become more interested in our perspective and more open to coming to agreements with us.

Notice Cues for When a Person Feels Heard

Invariably, people are not ready or don't want to develop solutions or strategies with you immediately. In fact, they often engage in a "yes, but" ritual, if they do not feel understood and are not ready for solutions. If your colleague seems to be saying the same thing over and over, it probably means the person does not feel understood.

We are often like a cup full of liquid. When we are full, we are unable to take more in. By having another person listen to us, help us clarify our assumptions, give us empathy and validate our perspective, we release some of the liquid and can be more open to ideas and options.

In fact, once a person feels heard, he often seems to shift focus and ask the listener for suggestions or ideas. If you pay attention, you can notice cues that the other person feels heard. The person usually relaxes, his voice may calm down, and he is likely to make statements or ask questions related to solutions. For example, a person may say, "What can I/we do?" "What do you think?" "What are the options?" or "What's your view?" Often, a person repositions his focus when he feels heard. In practice, so few of us experience being heard that it usually doesn't take too much empathy or focused attention for us to experience being understood.

If you are not sure that the other person has been heard, you can inquire. For example, you can ask, "What else?" or paraphrase in your own words and ask, "Do I understand?" or "...is that right?" When you believe you understand the other person and she seems more relaxed, you can ask questions such as "What would be ideal?" "What are some options?" or "What is possible?" Then be silent, giving the person space to go inward and identify possible options.

If the person has not naturally asked your view and about your needs, you can begin to share your perspective. Sometimes, I ask permission to share my perspective. I might say, "I would like to share my perspective, okay?" You can also say, "I would like to listen to your perspective, and then I would like to share mine, okay?" You might ask, "Are you ready to hear my view or needs?"

If you are experiencing differences with a person, it is important that you first listen to the other person and then share your perspective regarding what is important. After doing so, you can use the reframing statement, "Given your need for X and my need for Y and our joint need for Z, what are our options?"

Summary

In this chapter, you learned the critical skills for listening to another person. These skills help identify what is important to a person and what is mutually important. They include Mirroring, Empathizing, Empowering questions, and Tracking the mode of interaction. You can use the acronym "MEET" to remember them. More importantly, have the intention of understanding the other person's perspective. Practice listening in your interactions. The more you practice, the more natural it will become.

Next, we will learn how to build on the understanding you create and to explore options and agree on solutions. S for Solution is the last move in the OASIS Conversation process.

CHAPTER 9

S Is for Solution

Building Agreements for Results

*"If I had an hour to solve a problem, I would spend fifty minutes
defining the problem."*

— Einstein

OASIS Conversations

Have a clear intention, plan when possible, and build rapport.

    O = **Observation**

    A = **Awareness** (of assumptions, emotions, and
        background)

    S = **Shift** (to being open)

    ⌐ = **Importance**

    S = **Solution**

The final move in the OASIS Conversation process, S for Solution,
is to identify options, strategize, and agree on solutions. You have now
listened and come to understand what is important to the other person,
and you have shared what is important to you. Now that you know
what's important for you both, you are ready to explore options and
agree on actions.

The purpose of separating the I move of understanding what is important from the S move of agreeing on a solution is to emphasize the value of slowing down and building understanding before moving into action. When you take the time to understand, without the pressure of immediately jumping to solutions, you can focus your energy. Research demonstrates that once a problem or issue is clearly defined, as is done in the I move of the OASIS process, the effectiveness of finding solutions increases by 85 percent! Also, when we feel understood, we relax, and then finding solutions and identifying agreements are much more available.

Cue: Remembering the Final S for Solution

The cue for the final S of the OASIS process is to imagine yourself and others choosing a path and taking steps toward a goal. You are agreeing on actions that will support you in creating satisfying relationships and results. You may viscerally feel your feet striding into the future. This move supports joint ownership and accountability.

Questions for the S Solution Move

The purpose of this move is to explore options and agree on next steps. Questions you are likely to ask include:

"Given what's important (to you, me, and us), what are our options?"

After exploring options, you will identify agreements: "What am I going to do? What are you going to do? What will others do? When? How will we know?"

Reframing Statement

In the scenario from the chapter on Importance, Rita, the manager, and Indru, her staff member, were able to make a reframing statement after listening to one another and sharing their perspectives. Remember: the formula is, "Given that X is important to you, Y is important to me, and Z is important to both of us, what are our options?" For best outcomes, put the statement in writing when working with a team or a group. The written statement ensures that those involved are centered on the same issue. People can read and reread what their focus is supposed to be. You would be surprised by how many times I've seen groups come to a solution without being clear about what they are working to solve!

Clarify words and concepts early in the strategizing process. This will help assure you are in agreement. Where possible, define terms using observable data. For example, you might define the term "efficient" to mean that clients receive feedback on their project's status within twenty-four hours of making a request.

Solution Focus

Many of our interactions lead to agreements and the need for taking action. After you have clarified what is important to you and your partner, you will often want to consider what you will do next. It is useful to focus on the solution you want to achieve. Have a positive mindset and believe that solutions abound. This will support you in identifying options. Considerable research has shown the value of a positive mindset about what is possible. The fields of positive psychology and practices like appreciative inquiry support this approach. In this way, you direct your attention and energy toward the future.

An open mindset involves welcoming "what is" and what is possible. We have focused on "what is" in the previous components of the OASIS Conversation process, which enables options and solutions more easily to emerge.

Carol Dweck[13], a psychologist at Stanford University and Harvard University, has conducted research on the impact of people's mindsets. She's found that those who have a fixed mindset focus on problems, and care more about being right, and less about finding a solution. They are also less successful and less creative. Those who have a growth mindset focus on finding solutions. They incorporate an open mindset and are open to learning and experimenting. They expect to find solutions, and they usually do. A hallmark of a leader, especially in turbulent times, is being optimistic and focused on finding solutions—no matter how difficult that may seem. The leader's expectation of success inspires and supports others in taking action toward goals.

Identify Options

Rita and Indru, from the earlier case study, were able to suggest several options after they identified what was most important. For

13 Dweck, C.S. *Mindset: The New Psychology of Success*. New York: Ballantine Books, 2006.

example, they could schedule regular project meetings to review the status of projects. They could use an online project management system to track progress; they could keep abreast of projects on a whiteboard in the main office by hand; they could leave messages on the status of cases by voicemail or e-mail. They could even assign a particular staff person to monitor overall progress and report achievements and challenges to the team.

It is useful to identify any constraints or imperatives when identifying options. Perhaps there is a defined budget, or maybe a manager requires an answer within the next week. Of course, don't close yourself to options too quickly. Just note possible constraints to consider. For example, you may not have a large budget for a new integrated computer system. Budget limitations would be one of the primary constraints. However, you might find an off-the-shelf package that could be modified somewhat for your needs. Another example of a constraint: perhaps three staff members are going to be traveling for work during the next month; since they won't be on site and will have another priority, that might impact your choice of option.

Explore Options

Consider the benefits and potential costs of each option. For example, Rita and Indru saw that a daily meeting would meet their goal of Rita having more up-to-date information; however, it wasn't workable due to the pressure of client service demands.

The criteria to select an option are based on what you identify as important for each of you individually and collectively. You could build a criteria matrix with the options down one side and the criteria along the other and rate each option against the criteria. You might decide to evaluate each option on a scale of 1-5 with 1 being a low satisfaction rating and 5 being a high satisfaction rating.

Brain Connection

As you are open, reflecting, and exploring options, pay attention to what neuroscientists like David Rock[14] call insight or "illumination."

---

14 Rock, D. *Your Brain at Work: Strategies for Overcoming Distraction, Regaining Focus and Working Smarter All Day Long*. New York: John Wiley & Sons, 2009.

This is where you get an idea or solution and then a rush of excitement. Think about the rush you experience when you solve a vexing problem, find just the right title for your speech, or solve a crossword puzzle. This experience is the result of new neural path connections in the brain. At the moment of insight, neurotransmitters such as adrenaline are released, resulting in the rush of energy. Other neurotransmitters such as dopamine and serotonin are also likely to be released. Having an insight feels physically positive and is one of the highlights of working and interacting with others.

According to researcher Mark Jung-Beeman, when you reflect on an issue before an insight, you relax and shut out some inputs from the outside world. The brain is giving off alpha-band waves. Then at the moment an insight occurs, the brain gives off gamma-band waves, which signals that new neural maps are being formed. This creation of a higher-level map links many parts of the brain and gives off substantial energy, which can mobilize action.

David Rock shares that during the state of illumination, you will see a face shift from looking up or slightly across with a dazed look, to the eyes racing ahead to action. However, the high-intensity energy rush of illumination passes quickly. Have you ever forgotten a great idea an hour or so later? If so, you recognize the value of making an agreement with yourself or others on the actions you plan to take after such an insight or "aha" moment. Note the idea and the agreement. When you make a commitment, you are more likely to take action and experience results.

Select Options

Rita and Indru agreed to coordinate by using a project management tool that could be accessed by themselves and the other staff members. Both would update information each day or call otherwise. They agreed to try this option, check-in about its success, and make modifications as necessary. Discussion about the new tool was planned for their next monthly staff meeting.

The goal of the OASIS Conversation process is to satisfy everyone involved and co-create winning solutions. An OASIS Conversation is not focused on finding compromises. A compromise is usually a situation where neither person is satisfied and each gives up something. However, our emphasis is on finding how each person's needs can be met. When you know what is important to each person, and perhaps what is behind that, then additional possibilities appear for finding satisfaction. The OASIS process is not just about meeting others' needs. If you attempt to do only that, you are likely to become angry. You must focus on being clear about what is important to you and the other and work to satisfy both needs.

Make Commitments and Agreements

Rita and Indru confirmed their commitment to the action of documenting the status of projects using a project management system. It is important to clarify and confirm your agreement. Assuming that an agreement exists may lead to trouble. Without clear agreement, new problems emerge.

Agreement Questions

Agreements should be specific and concrete using observable data. Clarify your commitment in terms that those involved can envision in the future.

Agreements include answering the following:

- What is each person (you, me, or someone else) going to do?
- When will it be done?
- How will we know it's done?

Also, consider possible contingencies or what will happen if the agreement cannot be satisfied.

Rita and Indru agreed to review available software programs to assess their appropriateness for monitoring client project activity. They agreed to decide on the best program by the end of the current month. Rita would purchase the program or secure it by the fifth of the next month. Rita agreed to begin inputting new client information on the sixth. Indru offered to input information on current clients with status updates by the tenth. By the fifteenth, they planned to meet and assess how the system was working.

In addition, Indru agreed to log project status updates two times a day and indicate the time of update. Rita could then check the status of projects and know she had up-to-date information.

Contingencies were considered. Rita and Indru agreed that if they could not update the information, they would call the other or leave a voicemail. The system was placed on their agenda for discussion in monthly staff meetings for six months to resolve any issues.

It is particularly useful to document your agreement. When it's written, clarifications and other modifications can be made. The written agreement supports people in recalling and following up.

A Word about Commitments

Making a decision to take action is important. Honoring agreements and doing what we say we will do is important for building relationships. Honoring commitments is an underpinning of building trust. When we stop trusting someone and others stop trusting us, significant consequences result. We often stop communicating effectively. Why tell our colleague about an important development if he can't be trusted? We justify our behavior. We then create a self-fulfilling prophecy. You don't trust a colleague, he doesn't feel trusted or included in information, and he stops including you. The lack of effective communication only supports an environment of misunderstanding and distrust. This situation takes energy away from results and getting things done together.

One of the challenges of satisfying our commitments is that often our action is dependent on someone else taking action. Since we can't accomplish much on our own, we need to be aware of whom we depend on. How will we manage when these people are unable to meet commitments?

One problem is that we may not be clear enough when we are asking others to make commitments. A part of us doesn't want to be dependent. So we might casually say, "Could you please find me the information on the X topic?" The other person might say, "I'll try." Since the person has not fully committed, you may or may not get the information. Perhaps someone makes a request of you. Often, we respond to a request without a real commitment by saying, "I'll see what I can do." These unclear responses can cause challenges in relationships. Your colleague may assume your response is a "yes" and be disappointed when you don't deliver. For both parties, this kind of unclear response can consume energy by causing confusion and frustration.

Clear accountability, however, will build trust and a greater foundation for a relationship and achieving mutual goals. When people are continuously reliable, have integrity, and honor their word, we can count on them following through. Likewise, when we follow through with an action that we have committed to, we support productivity and the relationship.

Making Requests

By definition, a request is asking someone to do something. For example, Rita could say to Indru, "I ask that you review these two software packages and provide me with your feedback on the viability, benefits, and downside of each by the fourteenth of this month." An effective request involves asking someone specific to do something specific by a specific time with the understanding of how you will know it has been done. Rita clearly stated that she was asking Indru to do something. She could say, "I request that you..." or "Will you...?" She could also make it more of a demand, "Do..." or "Review...".

Your goal is to make a clear request and receive a clear response. I know that sometimes I hate to ask things of others, yet part of life is making requests and also giving people the opportunity to respond. Once you make a request, such as "Will you complete the report and distribute it by 5 p.m. today?", you can wait for a clear confirmation. If you do not get back an answer, you can ask, "Do you agree?" Once you practice this kind of clean communication, you'll be amazed at the energy you save on worrying whether something will be done or managing yourself when your request is not satisfied.

When teams and organizations make clear agreements and honor them, things seem to work more smoothly. When agreements are not clear and not honored, organizations and teams suffer. A lack of trust and a feeling of disrespect then results.

Responding to Requests

You do have a choice about how you respond to a request! Some people have a hard time saying "no." If you pay attention to your habitual response to requests, you can practice being more at choice. When I coach people, I often work with them to practice the full range of responses so that their answers of "yes" and "no" can be stronger and more authentic. If you feel at choice to meet what is important to you and to others, you will feel better about choices and relationships. If you are only responding "yes" automatically to meet others' needs, at some point you will feel resentful. This will impact you and your relationships. If you only say "no" to others, you will be missing opportunities and also may hurt some relationships.

We each have habitual patterns about how we make commitments. Some readily say "yes" to requests and have a hard time saying "no." Others find it easier to say "no" first. Pay attention to your body and how you respond to requests. Then experiment and flex your muscles to have more choices available to you.

If a colleague asks you to find some information for him or do him a favor such as attend a meeting for him, you have a range of possible responses.

- Commit: "Yes. I will do it. I promise."
- Decline: "No. I will not do it."
- Commit to commit at another time: "No, I can't commit now. Let me get back to you after I check with…" or "Let me check on my available resources. I will get back to you by a certain date. I will let you know after.…"
- Slow down: "I have some questions before I can commit: What do you need and by when?"
- Counteroffer: "I can't agree to your request as is, but I suggest the following alternative. Would X be an alternative you can accept?" For example, "I can meet your need if you accept delaying another project."
- Contingency: "If I can't meet my agreement, I will let you know and find a backup."

Sometimes you may make an offer to someone before she makes a request. If you anticipate a need, you can make an offer. It would have been an offer if Indru had volunteered to review the software packages before being asked to do so. Or a staff member can offer to take notes at a staff meeting. "I'll take notes today." You could then make sure you understand the offer by saying, "So you will take notes and e-mail them to the group today?" You will know if it is done by receiving and reading the e-mail (or not).

Use Observable Data When Making Agreements

Observable data can inform our decisions. At home, for instance, I may think you understand that I want you to do the dishes because I said, "The kitchen is a mess." If so, I am likely to be disappointed when I return home and still see the dirty dishes. However, I did not make a clear request of you. You didn't agree to wash the dishes either. It could also be that I was not asking you to do the dishes—just making a comment. Not being clear is the source of much frustration in relationships.

Consider what the observable data would be in this "cleaning up the kitchen" example. For instance, "I will do the dishes and clean the kitchen by 11:00 a.m. When you return from shopping, the dishes will be washed and put away!" The more specific you can be, the more you will ensure agreement. If you don't ask to have the floor washed, for example, maybe the dishes will get washed and the counters tidied up, but the floor won't get mopped.

I remember wanting to surprise my mother by cleaning the house as a young girl. When my mother came home, rather than expressing appreciation, she was disappointed that I did not wash the kitchen floor. Since I wanted to please my mother, I would have cleaned the floor if I had thought about it. Her reaction did not motivate me to volunteer the following week—or the week after that.

Honoring Our Commitments

Once we make a clear commitment, ideally we satisfy our agreement and support the relationship. Situations may arise when we can't, however. Be sure to let the other person know as soon as you can if this happens. It is important to consider possible factors that may impact whether you can fulfill your commitments before you make them. Guard your integrity. You may not be able to win it back if you lose it. When you are not able to deliver on a promise, ask the other person what the impact will be on him. Figure out how you can support the other person in getting his need met.

Closure and Reflection

Finally, in the Solution move of the OASIS process, consider the interaction. A conversation should support building the relationship as well as taking actions on tasks. Open-minded OASIS Conversations support addressing immediate needs and long-term concerns. It is useful for you to reflect on each when using OASIS. For example, the agreement made by Rita and Indru supported their current relationship and addressed the misunderstanding they were experiencing. Rita came to understand that Indru was very committed to serving clients efficiently. She had questioned this before. By working together on this issue, they built a foundation for their long-term relationship. The conversation also supported the ongoing task of keeping clients informed. In the precipitating situation, remember the client casually asked for an update unexpectedly. That took Rita off-guard since she didn't have an answer.

The result of Rita and Indru's OASIS Conversation is that the team now has a more efficient system. Rita and Indru will be communicating more quickly and easily so this should help the entire team improve in client responsiveness—not just Indru.

While some of us focus first on the task or productivity and the relationships later, others are primarily concerned with relationships. Actually, each one builds on the other. A good relationship serves as a foundation for creating agreements and being productive together. Successful productivity serves as a foundation for building a relationship. At the end of your conversation, reflect on what you have achieved with the other person or group. For example, consider these questions:

- What are we leaving with?
- Has anything shifted as a result of our conversation?
- How do you feel about our conversation or our work together?
- Is there anything we need to attend to now or in our next conversation?
- What have we learned?
- What is not finished?
- How are we progressing on meeting our shared goals? Short-term goals? Long-term goals?
- How is our relationship? What will support us in the short-term and long-term?

I have come to value closure from my coaching work. A simple statement, "What are you leaving with?" or "What stands out for you?" allows for making the meaning and the results clear. Asking "What is not finished yet, or what still needs our attention and discussion?" might yield results, too. If Indru had concerns about a project that he and Rita had not discussed yet, he could bring it up so they could.

Practice

Reflect on your day or week. How do you respond to requests made of you? Do you usually comply or decline? Would you like to practice the other forms of responding? If so, stop and reflect before giving an answer and try out some alternatives.

Notice when you are making requests or offers. Be specific about what will be done and when and how you will follow up. Pay attention to when you or others are vague in your requests, offers, or commitments.

Summary

The last move of the OASIS process, Solution, evolves from stopping, becoming open, and learning what is important to those involved. From this place, identifying options and agreements that will support the relationship and being productive is easier. It is valuable to have an open mindset and expect to identify creative options. After evaluating options against the needs identified, a decision can be made. Then clear requests, offers, and commitments are needed to build and sustain trust. It is helpful to know the next steps, who will do what and when, and how you will know.

We have carefully reviewed the OASIS Moves in detail. Let's use the case in the next chapter to put it all together. We will also explore resistance and how to work with it using the OASIS Moves.

CHAPTER 10

Putting It All Together

A Successful OASIS Conversation

*"What is needed, rather than running away or controlling or suppressing or
any other resistance, is understanding fear; that means watch it,
learn about it, come directly into contact with it. We are to
learn about fear, not how to escape from it."*

— J. Krishnamurti

OASIS Conversations

Have a clear intention, plan when possible, and build rapport.

> O = **Observation**
>
> A = **Awareness** (of assumptions, emotions, and background)
>
> S = **Shift** (to being open)
>
> ꙮ = **Importance**
>
> S = **Solution**

Case Study: Tackling Resistance

Jean, a manager in a major global organization, recently learned that Matthew, a senior member of her team, has not signed up to attend a computer software training workshop. At next month's end, a new computer system will be operational and no support will be offered for the old system. Jean's department members won't appear to be team players if they are not all using the new system. Because Matthew is older and has been in the organization years longer, Jean believes he should set a good example for the rest of her team. She's worried that others might think they don't need to adapt to the computer change either. Jean also wonders whether Matthew respects her position and authority as the manager.

Jean noticed her judgment signals, tightness in her stomach, and an internal voice saying, "He should learn the new system. Why doesn't he follow directions? Who does he think he is?" While she wanted to yell at Matthew, Jean respected her signals and stopped herself. She internally stepped back and reminded herself to "assume positive intent." She recalled that Matthew is a good person and a major contributor to her team. She took a deep breath and shifted to a more open stance. She felt calmer. Then, she set the intention to have an open-minded OASIS Moves conversation with Matthew. She's positive and thinks their relationship may even be enhanced if they talk openly.

In this chapter, we will review how Jean prepares for her conversation with Matthew, and we will listen in on the actual conversation. We will review the OASIS Moves process and consider how to manage a situation where someone appears to be resistant.

Planning for an OASIS Conversation

Jean carefully prepared for her OASIS Conversation. While we'll look at how she planned for it by using each letter of the word OASIS, note that it is not necessary to plan for each move in the order of the letters in the word. In fact, usually the place to start is the first S—Shift.

S Is for Shift (to Being Open)

First, Jean noticed the signal of her stomach tightening. She judged that Matthew should be responsible and attend the training as asked. Did he think he was better than everybody else? Every fiber of her body believed she was "right" and Matthew was "wrong." She caught her signal and recalled her intention to be mindful (present and non-judgmental). She stopped, stepped back, and suspended acting on her judgment. Her instinct was to go to Matthew's office and demand that he attend the computer-training workshop. She took a deep breath and gave herself a little time to prepare. Matthew was a valuable team member—she didn't want to say something she'd regret.

Jean recalled that when she thinks she is right and someone else is wrong, it is time to stop and pay attention. She imagined a red stop sign with a judge's gavel and stopped herself. She gently coached herself onto the OASIS path. Jean wanted to speak with Matthew from an open state. She understood that emotions are contagious, and that if he detected her judgment, he was likely to become defensive.

Jean reminded herself of the oasis image she's created for herself. In it, she is relaxed and peaceful, as she holds her sleeping, young child. She is fully present and curious, and life feels in harmony. She used that image to create compassion for Matthew, remembering and appreciating that he works hard. Jean focused on being optimistic that they could work through this issue together.

O Is for Observation

Jean identified her observable data. She had reacted when she read an e-mail from Jordi, the training department manager. The e-mail said Matthew had not signed up for or participated in any of the many computer workshops they offered on the new system. Jordi provided the dates of the remaining sessions. He also reminded Jean that the system would be fully operative in the next month and that no support would be provided for the old system. Jordi copied Jean's boss, Beth, on the e-mail.

Jean's observation for Matthew would be, "I received an e-mail from Jordi in the training department. He indicated that you have not signed up for or participated in one of their workshops on the new system." She may want to remind him that soon there will not be support for the current system.

A Is for Awareness (of Assumptions, Emotions, and Background)

In a few minutes, Jean became aware of her emotions. She felt embarrassed that her boss would see that her star senior staff member had not complied with the training request. She felt annoyed and frustrated with Matthew. Why did he have to be so difficult about this? She was also upset with herself for not checking on compliance earlier. How frustrating! Didn't he respect her authority?

She assumed that: 1) Matthew did not intend to take the course and learn the new program, 2) he didn't respect her as the boss since he had not complied with her direction, and 3) he must be aware that he'd be setting a bad example for the new staff members and he didn't care. She worried that her boss might think she couldn't manage effectively. She also assumed that Jordi and the training department would have a negative view of her department for not fully participating in the training. She fretted, wondering whether this situation would negatively impact her upcoming performance review.

Jean's background was that she had been the youngest female manager in her previous organization. She had not worked well with an older, male staff member there, so she wanted to make sure things went well with her relationships in this job. When Jean realized this history was influencing how she reacted to the e-mail, she reminded herself that this work situation was much different than the earlier one. Also, she was able to acknowledge that she had a relatively positive relationship with Matthew. Her current boss seemed satisfied with her, too. Jean understood that implementation of the new system was important to her boss and the organization. She really wanted her department to be perceived as supporting the change.

I Is for Importance

Jean listed what was most important to her in the situation:
- She wanted her department to be perceived as supporting the computer system change.
- She wanted a positive relationship with Matthew in this discussion and in the future.
- She wanted to make sure her department would be able to communicate effectively with other departments using the new system since the old system would not be supported.
- She wanted to ensure positive relations with her entire staff.
- She wanted to be perceived as a competent manger by her boss, her staff, and other organization members.

Notice that she considered both task and relationship issues and immediate and long-term areas of importance.

Jean didn't know what was most important to Matthew, and she would not know until she talked directly with him. She guessed some possibilities based on her history with him that she could explore when she spoke with him, including that he might:

- Be focusing on other projects
- Consider himself senior and exempt from the training workshop
- Not value the new system or realize he won't have support for the old system
- Not like the training programs offered by the organization
- Believe his expertise with the old system soon would be valueless, and therefore, would experience a loss of status
- Feel embarrassed in training programs and not want to look silly compared to others who were more advanced with new technology
- Think he could avoid the switch to the new system and not realize it was mandatory
- Feel angry that he didn't get the promotion to the management position she now holds
- Not like working for a woman much younger than he is

Thinking about these possibilities helped Jean prepare for her OASIS Conversation. She realized she could best identify what was important to Matthew by asking him and paying attention to his response. She recalled that status was important to him. He had, on more than one occasion, underlined in staff meetings that he had extensive experience and longevity with the company. She also recalled that he had expressed negative feelings about yet another change to a new master computer system in the organization.

S Is for Solution

Jean could not predict what would be the best options for action in this situation. She realized that she would like Matthew to take the training course and show support for the change. Perhaps he could learn the new system in another way. She was also open to looking at his workload. He might need some support. Did he need more information about the change to be comfortable with it? Perhaps she could offer him a more visible role, supporting his need for status and her need that he show support for her as his manager. Jean realized she had several options for supporting him in learning the new system. She wanted to make sure she used this opportunity to build their relationship.

After planning for the conversation, Jean felt ready to speak with Matthew. She set her intention by imagining an oasis in the desert and visualizing having an oasis experience with him as they engaged in an open-minded conversation.

Resistance

At first, you may conclude that Matthew is resistant to learning the new computer system. From Jean's perspective, he is not doing what she wants him to do. Our natural response to someone who is resistant is to push him or her. However, if Jean inquires rather than pushes, she is likely to make more progress with Matthew. From Matthew's viewpoint, he is not being "resistant" but doing what makes the most sense to him.

When I notice what I consider to be "resistance," I think, "resistance is my friend." I address the presented concerns when I become aware of them. That is, I don't need to shy away from my resistance. Rather, I try to understand where it is coming from and trust I can work with it. You can use the OASIS Moves to address resistance effectively. Become curious and open, and then ask questions and give empathy so you can learn more.

OASIS Conversation between Jean and Matthew

First, Jean builds rapport and finds common ground with Matthew. This helps create safety and openness in the conversation.

J: Hi, Matthew, like this weather?

M: Not much! It sure is a rainy, cold day.

J: How is your day going?

M: Fine. I'm working on the Ridge project. It's taking a lot of effort.

J: I appreciate your focus on that. I've heard you've had some challenges with the client.

M: Yes, they gave us some new specifications and requirements last week. We'll really be pushing to meet the deadline.

J: That's quite a lot to do. Do you need some support?

M: No. Joe and I are working on it. We still expect to meet the deadline.

J: Thanks for your commitment. I appreciate it. Do you have a few minutes to talk with me this afternoon? I want to talk with you about the new computer system.

M: Yes, I have time open at 2:00 p.m.

J: Thanks. That works for me, too. Let's meet for coffee in the cafeteria.

Later that day, they meet and talk.

J: Hi! What's the latest?

M: We had a breakthrough late this morning! We figured out a solution. We're using the same calculations we used for the Trumpet project last November.

J: Great! That makes sense. What a relief! I appreciate you sticking with the challenge. Of course, you're known for that.

M: You wanted to talk about the new system?

J: Yes, I got an e-mail from Jordi in the training department. He said you had not signed up for the training workshop on the new system. Beth, my boss, was copied on the e-mail.

[Jean begins the conversation with her observation. Matthew has been clued in and knows her focus. He doesn't need to be defensive.]

J: I am wondering what to say. I have been a bit worried that you might not be planning to take the training workshop.

[Jean decides what assumptions and feelings to share with Matthew as she begins their conversation. If she only shares the observable data, Matthew is left to assume her emotions and response. He could assume she is angry and react. It's an art to decide what to share.]

M: Yes, I have not signed up. I don't think we need another system. This will be the fourth system in five years. Why even bother? My buddy in the Finance Department says he has already found bugs.

[Here, Jean has to catch herself and notice her signals again: the tightening of her stomach and fist. She reminds herself to stop and remain open and curious. She listens and provides empathy. She does this even though she wants Matthew to attend the workshop and is nervous that he may refuse to learn the new system.]

J: So you question whether it is worth switching again?

M: Yes. It just doesn't make any sense to me.

J: I can imagine your frustration. You've endured four computer system changes.

M: It really is frustrating and tiring.

J: So you are fed up with changing computer systems and tired of being asked to change systems again. It's got to be even more aggravating since you have already heard the new system still has bugs.

[*Besides using words to describe how she guesses Matthew is feeling, Jean tries to sense his frustration. Matthew sees that Jean understands how he feels and his view of the changeover. Jean remains patient to make sure she has understood how Matthew feels.*]

M: Yes, but I know we have to switch.

[*Jean notices that as Matthew receives her empathy, his tone changes, he relaxes and takes a breath, and his shoulders drop. She continues to give him empathy until he signals he is ready to consider alternatives. It doesn't take long. However, sometimes it might take more time—even more than one conversation.*]

J: Yes, they are eliminating support for the current system by the end of next month.

M: Wow! I didn't realize they would push that. They haven't in the past.

J: Well, that's what they've said. Beth assures me they really mean it.

M: I guess I need to learn the new system then. Quite frankly, I hate those training programs they offer.

[*Again, Jean needs to catch herself. A part of her wants to order Matthew to just sign up! This would be okay in some situations, but she knows Matthew would resist. She keeps herself open and curious and empathetic.*]

J: Really? What don't you like about the training?

M: Well, the kids—the twenty-somethings—in the sessions are a lot quicker with the computer than I am. Don't get me wrong. I am not afraid of using a computer, obviously. I just don't feel like the courses are directed toward me. Anyway, I've been so busy on the Ridge project and a couple of others that I just haven't had time to think about much else.

J: Yes, I know you've been swamped.

M: Yes, I've been focused on what I think is most important.

J: So, let me see if I understand. You are not in favor of another system change. You have already heard about some bugs in the new system, which upsets you. You have been focusing on the most important projects with critical demands and attending the training has not been a priority for you. Finally, you don't enjoy attending the computer system workshops put on by the training department. Anything else?

[*Here Jean is capturing what is important to Matthew. She has not yet identified what is important to her.*]

M: No, that's about it. How do you feel about it?

[*Once Matthew feels understood, he naturally turns to Jean to hear what's important to her.*]

J: This is my first experience with a computer system change here. I am not really sure that they'll soon cut off support for the old system, but I want us to be able to deliver our reports to the other departments. I want our team to be perceived well. Since I'm new here, I don't want it to look like our department is not complying. I want you to feel supported, and I want us to meet our other deadlines. Does that make sense?

[*Jean has stated what is important to her.*]

M: Yes. I don't want you to think I'm giving you a hard time because you're new.

J: I have to admit the thought had crossed my mind. I know it can't be easy for you to have me come in from the outside to manage the operation.

M: I was upset about it when they brought you in. I don't hold it against you, personally. I know that I work hard. I don't know why they brought in someone from outside. They could have promoted me.

[*Again, Jean remains open and trusts that she has the OASIS Moves skills to have this conversation with Matthew. She recalls that it is better that he is comfortable saying these things than not. Empathy means understanding, not necessarily agreeing. Jean wants Matthew to learn the new system. She also wants to build a good long-term relationship with him.*]

J: I appreciate your talking with me about this. I know it must be difficult with your years of service. Sounds like you don't have clarity about why the decision was made to bring me in from the outside. You have a strong reputation. I know you are committed to the clients and I want to support you. I will do my best to make sure Beth and top management see your efforts.

M: I would appreciate that. Did you know that your predecessor and I did not get along well? He was only interested in his own career. He didn't care about the rest of us.

J: Oh. What would you like from me? Have you thought about specifics?

M: I could use more visibility at some of the leadership meetings. The top few people don't really know me. I feel like I have been hidden.

J: I can help you with that. Let's go together to report on the Ridge project at the next management meeting.

M: Thanks. I think they will like hearing how we addressed the challenges.

J: So, let's consider our options. We are both committed to serving our clients and doing excellent work. It's important for you to get visibility and be efficient with your time and energy. It's important to me that we are positioned as supporting the organization and complying with upper management's requests. In addition, I need to feel like we are a team. I want the staff to see that you support me.

[*This is the Importance reframing statement. Given what is important for you and what is important to me, and what is important to both of us, what are our options? While some agreements on actions have been made, now it's time to find a solution and select additional actions and confirm agreements.*]

M: Well, I understand that I need to learn the new system so we will be in compliance. But I really do hate those workshops!

J: Want a tutor, instead? How about Mark?

M: Yes, we work well together. We could meet after we finish the Ridge project.

J: We also have the issue of your full plate of work. Could I assign the new intern to work with you? He could help you with some of the routine work.

M: Well, I haven't been interested in working with interns. It takes too much of my time for what gets produced!

J: It's really important for you to be efficient.

M: Yes, and I do get a lot done.

J: Okay. How about working with Vanessa? I know she is a strong worker. She has a two-year contract. This way you can feel like your investment is worth it. I would like you to let Michael, the newest intern, tag along with Vanessa. He is reporting to her and he needs a challenge. I think they will both learn a lot from you.

M: Okay. I'm not sure about the timing with this deadline, but I'll give it a shot.

J: When can you begin working with them?

M: Hmmm. Now that I think about it, they could help me with the project summary on the Ridge project. We are using the other prototype and they could follow it. Should I meet with them in the morning after the staff meeting?

J: Great! I will talk with them today and remind them that you are under deadline pressure so they should try not to slow you down. If you find them slowing you down rather than helping, get back to me. We will review how it worked at next week's one-on-one meeting.

[*Jean was specific with agreements. She has identified who is going to do what, when and how it will be known. She addressed the contingency that Vanessa and Michael's assistance might be more of a hindrance and asked that Matthew let her know. Finally, she added a time for follow up and evaluation.*]

J: Okay. When will you be fully trained in the new system?

M: I could start working with Mark this Thursday at the end of the day. If he's free and if we can meet a couple of times next week, I will plan on being up to speed by next Friday.

J: How will we demonstrate you know the system without having taken the workshop?

M: I'll take the proficiency test that they routinely give at the end of the workshops. I can get one from Jordi. When I pass it, I'll have Jordi write an e-mail saying that I have satisfied the requirement.

J: Okay. I will inform Jordi that we are taking this alternative. Now, just so we're both clear, let me summarize the plan.

Matthew, you plan to work with Mark beginning on Thursday and be trained on the new system by next Friday. You will take the proficiency test from Jordi and have him send an e-mail to me and the head office verifying that you met the requirement. I will then forward a note to Beth letting her know that our department is in full compliance and ready to use the new system.

We agreed that I will assign Vanessa and Michael to work with you. They will start with drafting the summary for the Ridge project. I will talk with Vanessa and Michael and then the four of us will meet briefly after our staff meeting tomorrow. I will put a meeting on the calendar for two weeks from now to review how it's going.

Finally, you will attend the next management meeting with me to present the challenges and results of the Ridge project. I will schedule us to meet a few days in advance to review the presentation. This will support you in getting more visibility and support me in demonstrating my commitment to working well with you and this department and the organization. Anything else?

[*Solution—here they agreed to specific actions that each would take, by when, and how they would know they occurred.*]

M: No, that's more than enough! Thanks, Jean. I am looking forward to working together. Thanks for your understanding. I appreciate it.

As you can see, this potential problem of a resistant staff member allowed Jean and Matthew to enhance their relationship. Trust will be developed if they both follow through on their commitments.

Being effective does not mean only meeting the other's needs. Jean was able to satisfy what was most important to both Matthew and herself as well as meet what was important to both of them.

Summary

In this chapter, a case study of a manager's OASIS Conversation with a resistant staff member was provided. Preparation is useful for challenging conversations. Then, it is helpful to be aware of what phase of the OASIS process you are in during a conversation. When in doubt, catch yourself and shift from a closed to an open state. It is always useful to give empathy and understanding to others. Finally, close with clarity on solutions by identifying what you each will do, when, and how you will know.

In the next chapter, we will consider some particularly challenging situations.

CHAPTER 11

Using OASIS Conversations in Challenging Situations

*"The capacity to be puzzled is the premise of all creation,
be it in art or in science."*

— Erich Fromm

OASIS Conversations

Have a clear intention, plan when possible, and build rapport.

O = **Observation**

A = **Awareness** (of assumptions, emotions, and background)

S = **Shift** (to being open)

⌢ = **Importance**

S = **Solution**

You might be wondering whether the OASIS Conversation process may be used in long-term relationships where deep patterns have developed. The short answer is "Yes!" The OASIS process is useful in any relationship that will benefit from understanding the needs of those involved and identifying agreements.

The OASIS Conversation process has been effective in many interactions across the world. It is a rational process and, unfortunately, is more challenging when someone is under the influence of drugs, is not mentally sound, or simply intends to hurt others or not to engage. I have used the process with people in many difficult circumstances that seemed impossible. It is useful to be empathetic and open to understanding. However, sometimes it is best to disengage from someone or from circumstances that are abusive or may cause harm.

Power Struggles

I had just returned from a five-day business trip and had missed my then six-year-old daughter. As I put her to bed, my daughter fidgeted in the bed, bringing her feet to her head several times as if she were doing some kind of strength exercise. She kept pulling the covers up and down. She held my hand and asked me to massage her back. "Time to settle down and go to sleep," I said. She seemed restless and tired after a busy day of summer camp where she was learning about pyramids and mummies. I had hoped she would quickly drift off to sleep. Instead, she asked me a multiple-choice question.

"Mom, what is the right answer: A, B, C, or D? What do you do if the boys at school say, 'Nah, nah, nah, nah, nah: you girls are fat and dumb.' (I wondered whether that was why she didn't eat much at dinner?) A: Say 'Nah, Nah' back louder and call them names; B: Walk away and pretend you don't hear; C: Tell them you don't like what they are saying and to stop; or D: Tell the counselor."

I soon realized this was an after-the-fact discussion. My daughter let me know that she had tried each of the options that day and none of them had worked. "The camp counselor didn't help you?" "No. She just said 'Work it out among yourselves' and left us on our own." While my daughter had initially loved camp, she now asked, "How many more days of camp?" After I answered her, she groaned: "I have four whole days left?" After that, she demonstrated a new technique she'd developed for hiding tears. She rubbed her eyes and quickly wiped them away, so no one could see them. "It really works," she offered proudly.

My six-year-old was addressing the same kind of challenge I had been addressing with an executive coaching client that day. How do we deal with being locked into a struggle with someone else when it seems to be that person's fault?

Lynn, my coaching client, had just returned to work from an overseas trip vacationing with her family. Terrorist threats interrupted the trip, and in the midst of all that, she still worried about the behavior of her direct report, Terry. Lynn voiced her frustration during our coaching session, "How can I let her take up so much of my energy? She even ruined my vacation!"

Lynn and Terry were caught in an adrenaline drama. While Lynn was the formal senior leader, she knew that Terry interacted with leaders above her level. Terry's tenure with the company was longer, and she had built many strong relationships. Lynn believed she had done a lot to support Terry. She had even promoted her to another position on her team. Lynn explained, "There's no problem with Terry's work. She is competent. But why doesn't she come and speak to me? She'll send me an e-mail rather than get up, take two steps, and talk to me face-to-face. I typically hear it from others when she disagrees with any of my plans. She should tell me directly! I just got an e-mail from my boss that she sent him without copying me!"

Lynn could only identify Terry as the problem. She told me others concurred. Yet it was unlikely that Terry would leave the organization, and Lynn planned to stay at least another five years. Unfortunately, their struggle took most of the fun out of work for both of them. The stress spilled into Lynn's free time, too. "My son told me to chill out, and my husband agreed," she reported.

Lynn and Terry felt stuck. While the issues changed, the pattern remained. One blamed the other and felt aggrieved (like a victim) and vice versa. I worked with the team as a coach and both said they would like the struggle to go away. Terry feared that she wouldn't be given credit for her work so she went around Lynn. She avoided Lynn and spoke negatively about her. Lynn blamed Terry for the negative relationship.

As I spoke with each of them, I had the image of a tug-of-war rope strung between them. Each was claiming to be the aggrieved victim and justifying her action of pulling the rope on the other—being the aggressor. Neither was willing to let go of the rope even though the game cost a lot of energy, stress, and lost productivity. Occasionally, another colleague, Mark, would intervene. Often, his effort would exacerbate the drama and draw in other department members who felt compelled to take sides. Eventually, the department members who supported Lynn began having conflicts with those who supported Terry. In my work with organizations, I have seen this same pattern played out again and again.

When we are in such a drama, our adrenaline takes over, we have blinders on, and we are in judgment. We often experience an "amygdala hijack" where in a fight, flight, freeze, or appease response, we may attack or retreat. Later, we may not even recall our own behavior. Both of these intelligent and successful professionals lost their rational capacity when they participated in this kind of interaction. They could just as easily be my elementary school age daughter and her classmates saying, "Nah, nah, nah, nah, nah: I'm better than you!"

The Tug-of-War

We take on three basic roles when we fall into the tug-of-war adrenaline drama: the aggressor, the aggrieved, and the assistor. The aggressor, in a state of judging and in a fight response, freely exerts control over another and feels justified in her behavior. At times, both Lynn and Terry were in the aggressor role, doing something to hurt the other. For example, Terry often withheld important information from Lynn. At other times, both experienced being in the aggrieved role, experiencing a flight reaction. When Mark stepped in to assist the two, essentially he would move to the center to try to reduce the tension. Occasionally, he would take turns helping one or the other. Such assisters are also players in the drama who react by trying to appease. Like a drug, the adrenaline of blame and self-righteousness as well as helplessness can become addictive. The neural pathway for this behavior becomes like a swiftly flowing highway and can quickly fall into a pattern.

Imagine a time when you felt wronged by someone. Perhaps a colleague said something that embarrassed you in front of your boss. You felt aggrieved—notice your remembered sensations. Where do you feel your complaint? Imagine telling a friend how you have been wronged. Notice how you may stay in the aggrieved stance. Feel the righteous energy and your desire to fight back. Recall a time when you heard about a friend being mistreated. You may have wanted to defend your friend or jump in and fix the situation. While you are awash in adrenaline and the stress hormone cortisol in any of these roles, you lose focus on other possibilities. Yet you feel a sense of aliveness in the anger or righteousness. You can become addicted to the drama.

An alternative exists, however. We can catch ourselves in the heat of these dramas and make a choice to stop, step back, and quit judging.

We can name our emotions and give ourselves empathy and receive empathy from friends. We can move from our activated limbic brain to our neocortex and shift from the desert to the oasis to experience openness to possibilities. It is not easy, but with practice, we can learn to shift to being open. Assuming positive intent is always useful.

We Are Not Just Rational Beings

We are not just rational beings. Science and research are supporting that we all do things that do not support our conscious goals. We are not machines, so our emotions and unconscious feelings often drive our behavior. While we have free will, a growing body of research is showing that we have a limited amount and cannot always control our actions. Experts like Roy Baumeister[15] liken willpower to a muscle that can become fatigued by overuse. How many of us have broken diets or not achieved other goals despite our best intentions? It takes effort to manage ourselves, and we seem to have a limited amount of self-control. For this reason, it is useful to practice suspending judgment and make being open more of a habitual response. With practice, you will find yourself pausing and reflecting before saying and doing things that could be damaging.

Many of our behaviors are dictated by our past experiences. Often, we are not aware of why we say or do things that hurt others and ourselves. It takes effort to manage ourselves. We need to have compassion for others and ourselves, accept that everyone makes mistakes, and realize that, as humans, life is "messy." Each of us has been swept up in an amygdala hijack, and we may not be proud of our actions the next day. We need to forgive others and ourselves. Sometimes, I remind myself that people are often doing the best they know how based on their perceptions and conditioning. We also need to recognize that people do grow and can change when given the chance. I have had the good fortune of seeing many people forgive themselves and each other and create more productive and meaningful relationships at work and elsewhere. It helps when people use the OASIS Conversation process, give each other empathy, clarify what is important to them, and agree on actions that will be observable to all parties.

---

15 Baumeister, R.F. & Tierney, J. *Willpower: Rediscovering the Greatest Human Strength*. New York: The Penguin Press, 2011.

Stopping the Tug-of-War

How do you get yourself out of the adrenaline tug-of-war? First, notice your judgment signals. We feel like we are right and the other is wrong. We need to remember that we are engaged in a game and don't have full rational capacity. We need to stop and get ourselves out of the game. As we become objective, we can observe the interaction more clearly.

Who is in the position of being right and who is feeling wronged? You and the other person will switch between roles. Lynn will feel wronged when she recalls that Terry sent an e-mail to her boss without copying her. She will feel justified as the aggressor when she says that Terry should do as she says. (After all, *she is the boss!*) Sometimes, a third role, the assister, comes into play; here the expressed intention is to help the other. Lynn could indicate "I want Terry to keep me informed so I can make sure she doesn't look bad to other senior leaders since I know what they are looking for."

Realize that when we are locked in power struggles, we need each other to keep the fight going. You have control over how you respond to the situation.

Make the Choice

Choose whether you want to stay in the tug-of-war game or take responsibility and stop it. When you have stepped out of the game, ask yourself these questions: "Is this struggle serving me?" "What is the cost?" "What do I win when I win?" "What do I lose when I win?" Lynn knew that staying in the struggle with Terry was taking a lot of energy, affecting her peace at home, and depriving her of sleep at night. It was not serving her. Also, she recognized that she was not really in danger. She was performing quite well in her senior position.

The next question is: "What is my contribution to this struggle?" This is a hard question when we are playing the game. Who wouldn't take a few swings in self-defense if the other started it? Shouldn't you protect yourself?

Lynn often walked by Terry's office and purposely looked the other way. She didn't say hello when she saw Terry in the hallway. She talked negatively about Terry to other staff members who probably told Terry she was doing so. She even had important meetings with her team when Terry was out of the office. While Lynn felt justified for all of the actions, she knew she needed to change her behaviors.

She needed to ask herself, "What can I learn from this experience?" As we reflected, Lynn realized that what was most important to her was enjoying the years with her family before her children went to college. Peace was what mattered! The best way for her to experience peace at home and at the office was to shift the power struggle with Terry. When she gave it further thought, she realized that this interaction was similar to the struggle she experienced with her sister. Some of her reactions had been by habit and so were not really directed at Terry. She could acknowledge that she really did not need to compete with Terry. She also found more empathy and saw that her style—which was very direct—had probably been difficult for Terry.

I asked Lynn what she appreciated about Terry. She took a deep breath and began. "First, Terry is well-regarded in the organization. We have been well-protected and avoided a few lawsuits because she always does her homework. I can imagine how hard it is for her to know that I am not planning to leave this position any time soon. She doesn't have many other viable options for promotion. She is doing the best she can and probably has no malicious intent. I know she is hard on herself, too." Lynn's compassion for both Terry and herself opened up the space for them to have several OASIS Conversations. They made some agreements afterward. They agreed to have regular face-to-face meetings. Lynn, being the boss with more power and thus responsibility, took the lead to create an open climate and focused on showing respect for Terry. It took some time to build trust. Now, years later, both are working well together and both are positive about the other. Their improved relationship positively influenced their team and their large department.

Lynn accepted that Terry would probably always prefer written communication over verbal interaction given her introverted style. Lynn recognized that Terry has spent her whole career with the company and doesn't think she can leave it. She is a bright woman, works hard, does a good job, and has strong analytical skills.

Using OASIS Moves, Lynn asked Terry to copy her on e-mails that she sent to top management. She also asked her to meet for update conversations at least once a week. In addition, Lynn agreed to stop by Terry's office regularly to share news. Lynn committed to speaking positively about Terry and building their relationship.

When I work with couples, teams, and systems, I observe the unit as a whole rather than getting involved in the drama of who is right and who is wrong. Each party contributes to how the couple or team is interacting. You can think of it as a couple dancing. When one changes his dance moves, the other also shifts. When you look at the whole system, you don't blame one person or the other. I have noticed that when people work through such a power struggle, they often develop a solid relationship.

In my role as a consultant, I have witnessed many polarized relationships up close. Often when we try to analyze what happened, it seems to be something small, like a misunderstanding, that began the pattern. Then people take positions based on their perceptions, and soon enough, we have the tug-of-war. Remember, it is not one person's fault; everyone involved has contributed, and each can take responsibility for his or her behavior and agree to make a change.

In a client company, two department heads were in a major fight. Each was making harsh assessments of the other, and each had taken actions that affected many people. After facilitating a process of exploration with them, I helped them to see that they had been responding to some challenging conditions in the organization, including a conflict between their bosses. After a few OASIS Conversations, they put down the tug-of-war rope and treated one another with respect. Over time, they actually became good friends. Years later, they kept in touch and wrote letters of recommendation for each other. It is possible to get past such power struggles. It helps to practice having OASIS Conversations and have a third-party consultant or coach intervene, too.

At home, my daughter continues to talk with me about her role in tug-of-war matches. She is slowing down and monitoring her body language and tone of voice so others can see that she is open. She has found ways for the boys and girls to play together—for example, in a game of kickball. Making the suggestion to play together in a funny voice supported the kids in laughing and moving on. However, resolving conflict won't always be that easy for her. Like all of us, she will need to decide when to walk away and not fuel the fight with harsh language. I hope that her future teachers—and teachers everywhere—will guide children to use a form of the OASIS Conversation process.

Authority and Roles

A lot of conflict and tension occurs in relationships where there is not agreement on roles and responsibilities. In families and organizations, people adopt roles where each person has defined responsibilities. The real value in defining roles is that agreement exists about who will do what. Sometimes roles are defined on paper and available to anyone to review, such as job descriptions in organizations. Conflict occurs when agreement on roles doesn't exist and one party thinks the other should do something they are not. For example, a staff member is expected to follow the lead of his or her manager, and in return, a manager is expected to provide support and direction.

Most of us have learned ways to relate to authority based on our backgrounds. As a result, we may not fully live up to the expectation of our roles. Have empathy for others who may be stuck in a role that isn't working well. They don't always know the most useful behavior. You may use an OASIS Conversation to make requests for what you would like and ask the others about meeting their needs.

Practice Being Open-Minded

It can be more challenging to suspend judgment when you have significant background experience with someone. With a lengthy shared history, you may believe you can predict the other person's behavior and motives.

Perhaps we are able to remain curious about the intentions and actions of people we don't know that well. Interactions in which we have less investment and history are good opportunities to practice suspending judgment, shifting and becoming open, and noticing the impact. Participants and clients have reported doing so with great success.

For example, Joe suspended his judgment of a contractor he had hired to build a patio when he came home one day and saw a large ditch in his backyard! He was upset and surprised. He couldn't imagine a need for it, and he definitely hadn't agreed to have it dug. He felt his chest tighten. He assumed the contractor was incompetent and had failed to listen to his expectations. He was also concerned that he would be asked to pay more.

While he "knew" the contractor was wrong, Joe remembered to stop, step back, suspend judgment, and shift to an open state. He took several deep breaths, remembered that he was only seeing one perspective, and became curious. Joe learned from the contractor that there were actually few alternatives to the digging because a brick wall had been built under the ground. The two came to a mutually satisfactory agreement. In fact, Joe was pleased because he ended up getting more than he had expected. He also had maintained a good relationship with the contractor so he felt confident in knowing he could use his expertise for other projects.

Using OASIS Moves can be particularly challenging if you have not had a productive relationship with a person. For example, Eileen was so sure that she knew how Heidi, her peer, would behave that she didn't really give her a chance to be different. Eileen "knew" Heidi would not be open to a collaborative team process, so she didn't even offer Heidi the option. Even when Heidi took steps to demonstrate her openness to collaboration, Eileen would cut her off. Eileen's judgment prohibited her from seeing all of the observable data. Instead, she selected the data that supported her negative judgment. Eileen had created a self-fulfilling prophecy. It is useful to focus on forgiving others and ourselves, recognizing that we are all influenced by our conditioning and are often not aware of our impact. Finding our compassion can help us to forgive.

Equally important is to realize that the only person you can change is yourself, and that's not easy. However, as we change our perceptions and become open and curious, we unlock the other person from the cage of our assumptions, which gives that individual the freedom to make changes as well.

One option is to re-contract with someone or a team we find challenging. You can begin by saying that you recognize things can be smoother or more positive, and you would like to agree on what each of you can do differently. You can ask the other person (or persons) what you could do differently and what he may need from you. You can also make requests of the other person. Perhaps he asks you to share what you are working on and you ask him to attend certain meetings. Once you make a new agreement, you can agree to check on progress at a defined time and again make necessary adjustments. I have seen many relationships enhanced from this simple process. Using OASIS Moves, you will agree on the observable data that you will each see that will meet your needs and define success. It is a productive exercise for teams to define new operating norms.

Remember that emotions are contagious. If you are in judgment and don't like someone, that person is likely to sense it. A good idea is to look for common ground with the other person. You can talk about your common interests in sports, movies, or projects. Let the person experience that you are relaxed with him. Look for what you can appreciate about him. As you both feel more comfortable, you can have an OASIS conversation about what you both need and come to agreement.

I have saved many of my own relationships with others by accepting that it will take time to rebuild trust. Even if I have not fully trusted someone after a bad experience, I have been able to build agreements to work with him or her effectively.

Practice suspending judgment and shifting to being open. Notice how many times you are surprised or when your snap judgment would have been inaccurate. Recently, I was giving a workshop when a participant raised her hand to speak. I called on her, and as she spoke, I thought she was being critical of what I had just said. I noticed my signal (my stomach tightened); I caught myself and remained open. As I focused on her comment, I realized she was actually offering an example of how the OASIS process worked and expressing enthusiasm. If I had followed my instinct, I would have argued with her. Then, most likely, she would have become defensive. Our interaction would have played out differently.

Summary

In this chapter, we explored the challenge of power struggles that are a normal part of life. It is useful to recognize when we are engaged in such a tug-of-war (as the aggressor, aggrieved, or assistor), and to remember that we have control over how we respond to the situation. Ask yourself, "Is this struggle serving me? What is the cost? What do I win when I win? What do I lose when I win?" Consider your contribution to the struggle. Consider what you can learn from the situation. Suspend your judgment and work to re-contract with the other person on how you will go forward. Make it your intention to build trust by giving empathy, being transparent and following through on your agreements. Forgive yourself and others. Consider using a coach or mediator in particularly challenging interactions when necessary.

We have a limited amount of self-control and need to have compassion for ourselves and others. We have all been influenced by our background experiences, and we each see the world differently. We need to have compassion for ourselves and others. Apply the OASIS Conversation process to your most challenging relationships, as well as others.

It will take time for you to repair some relationships. You will have many opportunities to build your muscle for stopping, suspending judgment, and shifting to the open OASIS state. The next chapter will provide some additional ways to support you in leading with an open mindset and creating an oasis environment.

CHAPTER 12

Continuing to Shift

Stances to Embrace an Open Mindset

"If I regarded my life from the point of view of the pessimist, I should be un-done. I should seek in vain for the light that does not visit my eyes and the music that does not ring in my ears. I should beg night and day and never be satisfied. I should sit apart in awful solitude, a prey to fear and despair. But since I consider it a duty to myself and to others to be happy, I escape a misery worse than any physical deprivation."

— Helen Keller

OASIS Conversations

Have a clear intention, plan when possible, and build rapport.

O = **Observation**

A = **Awareness** (of assumptions, emotions, and background)

S = **Shift** (to being open)

ᐣ = **Importance**

S = **Solution**

If you only recall one thing from this book, I hope it will be asking yourself, "Am I open (responsive, expansive) or closed (reactive, contracted)?" or "Are we in an oasis?" Ideally, you will adapt an open mindset and recall the value of stopping, suspending judgment, and shifting to being open.

An open mindset is the belief, perspective, and behavior of being present and appreciative of "what is" and also optimistic about "what is possible." An open mindset involves being responsive and accepting rather than reactive and dismissive. An open mindset includes being curious (open-minded), compassionate (open-hearted), courageous (open-gutted), and welcoming or non-judgmental (open-handed). We benefit from being open to ourselves, others, and to larger systems (i.e., our families, workplaces, communities and environment).

A simple way of assessing whether you are embodying an open mindset is to ask yourself, "Am I open or closed?" or using our metaphor, "Am I in the refreshing oasis or the arid desert?" When you are closed, you will be aware of being contracted and resistant. You will be judgmental and believe that something or someone is wrong. When you are open, you will experience a sense of wonder and feel expansive. You will recognize that you may not be aware of a whole situation, so you welcome learning more. While we all naturally react to people and situations, it is useful to aspire to being open to learning more.

Given the fast pace of change and turbulence these days, we all will benefit from adapting an open mindset. Many of us realize that it is often an illusion to aspire to being in control, and that being flexible and resilient will support us in enjoying our lives and being more effective.

Having an open mindset is essential for leaders today. Whether you are in a formal leadership role in an organization or a parent, teacher, or someone who wants to make a difference, being open to the current environment and seeing what is possible will serve you in influencing and inspiring others. We can each take the lead in adapting an open mindset to make a difference in our spheres of influence. Ideally, our openness will inspire and support others in opening their minds and hearts and to be more welcoming.

The OASIS Conversation process will support you in having positive and productive interactions. An open mindset fuels the interactions and will support you in maximizing your potential.

An open mindset involves being welcoming and nonjudgmental and is supported by being appreciative, optimistic, compassionate, curious, and courageous.

Stances that Support an Open Mindset

So far we have been talking about how to notice an emotional response in the moment and shift to being more open. In addition to experiencing a range of emotions on a daily and hourly basis, we also experience moods, which can be longer lasting and less specific to a particular event. Moods can be more pervasive. We may naturally check to see the mood of our boss to assess the best time to ask for a raise or time off. We sense whether the person is open-minded or not or whether the person is in a positive or negative mood. Moods can last for a few minutes or predominate a person's life. We may not be aware of our current or predominant mood—it just seems the way things are for us. Our mood or stance impacts how we interpret our interactions. It is useful to check-in with yourself regularly and assess your mood. It is also valuable to know that by having a clear intention and shifting your thoughts and the way you are holding your body, you can shift your mood and energy and thus how you relate. Others infer your openness from your posture and nonverbal signals. They sense an energy that is inviting or not. People move toward or away from different stances or moods. Ideally, you will make it a practice to be in an open and inviting stance in your relationships.

We have focused on being nonjudgmental and welcoming (open-handed) throughout this book and particularly in the chapter on Shift. In this chapter, we will explore stances or moods that support an open mindset and a shift from judgment. They are:

- Curious (open-minded)
- Compassionate (open-hearted)
- Courageous (open-gutted)
- Appreciative of "what is" and "what is unfolding"
- Optimistic about what is possible

You can choose to focus on just one or all of these as you interact with others. I have found each to be valuable in moving away from judgment and onto the path to an oasis where we can see possibilities and actualize potential. I find that leaders are often drawn toward one of the stances. While one leader finds that being curious helps him to be open, another finds that focusing on being appreciative supports her in being open to other views. Ideally, we will experience each of these often.

Stances to Support an Open Mindset

Curious (*Open-minded*)	**Appreciative** (*Open to the present*)
What can be learned from this? What surprises are there? Wondering and being open-minded.	Being thankful and grateful for what is, appreciating strengths, and looking for what can be beneficial about a person and situation.
Compassionate (*Open-hearted*)	**Optimistic** (*Open to the future*)
What are others experiencing? Caring for and understanding others and the human condition and interconnectedness.	Being hopeful and resilient, trusting that things will work out even when it is not clear how. Focusing on potential and possibilities.
Courageous (*Open-gutted*)	**Welcoming/Nonjudgmental** (*Open-handed*)
What is needed? What risk or vulnerability is needed? What supports integrity and resilience?	Being responsive. Respectful rather than reactive. Being expansive instead of contracted. Creating space for differences.

Each of these stances is more than a thought. Each has an energetic body component. Research by HeartMath[16] suggests that when you feel negative emotions, such as anger and judgment, your heart's rhythm is disordered and jagged when measured with an EKG. The chaotic heart rhythm creates a chain reaction in your body in which your blood pressure rises and your blood vessels constrict. Over time, this reaction can cause health-related challenges such as hypertension and heart disease.

When a person is in a positive state—for instance, sincere appreciation—the heart rhythms are much more congruent. Shown on an EKG, they appear more balanced and even. In this situation, your immune system is stronger and your nervous system is functioning more

---

16 Heartmath Institute (www.heartmath.org) provides research related to emotions and heart intellligence.

smoothly, and according to Childre and Martin[17], you experience an overall state of wellbeing. Through a process called "entrainment," your state (a positive frequency of vibration) becomes contagious to others and they align with you. Christian Huygens, a Dutch scientist of the late 1600s, first discovered this process. The inventor of pendulum clocks noticed that when he placed two or more pendulum clocks near each other, they eventually moved to swing in unison. They had been originally set to different rhythms! In a similar way, humans naturally entrain to others.

By adopting these stances, we are likely to influence those we are interacting with to align with us. Emotions are contagious. If you are open-minded, those you are interacting with are likely to experience your stance and energy and become open to listening. They are likely to be willing to explore their needs and yours to create common ground and find solutions and agreements on future actions (the I and final S part of OASIS Moves).

Be Curious

In addition to being open in your body posture and heart to another person, you benefit by becoming curious and open for learning. The challenge with making a judgment is that we believe we know what is going on, what the other person's motives are, or how things should be. However, it is useful to remember: "We don't know what we don't know." This will encourage our curiosity.

By remaining curious about the entire packing process, Gary, the manager described earlier, learned much more than just why his two shipments were damaged. The packers informed him that the company had installed a conveyer belt for the boxes, with the aim of improving productivity. However, the packers did not have control over stopping the flow of boxes! When they tried to talk to their supervisor, they could not get his attention. Consequently, they had little choice but to continue to pack the boxes as they came off the belt. Since those at the other end of the conveyer had little understanding of the complete process, a chance existed that future shipments would also have problems.

---

17   Childre, D., Martin, H. & Beech, D. *The Heartmath Solution*. New York: HarperCollins, 2011.

Knowing this, Gary was able to address the packers' concerns and prevent more damaged shipments from leaving the warehouse.

Gary also discovered that in another situation, the packers involved did not understand the foreign language printed on the boxes, which said "This end up." Consequently, the packers guessed—incorrectly—and packed the boxes upside down! Gary found additional possible explanations for improperly packed shipments—more than he could have imagined. Most importantly, he realized that none of these situations involved incompetence on the part of the packing staff.

When we are curious, we ask questions like: "What can I learn?" "What can I discover about the other person and the situation?" "How can I be supportive realizing the other person may be locked in his or her own perspective?" "What are the options?" "What else can I find out?" "What's going well?" "What is possible?" "What are my choices?" "What is my contribution?" "How can this be a win-win opportunity?"

At its best, curiosity allows an experience to become an adventure rather than a continual judgment about how things could or should be. It involves having a sense of wonder and openness about a situation. Curiosity also entails a sense of playfulness and expectancy of surprises.

Identify a character or person whom you believe is curious. We have benefited greatly from the curiosity of many scientists and inventors such as Ben Franklin, Thomas Edison, and George Washington Carver, and as a result, we get to enjoy lighted rooms, books, and many conveniences. You may ask, "How would Thomas Edison or another curious inventor approach this situation?"

Unfortunately, we've been trained to limit our curiosity. In some school settings, the focus was on getting the right answer, and we were discouraged from asking too many questions. Instead, we learned that "curiosity killed the cat." If we overthrow this early training, suspend judgment, and remain curious, we create unimagined possibilities for understanding others and for effective communication.

However, curiosity is not about interrogating. If we come from a judgmental place, the other person is likely to experience our questions as an interrogation, which leads to greater defensiveness. The difference is that from a state of curiosity, you are not the expert, but instead, you are learning with another person or group. You demonstrate interest in other possibilities and are willing to be in the state of not having the answer.

Allowing yourself to "not know" may take some practice, since many of us have been conditioned that we must have the answer. In a state of exploration, learning is possible for all parties. Often, if we make the first move and become curious, we enable others to join in the exploration. I am an avid learner. By being curious, I am always discovering new things, which makes life more enjoyable.

Practice

One way to experience curiosity and practice it as a skill is to begin some of your questions with the phrase, "I'm curious...." If your tone of voice is congruent with genuine interest in exploration, people are less likely to feel threatened. True curiosity is likely to evoke responses that include not only the facts, but also how the other person is feeling, his or her assumptions, and his or her needs.

In workshops, I ask participants to work with partners to help them experience and develop their curiosity and openness to learn. Each begins a conversation with the other by stating, "I'm curious... about your work, your hobby, your comment"—whatever has generated their interest. The whole energy of the room changes in this exchange. People are laughing, smiling, and experiencing being open with each other. Afterwards, I ask them what it was like to be curious. Participants indicate that it is enjoyable, they feel open to the other person, they learn new things, and they feel more connected with their partner. People often seem different after practice. The individuals who are the recipients of the statement "I'm curious..." are surprised by how much they share. They also feel better understood and seen by the people asking the questions.

Occasionally, though, a person on the receiving end of the statement does not have that experience. When we stop and explore this, the person asking the questions may share that he was not really curious; he was closed and just doing the exercise. So, being curious is not only about the words we use, but how we are genuinely feeling and our physical stance of openness.

How to Develop Your Curiosity

To develop and nurture your sense of curiosity, notice what interests you and how you experience curiosity in your body. As for me, I feel a sense of openness in my chest, I feel a bit playful, and I expect surprises. By becoming aware of this response, I am more easily able to notice whether or not I am being curious. The rewards can be a surprise and delight, like how we feel when we understand a riddle. Knowing that a delightful surprise is likely to be a part of our reward, it is easier to remain curious.

Curiosity was totally natural to you in childhood. Observe any child. My two-year-old niece continually asks others "Why?" She wants to know why her parents go to work, why it is raining, why they can't go to the park at night—her questions don't stop! Witnessing her raw curiosity and sense of wonderment is beautiful.

When I travel around the world and work with different people and organizations, I feel especially alive, curious, and open to learn. Travel allows me to enjoy the delights of new experiences and to explore them with curiosity. As I travel to new places, I feel curious about what I will discover. I feel enlivened, open, and joyful. I love to have a camera with me, and I am curious about what exciting images I may find. I am curious about the new foods I will try and all that I will learn. I am continuously surprised by other people's views. When I am curious, I feel my chest open, my posture straighten, and a sense of playfulness within the open space around my body.

When did you experience a sense of curiosity and openness to learn? How did you feel emotionally? What sensations did you feel in your body? Remember to call upon these feelings and memories when you want to access curiosity.

Identify what you are most curious about. Tell a friend or write about it. Notice how you feel as you reflect on your curiosity. Where do you notice your sense of openness? Are your facial muscles relaxing? Does your chest feel more expansive? How are you feeling? Do you have a metaphor for this state? What will help you remember how to bring your body back to this state?

Be Compassionate

A sense of compassion for others can be extremely valuable. Stuart was a client of mine whom most people thought was a very difficult manager. People felt intimidated by him. They became angry at how they perceived he treated them. For instance, he would often make people wait for scheduled appointments and did not look people in the eyes. People interpreted from his behavior that he felt above them. In return, his employees and others did not work well with him. To exert his authority further, he would become more demanding. He had locked himself into a vicious cycle that did not endear him to others.

In talking with Stuart, I learned that he was experiencing challenges in his family life. His spouse was ill and required a lot of his care and he was not getting much sleep. In addition, he did not feel confident and was trying to manage without real preparation for his job. His father was the role model he had been using for a boss. Unfortunately, because of his behavior, not many people gave Stuart much empathy. Since people were afraid of him, he was getting very little feedback. I could tell from our discussions that his intentions were positive. He was simply tired and did not have the skills to manage his life and employees effectively. After I showed compassion and empathy for him, he was able to relax and try some different behaviors. With time and effort, he improved in his relationship skills. He became a happier person, too.

How to Use Compassion

Compassion is a very strong stance that supports being open. It is hard (maybe impossible!) to be compassionate and judgmental at the same time. Compassion is the state of caring for others and being able to give them empathy for how they feel and see the world. Compassion is more than words. It is the experience of seeing how someone could be seeing the world in a certain way based on his or her background. While you may not agree with the person's perspective or behavior, you can connect with him or her as a fellow human with pain and emotions. With a sense of compassion, you are open to giving respect, support, and attention to a person, without expecting it to be reciprocal.

Nelson Mandela, a famous South African leader, had compassion and cared for those who held him captive despite his own challenges. He viewed his guards as real people with feelings and needs, which enabled the guards to become more open to him. Through his compassion and example, he opened up the possibility of leading South Africa out of apartheid. He understood the human condition and respected others. He did not hurt those who hurt him when he eventually gained political power. In his nineties, he continued to inspire people, despite no longer formally governing South Africa as president.

By putting ourselves in other people's shoes, we do our best to guess what it must feel like to be them. In this stance, we provide support and care for people. When people feel your compassion and empathy, they naturally become more open and compassionate themselves.

While difficult to hear, the challenging feedback I offer to many leaders is usually accepted. Beforehand, I typically collect data from their staff and make my own observations. Because these leaders know that I care about them and they need help, they become open to hearing and considering important feedback. I am confident in giving it because I want people to grow beyond behavior that isn't working well. I have compassion for them, knowing they are doing the best they know how based on their perceptions.

The most successful leaders I know are compassionate and care about the people who work with them. People working for them report feeling connected to them and being understood. In return, these leaders seem to get energy from their staff members. People want to follow and take action toward the vision of such a leader. Compassion is contagious and supports an oasis environment with lots of possibilities.

Practice Compassion

Compassion arises when we feel others' pain and have the desire to help them. It involves sending them "loving kindness" and wishing them well. Catch yourself caring for someone or a cause. Pay attention to your response. How would you describe your feelings? Do you feel open to the other person? Is there a person or a cause that connects you to this stance? I feel compassion for children, especially those in orphanages or in difficult circumstances. I notice that I really want to help these children and support them in having a better life. I have compassion for people who are different and don't feel valued.

Put yourself in situations where your compassion emerges. Be open to noticing when you watch movies, read biographies, or interact with people whose situations move you toward feeling compassion. Pay attention to what cause or individual particularly makes you aware of your compassionate nature. You may notice where you experience compassion in your body. For example, does your heart feel enlarged? You can then remind yourself of this person or situation to support yourself in being compassionate to someone else. Essentially, my natural compassion toward children supports me in remembering how I feel when I want to be compassionate to another group. Notice how our background experiences influence how we experience the world and relate. Ask other people when they experience compassion. Notice how their bodies shift and what emotions emerge. Reminder: You will benefit from being compassionate to yourself, too.

Think about someone you care about and appreciate that person's life situation and feelings. Think about what his day must be like. Consider the person's background situation and how that may be influencing her. Again, notice how it feels to care about this person. How do you feel in this open stance? I notice that I may have some judgment about why a person would approach a situation a certain way. However, when I search and am open to understanding the person, I can almost always see how it makes sense from his or her viewpoint. I then have compassion for the person and wish I could help and I do when I am able.

Research by positive psychologists such as Barbara Fredrickson and colleagues is showing the benefit of practicing "loving-kindness meditation" where you visualize sending kindness and support to yourself, your friends and family, your coworkers, and even those you may not favor. This kind of compassion helps us to see how we are united with others. Research identifies many health benefits of being compassionate and shows that compassion can be developed with intent and practice. A review of mindfulness-based interventions by Boellinghaus, Jones, and Hutton[18] found that loving-kindness meditation may be the most effective practice for increasing compassion for others and self-compassion.

Be Courageous

An open mindset requires courage. When we are open to new perspectives, our ideas, ways, and behaviors are likely to be challenged. Being open-minded involves examining our beliefs, facing our fears, and trying new things. Amidst the fast pace of change, we also need to maintain our integrity, even when being honest about our thoughts and

---

18 Boellinghaus, I., Jones, F.W. & Hutton, J. "The Role of Mindfulness and Loving-Kindness Meditation in Cultivating Self-Compassion and Other-Focused Concern in Health Care Professionals." *Mindfulness*. Vol. 5:2, 2012, p. 129-138.

feelings may not be easy. Being courageous involves pursuing goals in the face of obstacles and disappointments.

It takes courage to engage in open dialogue with others. We need to be open to hearing another perspective and be willing to consider new behaviors. For example, it takes courage to ask for and receive feedback about our performance. We need to respect that feedback is often as much about the one giving feedback and to be gracious and appreciative of the other's point of view.

Part of being open is paying attention to our gut. Often when we make decisions, we notice that we have a "gut feeling" to proceed or not. A growing body of research is finding that we have innate intelligence not only in our head or heart but our gut. Leaders who check-in with their guts are often seen as more adaptable and successful. Michael Gershon, in his book *The Second Brain,* shows that the gut has 100 million neurons and uses all the classes of neurotransmitters found in the brain.

It is useful to pay attention to our guts and notice when we are open or closed. Our gut gives us clues when we are reacting based on fear or taking action based on courage. It is valuable to take notice and appreciate our reaction.

A useful practice is to recall a time when you faced fear and proceeded to take action with success. Perhaps you were anxious about starting a project yet took the risk and experienced success. This memory will help you to notice your fear and be open to being vulnerable and taking action.

The more you are aware of your own fears and how to recognize and appreciate them, the more adept you will be in sensing fear in others. Giving empathy to yourself and others will be valuable. Winston Churchill noted, "Courage is what it takes to stand up and speak; courage is also what it takes to sit down and listen."

Be Appreciative

Recently, Lilly, a neighbor, told me about an especially great day. She spent it with a friend from Arizona. The two women talked the whole day, had a delightful meal in a fun restaurant, and enjoyed a walk in the sunshine along Lake Michigan. Lilly topped off the day with an outdoor concert at Millennium Park with other friends. Life felt good, and Lilly, a widow, smiled and said, "I feel good, and we are lucky to live in this beautiful city." A few days later, Lilly described the complete opposite kind of day to me.

She hated the traffic, had a surly waiter when she ate at a favorite restaurant with her sister, and was fed up. She described a car accident that kept traffic at a standstill for over an hour. She went on to tell about the loud noise from the nearby bandstand as they tested the sound system for a pending show. "I feel horrible. I want to move from this terrible city. I am lonely, and I'll never be happy."

I gently pointed out the difference in her perspective from a few days before. She considered a moment and said, "That must have been a fluke." She did not know how to get herself out of the state of feeling alone and judgmental of the city and those around her. I offered her the images of being open or closed. "Oh, I am definitely feeling closed right now," she said. I suggested she use appreciation or gratefulness as a way to shift to being open. "Oh, every day I say what I appreciate. I appreciate that I have my home, money, my health, family, etc. She was parroting a well-rehearsed list. She was not really shifting into a stance of gratefulness in her body. As she allowed her body to feel appreciative, I noticed that her shoulders dropped, she relaxed, her eyes opened wider, and a smile snuck out—the first one that morning.

When we are in the stance of gratefulness, our heart rhythm becomes more synchronized, which affects our body. Our vibration influences others around us. Lilly said this reminded her of the adage: "When you laugh, the whole world laughs with you. When you cry, you cry alone." We all have had the experience of wanting to move away from negative or closed people. We are drawn toward those who are open and positive. Through entrainment, we naturally align with this positive state of appreciation.

Gratefulness involves being thankful for all that we have and who we are. It involves counting our blessings and appreciating the small and large gifts of life. With practice, we shift our emotion to being positive. Gratitude research by Robert Emmons shows that people who practice being grateful for others and themselves increase their own sense of worth and happiness. When we are grateful for others, it enhances our relationships and we more readily connect with others. Given our selective attention, when we consciously focus on what we are grateful for, we will begin to notice even more things we are grateful for, and then our emotions will become even more positive. This emotion of positivity is contagious and shifts relationships.

Of course, most of us have heard that we *should* appreciate what we have. "You should be grateful for all I have given you!" shouts a parent. His child is acting entitled and the parent is feeling unappreciated in that moment. Using guilt to fix the problem usually works only temporarily, if at all. Being unappreciated disappoints us and takes our energy away. On the other hand, how do you feel when you do feel appreciated? Your energy jumps. You feel taller, more competent, and more satisfied. Life is good.

Organization development consultants and organizations have been exploring a process called "Appreciative Inquiry" that was first promoted by David Cooperrider. In it, managers notice and appreciate what a person or organization is doing well, and they use the energy generated from that appreciation to develop possibilities. Many corporations and non-profit organizations have benefited from this paradigm-shifting process. Most organizations tend to focus on what is wrong. This approach focuses on identifying strengths, successes, values, and hopes. You can feel the energy difference by answering a few questions: "What is working well around here?" and "How do we build on what is working well?"

Developing Appreciation

Margo was disappointed. Her boyfriend, Jason, did not ask her to go out to fancy restaurants and clubs and go dancing. This was her idea of a romantic time together. She said, "He is not very much fun. He does not like to do the things I do. I'm not sure he cares about me." Margo was feeling judgmental and not very enthusiastic about her boyfriend. She had grown up watching her father plan special outings for her mother. She had also seen a lot of movies where people in love are dancing together. So she interpreted Jason not inviting her to go dancing as Jason not caring for her. Jason, however, did not feel comfortable dancing and did not believe he could dance.

Margo could guilt herself into being appreciative. However, another approach would be to notice that she was feeling judgmental, stop, and then ask herself, "How am I grateful for Jason?" When I asked her to tell me, Margo listed the following: "I am grateful for his sincerity and his kindness. He supports me and is a great empathetic listener. He is true to himself, and he is not one to follow the crowd. He makes time for me, and we laugh a lot together. He is intelligent, and we have interesting conversations." She concluded by adding, "I am grateful he is in my life."

As Margo answered the questions out loud, her energy and demeanor shifted. She sighed and relaxed; she smiled and her eyes brightened as she spoke. Her heart seemed to open as she experienced a sense of gratitude for Jason. Margo had not directly told Jason that she would like to go out dancing. Once she understood what she needed, she had the confidence to have an OASIS Conversation with him.

You may not feel gratitude in a given moment, especially when you think you are right and someone else is wrong. However, with your intention to be grateful, you can make it a habit to ask yourself, "What do I appreciate about this person, myself, and this situation?" Then pause and allow yourself to notice why you are grateful. Put reminders where it is helpful and add becoming appreciative of "what is" into your routine. You can write what you appreciate in journals. You could even make it a habit to think of five things you are grateful for each day.

Practice Appreciation

Think of something or someone you are grateful for. Spend a few moments and reflect on the specifics of what you appreciate. Notice how you feel as you are in this state of gratefulness. Become familiar with this feeling. Do you notice feeling more open? Is your heart more open and feeling lighter? I notice that when I feel grateful, I feel an opening in my heart, like a flower that is blooming. What image comes to you?

You can also practice expressing your appreciation to others. According to *Gallup Management Journal*, when someone is acknowledged, his or her neurochemical dopamine is released. This release helps the person be positive. Notice actions people take for you and thank them. For example, if you are invited to dinner, you might say, "I am grateful for your kindness in remembering that I am a vegetarian and having some food that doesn't have meat sauce." Here we are using observable data to let people know what actions we appreciate.

John Gottman's[19] research on couples shows that a 5 to 1 ratio of positive comments, like those that show appreciation, predict a positive relationship. An even higher ratio of positive comments will support a great relationship. A higher ratio of negative comments does not bode well for a relationship. Another way of tapping into gratefulness is asking yourself and others appreciative inquiry questions. For example, "What are we doing well?" Do you notice your energy with a question like this? Another example is: "Think about your career; identify a moment when you felt engaged and effective. How did you feel? What made that moment possible?"

Have a mental photo album of these special moments. For example, I can easily shift into a time when I was facilitating a workshop in Europe. I was offering a new workshop that I felt good about. I loved working with the multicultural participants and hearing the positive experiences they had as they applied the tools. I had a lot of fun! I was very grateful to be fulfilling one of my goals. I had set the goal of working globally and making a difference in people's lives. As I imagine that experience and many others like it, I feel fully present and vibrant. I feel like my chest is open. I am grounded and I feel tall. At almost any moment, I can use this image to shift into a positive grateful state.

Be Optimistic

One of my first organization development clients taught me about optimism. John led a large division of a government agency. The organization had conducted an employee satisfaction survey of his division. The division received remarkably low scores. My role was to support John in creating a more productive work environment. As I conducted interviews and a more detailed assessment, serious issues related to fairness, respect, and even discrimination came to light. We held meetings and John spoke directly to many groups of employees. He continued to be optimistic and expectant of positive results in the face of major challenges. Immediately, we developed a strategy with employees and managers. John attended each meeting and openly talked about his part in creating the troubled environment. He continued to believe

---

19 Gottman, J.M. *The Science of Trust: Emotional Attunement for Couples.* New York: W.W. Norton Company, 2011.

that the environment could be turned around. He had to change his behaviors that people interpreted as him favoring his buddies. When asked, he described the experience of angry staff and the change process as "more painful than open heart surgery." However, he persisted with efforts to create a positive environment. His mission was to create a division that excelled in the execution of high quality customer service. Within a short while, his division received the highest scores on an organization-wide survey. In addition, his organization was receiving recognition across the country for its quality initiatives. It was praised for radically changing the work climate from the perception of discrimination to employee empowerment and participation. John and his staff inspired many other organizations to begin diversity and change initiatives. In the face of adversity, John remained optimistic that the situation could be turned around, so he devoted the effort to do so.

What Is Optimism?

Optimism is a positive stance of confidence about the unknown future. You don't really know what could happen next, yet when embodying optimism, you exude a confidence that things will work out. In the face of challenges, you hold the belief and take action to ensure that you and others will make it up the mountain. A person with optimism appears to have binoculars to see farther ahead and has the resilience to take actions that lead to success. Knowing that things will be okay, this stance allows you to be in the present and spend less energy worrying or being anxious.

Martin Seligman, a well-known researcher on optimism, found that the key predictor of success for those selling life insurance is optimism.[20] This predictor was even more important than personality or intelligence. Seligman's influence pervades a whole field of research related to optimism called "positive psychology." Results indicate that people who approach life optimistically tend to be happier, healthier, have better careers, make more money, and have better relationships. Not bad.

---

20 Seligman, M.E. *Learned Optimism: How to Change Your Mind and Your Life.* New York: Free Press, 1998.

In the past, optimism was considered a trait, meaning you already had to have the disposition. You saw the glass as half-full or half-empty. Now, research is showing that we can adapt the stance of optimism. Much of what we worry about is not worth worrying about. I know this from personal experience. My hope is that knowing you have the OASIS Moves available, you won't worry so much about relationships. You'll be confident knowing you have the skills to work through most relationship challenges.

Optimists tend to believe and demonstrate by their actions that an ample amount exists for all, rather than live with a sense of scarcity. Rather than adapting the view that there is just one piece of pie and you or the other gets it, optimists believe there is enough for everyone, and they are not fearful of being left out. Thus optimists have the capacity to be generous and supportive of others who often return the positivity.

Optimists see and act as if the world is friendly, and thus, they can relax and be open rather than constricted and fearful. The optimistic perspective supports resilience in the face of challenges.

Being optimistic is not just positive thinking. Those with an optimistic perspective believe they can do something to change a situation and make it better. They take action. Since they do, more likelihood exists that things will get better. Having an optimistic perspective becomes a self-fulfilling prophecy. Those who are pessimistic assume that nothing can be done to make a difference; then they do nothing and their perception is reinforced. In fact, research shows that an optimistic perspective literally supports a stronger immune system and better health. If you are in better health, it is easier to continue having an optimistic outlook.

Research by Seligman and others shows that when a person is depressed, some brain hormones become depleted and slow down immune system activity. Good news! Research shows that anyone can become more optimistic with the intention to do so.

Developing Optimism

We all have some optimism in us. It's what keeps us going even in the face of life's many curves. The first step of supporting this stance is to notice where you already are naturally optimistic. For example, Lisa, a new supervisor, didn't have confidence in herself in her new role. However, when we explored her areas of optimism, she said she is very optimistic about her ability to find places when driving. Not only that, when she has been someplace once, she will remember her way around, even years later. She connected to this natural competence. She realized that she never worried about finding her destination. In this state of optimism, Lisa had fun and the courage to turn the next corner when in a new city. She found the roadblocks and one-way streets to be like some of the computer game challenges she enjoyed. Lisa had a smile on her face and a glint in her eye. She sat up taller and was more relaxed in her body. She would say to herself, "I can handle this. I can figure this out. It will work out." She worked to transfer this sense of optimism to her new role as a supervisor and found that the same stance served her well. As Lisa trusted that things would work out with her staff, she found herself having a lot more fun with them. She also had the courage to take the more difficult actions required of a manager, such as giving constructive feedback and delegating.

Lisa learned to catch her pessimistic thoughts and then dispute them. When she caught herself thinking, "I'll never be able to run a staff meeting," she would stop and remind herself of other skills she had learned. She then selected and read an article about running a meeting to prepare for the new challenge. Then, she would reassure herself by thinking: "Okay, I can do this. It doesn't have to be perfect." If a coworker said, "I can never do this," you would likely show her how she has already succeeded, remind her she needs to take small steps, and encourage her.

You can apply this same process to yourself. Be kind. Remind yourself of the observable data—you probably have received good feedback from your staff. You were selected for the position and may have been told you have natural leadership ability. Consider some alternatives for your thoughts and feelings. Perhaps you are not confident about leading the meeting because you have not fully prepared. Do you need to read the report again? Are you remembering that last meeting when Charlie was disruptive? Could you plan to speak with him before the meeting to learn what is concerning him? For example, he may think he should have gotten the job and not you. To give yourself support, say something like, "I am learning how to manage and getting support to do so."

Practice Optimism

If you think the future will be mostly good, you will be motivated to persist through challenging times. So as you interact with others, remind yourself that things will work out. Visualize a beautiful oasis that is filled with abundance, nourishment, beauty, and support. Imagine yourself seated in a comfortable chair by the water with a cool drink, laughing with the other person. You feel safe and fully at ease. Trust that you are creating a place of connection.

Expect new possibilities in a given situation. Try to reframe situations that aren't working well. Faced with a potential conflict with another, the chance exists that you will end up closer to the person when you work through the situation.

Consider and take actions that will support achieving your goals. In the moment of a judgment, simply expect that you will work things out with the others involved. Go further and anticipate a more solid relationship and results. Stop, breathe, and approach the other with an open heart for a dialogue.

Welcoming and Nonjudgmental

By now, you know that the core of an open mindset and an OASIS Conversation is being welcoming and nonjudgmental. The more we are welcoming and respectful of ourselves and others, the more we create an oasis environment.

Find your place in the oasis. What if I told you that you have a place with your name on it in an oasis? Lush, green palm groves and numerous streams of fresh water and many natural hot baths and spas surround you. The fertile ground yields mountains of fruits and vegetables. You smell the fresh scent of the fruit and the colorful flowers. Feel the breeze and the warm sun on your skin. Space and open air surround you. You fit in here and have fulfilling relationships. You have a life of ease and comfort. There is nothing for you to control. You can come here anytime you choose, and you can bring others with you. It's all paid and guaranteed. No one will ask you to leave.

As you imagine this, how do you feel? Do you find yourself relaxing and trusting? Take a deep breath and notice that the tension in your stomach, back, and neck relaxes. How do you feel in this oasis?

Some say they feel relaxed and free. Others report feeling happy and alive. For some, this sensation is quite new. Others say they feel more compassionate and creative. Most say they are more confident about having a conversation and are breathing freely and naturally. Without the burden of a sense of scarcity and the need to protect or fight for our needs, we have more energy for creativity and cooperation.

You have an open invitation. Remind yourself that you have free access to the open oasis state with an open mindset. Make the choice to be in the oasis and to interact from this state of ease and abundance.

I encourage you to select these stances (compassionate, curious, courageous, appreciative, or optimistic) to support you in being open and non-judgmental. Then notice the impact on your mood and those with whom you interact. In addition, I hope you experience more positive health and wellbeing.

Summary

In this chapter, we identified stances that you can practice to shift your body and mood to create an open mindset and accepting environment. Each of the stances enables you to become more open and to create a mood that supports possibilities.

It is useful to explore the following stances so you know how to assess your current state and shift into one of the following:

- Curious—being open-minded and exploring what you can learn and expecting surprises
- Compassionate—being open-hearted and caring for others and what they are experiencing
- Courageous—being open-gutted, willing to take risks, be vulnerable and resilient
- Appreciative—being grateful for "what is" and looking for what is beneficial about a person and situation
- Optimistic—holding a positive view of the future—trusting that things will work out even when it is not clear how
- Welcoming/Nonjudgmental—being respectful and expansive rather than contracted

As you explore these stances, you may be drawn to one or another. The more you practice accessing the stances, the more natural and easy it will become to shift to an open mindset. In these moods or stances, others will become more open to you.

In the final note that follows, we will explore some ways for you to build the habit of leading with an open mindset and using the OASIS Moves in your daily life to enhance interactions and create unparalleled results.

A Final Note

Support for Your Journey

"We are what we repeatedly do."

— Aristotle

"There isn't anything that isn't made easier through constant familiarity and training. Through training we can change; we can transform ourselves."

— The Dalai Lama

OASIS Conversations

Have a clear intention, plan when possible, and build rapport.

    O = **Observation**

    A = **Awareness** (of assumptions, emotions, and background)

    S = **Shift** (to being open)

    I = **Importance**

    S = **Solution**

I have enjoyed being on this OASIS journey with you. My wish for you is that you have many meaningful interactions that support achieving your goals and enjoying life fully. I hope that having an open mindset, being curious and open to different points of view, and using the OASIS Conversation approach becomes an embedded habit.

So, now that you have the intention of being open to others and using the OASIS Moves in your interactions, what will support you in that intention? Building new patterns of behavior requires intention, practice, and support.

Habits

According to Neale Martin and other researchers, about 90-95 percent of our behaviors are habits. We automatically do many things that don't take conscious thought. Our habitual thoughts, emotions, and behaviors have developed throughout our lives based on our background experiences and conditioning. We have developed habits around eating, hygiene, exercise, how we relate to people, how we organize our homes and lives, and how we communicate with others. Our unique constellation of habits forms our character or personality. Many of our habits are deeply ingrained and are just the way we do things. Some are still serving us, however, and some are not.

Our habits may feel so ingrained that we cannot imagine another alternative. Brain and neuropsychology research, however, demonstrates that we are capable of building new neuropathways in our brains.[21] These correspond to new actions we take in our lives. Doing new things may keep us alive and active longer.

Picture a habit as a path formed in a meadow. At first, the meadow is full of tall grass. You need to get from point A on one side of the meadow to point B on the other, so you begin to walk through the grass. As you repeat the path to point B, it becomes more worn, and soon enough, the pathway is clear. Over time, you naturally take the path when you get to point A, without thought. The path becomes easy and comfortable for you. Eventually, you don't even notice a choice exists and you don't devote much energy to considering which way to go. Scientists say that over time neural paths are built, and a habit is supported by the basil ganglia part of the brain.

The value of such a habit is that you don't need to devote much energy or will toward taking the action. You are conditioned to take the established route. This leaves more energy for other creative opportunities. Research by Baumeister[22] suggests that we have a limited

21 Hanson, R. *Hardwiring Happiness: The New Brain Science of Contentment,- Calm and Confidence*. New York: Random House, 2013.
22 Baumeister, R.F. & Tierney, J. *Willpower: Rediscovering the Greatest Human Strength*. New York: The Penguin Press, 2011.

pool of will and discipline. If we exert a lot of our will for one action, we seem to get tired and have less for taking other actions. For example, a study had participants who were deprived of food and then were exposed cookies and asked not to eat them. Another group, who hadn't eaten either, were offered and allowed to eat the treats. The first group, which had to refrain from eating the treats when they were hungry, was less persistent in the next task of trying to solve insoluble puzzles. It appears they used their limited willpower. (It sure doesn't sound like it was a fun study to be in.)

You want to develop habits for the behaviors most important to you, so you are not required to exert your strong will and thought for each decision. By practicing the OASIS Moves, you will develop useful habits that will serve you in your interactions. With intention and practice, the moves will become habitual and easy for you. My clients and workshop participants report easily incorporating the moves into their daily interactions. In fact, you probably naturally use many of the skills in interactions that go well for you. It is those more challenging interactions that require a little more intention and practice.

Forming New Habits

One habit that many of us have formed is driving. Before I learned to drive, I was unconsciously incompetent. I didn't think about driving and did not have the skill to drive. I remember when I first started to learn. I had to think about each detail from adjusting the seat and mirror to remembering where the turn signal was. I had to think consciously about moving my foot from the gas pedal to the brake. It all seemed awkward and unfamiliar. So initially, I was consciously incompetent. I knew I did not know how to drive when my classmate stopped in the middle of the road because she suddenly saw a bird land there and I didn't know what I would have done if I were in the driver's seat. Over time, I grew to be consciously competent. I paid attention to the road and was aware of putting my key in the ignition and buckling my seatbelt. I was a careful driver. As I had more experience with driving, I became unconsciously competent. I no longer think much about driving and am comfortable driving the car from one place to another even when I am engaged in an interesting conversation with a passenger. I often have the experience of getting in the car and driving to a place without a lot of recall regarding the path I took.

Habit formation of the OASIS Conversation process takes a similar path. Some of us naturally and without effort ask questions and listen to how others respond. Some of us have developed the habit of talking first and perhaps not paying attention to how others are listening. Some of us have developed the habit of interrupting, while others have developed the habit of being curious and open. As with all habits, some serve us at this point in our lives and others really do not serve us.

Emily, a manager in a Fortune 100 company, received feedback from her staff and peers that she was not empathetic and appeared to be uncaring and autocratic. She was shocked. In fact, she was quite aware of the challenges of her staff and even felt empathetic. As I coached her, I realized that she had understanding and empathy for people. However, she did not express her understanding and quickly moved to telling people what to do. She realized that in her haste to move quickly, she had developed the habit of jumping right to talking about solutions and skipped over the I component of finding out what was important and demonstrating understanding and giving empathy. This path in the meadow was well worn and out of her consciousness. She learned that she had the same pattern of behavior at home as at work. She became aware that it was costing her satisfaction in her relationships. People had begun not sharing information with her. They perceived her as uncaring.

Emily decided to build a new pathway that involved slowing down to understand what is important (I) to others and to express her caring and empathy before moving to offering a solution (S). This shift in behavior improved her relationships with all those around her. In turn, she felt more supported by other people. She moved through the same pattern of new habit development. At first, she was totally unaware of the impact of her behavior (unconsciously incompetent). She began practicing expressing empathy and understanding what was important, but it was not fully smooth. She felt a bit uncertain and had to practice in our coaching sessions and with staff. This took some effort (consciously incompetent). She knew her comments felt a bit jarring and not really natural. With practice, however, the words began flowing more easily and she got feedback from her staff and family that they felt understood by her (consciously competent). The empathetic statements became easier for her to say aloud. Finally, she was able to give empathy and express her understanding without much effort (unconsciously competent). In fact, she was surprised during one coaching session when I pointed out that she was giving me empathy and understanding. She was able to do so without conscious effort.

As Emily worked to make empathizing a habit, she was strengthening the neural pathways for empathy. These circuits were becoming stronger and were quickly activated. As she refrained from jumping to giving advice, those wires became thinner and less activated.

Building New Habits

How was Emily able to develop her new habit of giving empathy and expressing understanding about what was important to others? You might think that we spent a lot of time working on changing her old habit. In fact, once we understood her current habit, we spent little time reinforcing what was no longer working for her. Certainly, her habit of moving quickly to action supported her in being effective. It probably worked in her family since there was a strongly reinforced feeling of connection with her parents and siblings. In the workplace and in her role as a product manager, the need was to focus on speed and taking action. She became skilled in moving projects along, and this served her well. In her new role, however, she functioned as the leader of a team that was working cross-functionally. She worked with people in different roles, with different agendas. A sense of mistrust and discord marred the cross-functional team's productivity. Emily needed to slow down and make sure the various people involved felt understood about what was most important to them.

Neuroscience research[23] is showing that our brains are constantly making connections and building maps of connections. We are continually building neural pathways as we are exposed to and learn new things. While at one time scientists thought that most of our personality and behaviors were established by the age of six and that we stopped learning new things as we got older, research is showing that we are building neural pathways throughout our days. The brain's neuroplasticity is now understood. The brain compensates and is continually building new neural pathways and connections throughout our lives.

---

23 Rock, D. & Page, L. *Coaching with the Brain in Mind: Foundations for Practice*. New York: John Wiley & Sons, 2009.

Our brain tries to order and make sense of all the data and stimuli we are exposed to. We naturally make connections between things we know and new things. Over time, these connections become "hard-wired" and well-worn paths. In fact, the ways we talk, listen, and interact have become hard-wired and habitual. We all know people who talk much more than listen and vice versa; some habitually talk about themselves, while others habitually talk about others. Our interaction styles become habituated and automatic. We tend to be unconscious about how we are communicating. I am working with an executive on his leadership presence. He is unaware that he tends not to look at clients, trails off, and becomes quiet when talking to a group. He has had to become more conscious and commit to building new habits that serve him more in his role of partner in a large firm.

What we pay attention to is what forms new neural paths. Habit formation requires repetitive attention over time so that new wiring can be established. What we pay attention to is repeatedly reinforced. Reminders and support from others is useful.

My coaching client made the commitment and developed the habit of looking at the people he was talking to in meetings. He developed supports to keep him on track. He had reminders in his calendar and notebook, and he talked with me, his coach, who reminded him and reinforced the behavior. In addition, he had colleagues who reminded him and noticed when he gave eye contact. Within a short while, my client was giving eye contact as he spoke to his clients. Over time, the habit became more embedded and he became unconsciously competent in interacting with clients and colleagues.

Be sure to focus on what you want to create or do. I find if I focus on what I don't want—such as not eating sugar—that's about all I want to do.

Connections that are used become stronger while those not used become weaker. If you have not focused on a subject for many years, you will find it hard to recall how to do algebra or physics. The pathways have become less worn and less strong. Don't give any attention to the habits you don't want. Instead, focus on the behaviors you want to develop and allow new neural paths to form. Let the old paths wither away without attention.

Reinforcing OASIS Habits

You can build the muscle of choosing to be open and curious rather than closed and judgmental. You can build the habit of realizing that there are multiple realities based on our different backgrounds and experiences. You can make choosing an open mindset and the OASIS pathway a habit.

How do we build and reinforce new habits? First, we have to recognize our current habits and appreciate them. Then we need to notice how our current pattern is still serving us and make the choice to keep it or make some changes. If we want to make a change, we then need to choose to build a new habit and plan how we will do so. We need to find ways to support ourselves. We need to be kind to ourselves. It is not easy to build a new path in the meadow; it takes the conscious decision to do so and also effort. We need to practice each day and trust that we can create the new path or habit.

I would love for you to walk away from reading this book with the habit of being open and creating an OASIS in all relationships. In fact, I hope you have the intention of being open to yourself and others. This intention is critical and will serve you well. I believe people are quite forgiving if they believe your intention is to be open.

In the same way you are not a cook after reading a cookbook or a swimmer after reading a book on swimming, it will be valuable for you to practice and find support for this effort. You will have a lot of opportunity to practice since you interact with all kinds of people each day.

Take any component of the OASIS Conversation pathway and work on practicing the skills that will serve you best. For example, you can:

- Remind yourself of your intention to create an OASIS in your interactions and to be open-minded and present
- Focus on separating your observations from assumptions
- Become aware of your assumptions and emotions and name them
- Consider the impact of your background conditioning and experiences on your perceptions
- Catch yourself in judgment, stop, step back, and shift to being open
- Focus on "assuming positive intent"
- Remind yourself that "you don't know what you don't know"

- Notice your mood and shift to an open mindset by being compassionate, curious, appreciative, or optimistic
- Practice actively listening and mirroring others
- Practice giving empathy
- Ask empowering questions
- Practice tracking modes of listening (tell, sell, gel) and taking others' perspectives
- Focus on understanding what is important to you and others, and finding common ground
- Ensure you have listened and understood before offering solutions
- Explore options for solutions
- Make clear commitments
- Follow up on agreements
- Check if you are "open or closed" and shift to an open mindset

Ideally, you will participate in a workshop where you can practice the OASIS Conversation skills, adapt an open mindset, and receive feedback and tips on how best to have open-minded conversations for unparalleled results. Also, coaching will support you in honing the skills. You can learn more about building the OASIS skills and other tools to remind and support you on your journey at www.OASISConversations.com.

I hope that as you reinforce your habits of being open to others and using the OASIS Conversation pathway, you will enhance your energy for creativity. I hope you will have more meaningful conversations and relationships, achieve your goals, and support others in doing the same.

Please email me at Ann@Potentials.com and let me know your successes, challenges, insights, and questions. Read my blog, and keep current with new findings and progress related to the OASIS Conversations process. Visit www.OASISConversations.com for tools and reminders to reinforce this book.

Thank you for being on this journey with me. I wish you positive connections, engagement, and innovation. I believe that creating open-minded conversations is an essential skill for leaders. It is through effective conversations that we impact organizational climates and create the space for realizing opportunities. May we each create an oasis for mindful conversations where there will be more productive interactions with more results and more joy.

Resources

You can explore the following resources for more information on brain research and related areas. See also www.OASISConversations.com for additional information.

Baumeister, R.F. & Tierney, J. *Willpower: Rediscovering the Greatest Human Strength*. New York: The Penguin Press, 2011.

Boellinghaus, I., Jones, F.W. & Hutton, J. "The role of mindfulness and loving-kindness meditation in cultivating self-compassion and other-focused concern in health care professionals." *Mindfulness*. Volume 5:2, 2012. p.129-138.

Dimoka A. "What does the Brain Tell Us About Trust and Distrust? Evidence from a Functional Neuroimaging Study." *MIS Quarterly* (34:2). 37-396.

Emmons, R. *Thanks: How the New Science of Gratitude Can Make You Happier*. New York: Houghton Mifflin Company, 2008.

Frederikson, B. *Positivity: Groundbreaking Research Reveals How to Embrace the Hidden Strength of Positive Emotions, Overcome Negativity, and Thrive*. New York: Crown Publishers, 2009.

Goleman, D. *The Brain and Emotional Intelligence: New Insights*. Northampton, MA: More than Sound, 2011.

Gottman, J.M. *The Science of Trust: Emotional Attunement for Couples*. New York: W.W. Norton Company, 2011.

Hanson, R. *Hardwiring Happiness: The New Brain Science of Contentment, Calm and Confidence*. New York: Random House, 2013.

Hatfield, E., Cacioppo, J.T., & Rapson, R.L. *Emotional Contagion*. Cambridge: Cambridge University Press. 1994.

Heartmath Institute (www.heartmath.org) provides research related to emotions and heart intelligence.

Hewlett, S., Marshall, M. & Sherbin, L. "How Diversity Can Drive Innovation." *Harvard Business Review*, December, 2013.

Kahneman, D. *Thinking, Fast and Slow*. New York: Farrar, Straus and Giroux. 2011.

Lewis, T., Amini, F. & Lannon, R. *A General Theory of Love*. New York: Random House, 2000.

Rock, D. & Page, L. *Coaching with the Brain in Mind: Foundations for Practice*. New York: John Wiley & Sons, 2009.

Rock, D. *Your Brain at Work: Strategies for Overcoming Distraction, Regaining Focus and Working Smarter All Day Long*. New York: John Wiley & Sons, 2009.

Shermer, M. *The Believing Brain: From Ghosts and Gods to Politics and Conspiracies—How We Construct Beliefs and Reinforce Them as Truths*. New York: Times Books, Henry Holt and Company, 2011.

Siegel, D. J. *Mindsight: The New Science of Personal Transformation*. New York: Bantam Books, 2010.

Siegel, D.J. *The Developing Mind: How Relationships and the Brain Interact to Shape Who We Are*. 2nd Ed. NewYork: Guilford Press, 2012.

Stone, T. *Pure Awareness*. Carlsbad, CA: Great Life Technologies, 2007.

The Consortium for Research on Emotional Intelligence in Organizations (www.eiconsortium.org)

Van Hecke, M. et.al. *The Brain Advantage: Become a More Effective Business Leader Using the Latest Brain Research*. New York: Prometheus Books, 2010.

About the Author

Ann Van Eron, Ph.D., MCC, is founder and principal of Potentials, a global coaching and organization development consulting firm coaching leaders and teams all over the world for over twenty-five years. She specializes in creating positive environments where people have open-minded and productive conversations for greater results.

Her clients include Fortune 100 corporations, nongovernmental organizations, healthcare agencies, and non-profit and privately held companies. Ann promotes leadership development and teaches managers how to be effective in coaching their teams. She assists organizations in creating cultures of respect and openness for unparalleled results. She engages people in having mindful conversations for impact using her proven OASIS Conversation process. She is an author and speaker and offers training, coaching, and consulting to leaders, teams, organizations, and coaches. She is certified as a Master Coach and has a doctorate in Organization Psychology from Columbia University. Ann is committed to assisting people in fulfilling their leadership potential and enjoying life.

Ann lives in Chicago and enjoys photography, art, nature, traveling, and learning new things with colleagues, friends, and family. She is committed to being of service and making a difference.

www.Potentials.com

About OASIS Conversations Coaching and Consulting

If you are looking for a dynamic coach and facilitator to guide you through the OASIS Conversation® process with your team or organization, look no further than Ann Van Eron, the OASIS Conversation creator and her team of certified coaches and facilitators.

The OASIS Conversation process has been tested all over the world with much success in such organizations as the United Nations, New York-Presbyterian Hospital, Cleveland Clinic, GE Capital, Ford Motor Company, the World Bank, and other corporations.

When you hire Ann Van Eron to support your team in learning to be more open and find an oasis of agreement, you will find your workplace changing into a friendlier, more productive, and more understanding place within a short time.

OASIS Conversations produce results, improve relationships, save resources, enhance innovations, create efficiencies, spur rapid problem resolution, improve employee and customer engagement, and enable organizations and teams to share a common language and process for identifying common ground and creating agreements.

Benefits your team will experience by using the OASIS Conversations program are:

- Leaders will experience being more confident, centered, and present in the midst of turbulence.
- Participants will be able to cultivate the emotions related to high performance.
- Team members will be able to create positive climates and cultures that support open conversations for impact.
- With the conversation skills and open mindset, leaders and others will experience more engagement, innovation, and real results.
- Team members will be more emotionally and socially competent.

Besides workshops and webinars on OASIS Conversation skills and the value of an open mindset, customized options tailored to your specific organization and needs are available. We interview team members in advance and facilitate unique experiences to suport high performing team develoment.

Also, personalized coaching is available. Learn your strengths and areas of opportunity for creating positive and productive interactions for unparalleled results.

In addition, online and in person workshops are available for participants to experience the OASIS Moves.

Coaches and managers can choose to be certified in the OASIS Conversation process. See more details at www.OASISConversations. com or www.Potentials.com.

Also, consider booking Ann to speak at your next event on the importance of an open mindset and how to create OASIS Conversations for more positive and productive interactions.

You are also welcome to join a practice group to learn the OASIS Conversation process more fully.

To discover how Ann and her team of certified coaches and facilitators can help your organization and its members reach an oasis, contact her for a complimentary consultation:

Ann@Potentials.com
www.Potentials.com
312-856-1155

91109655R00144